Eber & Wein Publishing's

Who's Who in American Poetry

John T. Eber Sr.
MANAGING EDITOR

A publication of
Eber & Wein Publishing
Pennsylvania

Who's Who in American Poetry: Vol. 1

Library of Congress
Cataloging in Publication Data

ISBN 978-1-60880-730-7

Proudly manufactured in the United States of America by

Eber & Wein Publishing

Pennsylvania

Who's Who in American Poetry

A Walk with Death

They say that when you are about to die
That your life flashes before your eyes
The good, the bad, and the ugly
Each memory spread out for you to examine closely
In those brief moments before the reaper comes calling
You begin to remember everything
But for her it was different
There were no happy memories to look back upon
No flashes of life before the end
No sunshine and rainbows or white lights
For her there was only the constant pain
So many regrets and shattered dreams
She was glad for the end
For it was an ending to the pain
She would step through the threshold
And walk with death to the bitter end
The machines stopped pumping life into her body
The incessant beeping drowned out everything else
She was not alone for she had Death to walk with her
His black robes and skull mask a stark contract
He held out his hand—the time was now
As her soul fled her body, she took his hand
The pain a distant memory

Brittany Sarkozi
New Boston, MI

[Hometown] *South Lyon, MI* [Ed] *graphic design* [Occ] *Nissan parts specialist* [Hobbies] *music, writing, playing bass clarinet, ballet* [GA] *being published in a ton of these books*
I remember in twelfth grade my English teacher gave me an entry form to one of these contests and I will always be grateful to her because since I submitted that first poem I have been featured in a dozen books like these. I enjoy writing and poetry and never want to stop.

Loving Memories

My Earl has now left me
The days are lonesome and long
After sixty-eight years of life together
It's so hard to believe he is gone

Our lives becoming as one was meant to be
We made it through all kinds of weather
Bright sunshine always chased the dark clouds away
And we spent a lifetime of love together

Since God took you away
My days are lonely and long
I was left with a broken heart
But the Lord has kept me strong

Memories are all I have left
We are together still in my heart
Nothing can ever change my love
That we had from the start

You were always my one and only
Our hearts melted together when first we met
Love has a way of its own
Loving memories of our love, I will never forget

Mary Carr
Sevierville, TN

[Hometown] *Sevierville, TN* [Ed] *12th grade* [Occ] *retired* [Hobbies] *bird watching* [GA] *caregiver, being able to keep my husband at home*
Memories inspired my poem. I was my husband's primary caregiver for sixteen months. With the help of home healthcare and a nurse practitioner I was blest to care for him at home. He passed away at age ninety-two—January 8, 2022. Nurses are angels; God bless them.

Buttercups

While idly walking one day
Suddenly in front of me huge a field full of buttercups
Instantly Wordsworth's "Daffodils" came to mind
How he "gazed and gazed"
Buttercups, there were passers-by who simply passed you by
They missed a lovely memory
For I ever remember you
Beautiful field of buttercups

Bridget Ingraham
Phoenix, AZ

A New Concept

You know there is a Creator, right? All you need to do is follow the Creator's rules. Your life will be enjoyable. Talk to Thee as your best friend. Say good morning, then talk to Thee during the day. Ask for help, or assistance. Keep a positive attitude, be happy, Don't let your mind get stuck on something that isn't really necessary. Think about what you're thinking about. If it isn't positive, delete it before you focus on it. Remember to forgive and forget. Move forward with your life. You're here on Earth for a reason. Be cheerful, help others, even with something small. The blessings are amazing.

Skip Canfield
Wapato, WA

[Hometown] *Wapato, WA* [Occ] *retired*

Personally

Personally, I've been bitter in the past of bad luck I never deserved. And still unknown answers aren't clear. To those who have been robbed of their peace and pride—hate can build up inside! Satan comes to steal and destroy! He sets stumbling blocks by the wayside. Personally, when a baby is born to be loved evermore and in time their future seems unsure. Why aren't folks friendly as they used to be? America wake up and be what we need to be! When streets were safe for you and me. Why have places had tragedies of things that should have never taken place? For a child to be in sudden fear and pain brings heartbreaks of tears of "incidents insane." Personally, when I'm inspired to write a poem such as this, let's pray God will protect everyone near and far, in towns and places, all around! And make as concerned when we need to be. Let's respect the young and elderly. So love your children as you're supposed to do. And trust God to see you all through!

Frances Elaine Camp
Americus, GA

[Hometown] *Wellston, OH* [Ed] *11th grade at Jackson High School* [Occ] *homemaker, military widow* [Hobbies] *being an author, home karaoke, and 2022 craft beautiful jewelry* [GA] *former "Willow Grove Lane Story"*
The Bible has told us we are in the world but not of the world. Weather and news can affect our daily lives. God is to love us all and we are to love others as He loved us. But He isn't always pleased by mistakes that are caused by so many stumbling blocks and etc. Some sins can be forgiven and others hold years of grudges! The golden rule used to play a role in several lives—"Do unto others as you want them to do unto you!" God bless all.

Only a Moment

What's in a moment tucked away in one's mind?
Perhaps, a margin of delight that goes back through time.
What's in a thought that last only a moment?
A treasure like gold stored deep in one's mind.
What's in a dream that last only one night?
A fragment of slumber till dawns early light.
What's in a heart that beats so violets?
Ice cream and cake and bouquet of violets.
What's in a kiss? It makes one wonder.
It arouses one's sole like roaring thunder.
What's in a smile form some distant friend?
A time to remember, over and over again.
What's in a lifetime of one hundred years?
A treasure of love, laughter, and tears.
What's in a hug, from you for me?
Just think what it means and it's always free.

Charles H. Norman
Uvalde, TX

[Hometown] *Lubbock, TX* [Ed] *some college—chemistry* [Occ] *retired locksmith* [Hobbies] *stamp and coin collecting, writing books and poetry* [GA] *safely returning from Korea '50–'52*
*I am an ex-marine, Korean Chosen Reservoir Survivor, 1950–52, and am ninety years old. I have been writing since I was a senior in high school. I have written eight books and one book of poetry (300 poems). I got the inspiration to write this poem from Jerry Lewis, the actor who had the program on TV—*My Children. *He received a copy—I received a letter from him, and it is in my book of poetry.*

If Only

If only . . .
The sun always made you happy
Smiles came to sad faces
Love came to broken hearts
Food came to the hungry
The rainforests always have rain
All animals loved people
All people loved all people
Death was joyful not sad
Lush green would last forever
Blue skies and white clouds lasted all night
Ocean waves became calm and silent
All people were the same color
We could all be forgiven
All our loved ones could be returned to us
Money meant nothing
Tears never fell
Being young never went away
Hopes and dreams lasted forever
Forever meant forever
There was no sickness
The skies above would open
They would come
If only . . .

Noel Ciolino
Westhampton, NY

[Hometown] *Lindenhurst* [Ed] *BFA* [Occ] *artist, writer* [Hobbies] *walking* [GA] *love of family*
This inspiration for this poem came when I was listening to John Lennon's CD Imagine.

Miracle

Miracle gives
positive surprise.
Miracle helps
you rise.

Miracle is
considered wonderful.
Miracle always
follows rule.

Miracle fulfills
your desire.
Miracle is
always to admire.

Amar Mistry
Grand Terrace, CA

[Hometown] *Grand Terrace* [Occ] *computer science, mathematics* [Hobbies] *reading, volleyball, writing*
I write spiritual poetry that is inspiring and motivational. My poems give spiritual knowledge and help you become more efficient in dealing with life problems. The poems can be read three times as suggestion to have the quality indicated by the title.

Violets, Roses, and Orchids

The unassuming, profound beauty of a wild violet brings unexpected pleasure as you come upon it surrounded by a glistening grove of greenery. It speaks of God filling us with quiet beauty, grace, and strength in any situation. Like God, it never changes.

Although there are many colors of common roses and numerous types of hybrids, the fragrance is always the same. Thorns ever present as they grow can be removed when given as a gift. They speak of the body of Christ in diversity of Jesus spirited pathways and various levels of spiritual maturity, but all are a sweet smelling savor to God the Father.

The orchid is an exotic flower cultured in a controlled and restricted atmosphere. Within that atmosphere, it flourished as if in submissive acknowledgment that in so doing it will come to fruition as a delicately-robed, exquisite beauty worthy of royalty. It speaks of preparing ourselves in that we seek God's will in all we are to do for His glory, not ours. In this we put on our wedding garment, unwrinkled and spotless, awaiting the marriage ceremony.

Edith M. Funt
Gettysburg, PA

I'm eighty-four and usually write deeper and more controversial material, but this time it will still be spiritual-based but more uplifting.

Lost Love

I lost my love one fine afternoon
When she just bid me goodbye;
Now gloomy clouds hover over me,
I wish I could run off and die.

She took my love with her when she left,
She also left with my pride;
Once I was going to be her man
And she was to be my true bride.

But then she left with another man,
Never to return again;
My life no longer contains sunshine,
Only the dark clouds of the rain.

James W. Mayou
Mashpee, MA

I wrote this poem during one of my lowest times. I was going through a divorce of "irretrievable breakdown" from my first wife. This was before I met my second wife.

Happiness Is...

Some think happiness is a constant state of bliss;
However, contentment overcomes this!

If your life is fairly stable,
And your family's around the table,
There's nothing else in this world each day
That can chase the sadness or the blues away!

If you can deal with life's tragedies,
And that includes fatalities,
And you can keep your equilibrium,
Through all of this, and then some,

You've achieved the goal of life
Which is contentment in spite of strife!

Shirley Stevens
Merrill, WI

[Hometown] *Crandon, WI* [Ed] *one year of college* [Occ] *manager, medical van service, retired* [Hobbies] *collecting milk glass and recipe books* [GA] *my children*
I am a collector of milk glass and recipe books. I've hunted rummage sales and second-hand stores and am thrilled when I find a particularly pretty piece of milk glass. Also, my favorite recipe books are those compiled by churches or other organizations. People submit their best! I've had good times and bad. I've lost my husband and two sons, but my faith has carried me through. I was sitting in my sunroom one day when I realized I was content with my world. That's when I wrote this poem.

A Renewed Tomorrow

A never-ending psalm portrays itself
On a long winding road
Emptying it on a gulf of love and wisdom
To be reconciled among the hope of revival
Entering a plea of immense sorrow
On a rainbow of strength to begin
A testament for a renewed tomorrow

A blue bird captured into the fold of doubts
Answering the call of a mended wing
The trial of subversions for all to sing

It empties itself of happiness and submission
Challenging the song of a welcomed transition

Colleen S. Johnson
Salisbury, MD

Embrace the Darkness, Never the Monsters

Darkness, my first true friend, they have always been there for me since birth. Just as when I thought about making an end, they will remind me of my worth.
Girls wore skirts and dresses that doesn't want to play rough. Boys prefer playing with their guy friends and think we have cooties. I just did my own stuff and tried to be a cutie.
My body grew bigger, but I try to play as much as possible. Everyone didn't want to be with the cow. I wouldn't feel happy because it was impossible, and I didn't know how.
As the years go by, my clothing grew darker while my skin goes paler. I withdraw myself from others because I strongly believed that I should be the only one who suffers.
One year in high school helped me slowly realize something was wrong. People showed me a light within the darkness. What I saw was strong and dangerous.
They consumed me and began making my friendship unhealthy. Telling me that I am worthless, and I should obey them. The monsters love treating me as their precious little gem.
I needed to escape, but I will be leaving my dear friend. Is it too late or is it the end?
My head is in my arms as I sit on the ground crying. A gentle hand placed itself on my shoulder, causing me to look up. Our eyes stare at each other connecting and he pulls me up.
"Embrace the darkness, never the monsters," was all he said before taking my hand. He's going to help me recover and I finally found someone who understands.

Kat Madison
Anaheim, CA

When people think of darkness, they will mistake it for inner demons. Monsters will hide in darkness because it's quiet and peaceful. Everyone finds comfort in strange places. My comfort is within darkness because they never judged me for being me. I always knew I was different, even from my family. My soulmate taught me that phrase, "Embrace the darkness, never the monsters!"

Do Not Forget Us

A good many years ago
I left home and hearth,
and all I had ever known
to serve my country as a marine.
During my years of service
to the nation of my birth,
I served in various locales.
My departure from the US
is what I remember the most—
a year-long deployment to Okinawa.
I remember most vividly,
watching from an airplane window
as the coast of California
disappeared in the distance.
People were speaking in muted tones
or not at all—hushed, and sobered,
watching the lights of the cities
recede lost in darkness, and distance.
If you have ever been in uniform and served,
then you will understand.
To serve one's country in a foreign land,
separated by a vast ocean
and surrounded by strangers,
persons as different from you
as you are from them,
is a maturing experience.

Steven M. Lambert
Warsaw, IN

[Hometown] *Warsaw, IN* [Ed] *high school, trade school* [Occ] *armored truck driver* [Hobbies] *documentary devotee, reading history books, taking drives in the country* [GA] *published author; 20 years military service*

As a young man I served in the USMC. In the fall of 1978, I deployed to the island of Okinawa, south of mainland Japan. My year I spent over there was quite a learning experience. While there I went by naval vessel to Subic Bay, Philippines. I also underwent cold weather training in South Korea. I learned so much while over there. I believe everyone should travel, if possible. Military service is the best way!

The Circle

The circle is an entity
we try to comprehend; it
has no beginning or apparent
end.

The circle is part of a dimension
where a God we contend has no
beginning or apparent end.

Our minds are programmed to
comprehend that everything
has a beginning and apparent
end.

Religions thrive on the premise
that this God we contend is an
entity in the dimension and
one on which most of us depend.

Hold on to the circle, because
it is our contention that the
circle is the link to this next
dimension.

Howard H. Mackey Jr.
Edgewater, MD

[Hometown] *Edgewater, MD* [Ed] *bachelor of architecture* [Occ] *retired architect* [Hobbies] *writing poetry, fishing, Lladró collecting, (non-firing) gun collecting* [GA] *raising four successful children*
I was born in Washington, DC and married Anna Catharine Thompson, my childhood sweetheart. We raised four children, Howard III, Stanford, Karen, and Adrienne. I am a WWII veteran, having served in the United States, Belgium, France, and Germany from 1945–1947. I studied architecture at Howard University after my army service. I married while in college and graduated in 1953. After thirty-five years of marriage and the passing of my wife, I moved to Annapolis, MD. I retired and married Ernestine Mebane, who passed after nineteen years. I move to Edgewater, MD in 2001.

2020—A Moment to Remember

It's still a while I remember you and a transcendent time.
There are moments in life that one has never known that is sublime.
The memories that come to my mind of reciprocating soft kisses were fine.
The tender embrace and unique at the same time your manly passion.
You are a man stealthily discreet that I have to mention.

I have a fortune to enjoy your kisses in secret that became a victory.
Tall, light complexion, dark eyes, your ancestral Aztec and Taino gallantry.
When you smile, your aura reveals the unique human being in you.
One day I will show this poetry that I dedicated to the man in blue.
The best in me is to express the subliminal words to you.

Your name will never reveal, I will give my word.
When I see you on the streets caring to protect everyone, I feel proud of you.
Because you're a true hero, God cherishes the good people and you are, too.
There are moments in my life that I cherish and you are no exception.
I smile softly and say in my mind how fortunate it is a distinction.

Your parents gave you life, love, respect, and dedication.
You reflect and demonstrate the gentleman, I thank you.
I dedicate this poem to you with a soft discreet smile.
Life is breathing, break the rules, forgive, kiss slowly, laugh often,
be passionate, and never regret something that made you feel joyful.

Diana R. Gonzalez
Passaic, NJ

[Hometown] *Passaic, NJ* [GA] *learning to play the piano, community service, making homemade jewelry, reading and the inspiration in writing poetry.*
You could have goals in life, accomplished them, and never give up. Be humble, unique, different, and always put God first.

Silently

The silence of you
Is deafening…
I am going to send you
Some lonesome doves
To fly to you
Some butterflies to
Brighten your skies
An angel to
Carry my kisses to you
And to carry away my sorrow
Of being left behind
When you receive them
Let me know
That they made it over the rainbow
Come softly to me
In the stillness
And the loneliness
Of my nights….

Donna J. Shaver
Laurens, NY

[Hometown] *Laurens, NY* [Occ] *retired*
I dedicate this poem to John D. Robinson Phoenix Mills, Cooperstown, NY. We were teenagers in love for the first time, then we separated for sixty-two years. We were reunited once again in our love together for four and a half years. I lost John on July 4, 2021. We were our first love, last love, and our greatest love in this lifetime.

Twilight of the Common Dream

So it goes, and so it ever was,
And who's to say, and who knows
What will be, or when, or if
For that matter, ever. As once
A pessimistic poet of many years past
Was wont to pose lines like
"Don't bother me, I'm dying"—
As if she had any sense of what
She was saying or why she was saying it,
Other than being fed up with driving
Down the same old road, the reality being
We were all then, as most remain, merely
Bundles of bungling moods, either sharing
Or not, and mouthing what each knew
We all wished to be so in our leaning
Against the winds of change.

So, who's to say now what will be eventually,
Or not, in the face of so much and so many
Willing always to be less than they
Could have been had they not sacrificed
The small power they had over themselves
To the listless idols of time.

And so it is, most thrash and spin,
Like tops turned by hungry hands,
Yet running on empty in the absence
Of anyone willing to confront a stupid
Devotion to puerile righteousness that
Now infects and devours the mind—As those
Affect to despise what they cannot hope to find.

Gary F. Seifert
Falls Church, VA

[Hometown] *Upper NY* [Ed] *PhD philosophy* [Occ] *professor* [Hobbies] *writing, painting, drumming, cycling* [GA] *teaching philosophy in sign to the hearing impaired*

The Eternal Rose

The sculptor captured your crimson flame—
That triumphal moment in your career—
With every brilliant petal shown
Reaching upward and opened wide with cheer...
In startling suspended animation displaying,
With emotion and warmth aglow,
The glory of your longed-for and hard-earned success:
An example of nature's fabulous never-ending show.

Oh bloom, encased in a transparent plastic home,
Protecting your moment of beauty through the years,
A beauty reminiscent of our now forgotten youth
And its joys, its memories and its tears,
Your past life struggles are concealed completely...
And your future fate forever remains unknown.
Our senses are stimulated by your rosy present—
Unaware of the seed from which the bloom was sown—
And continually allow us to imagine,
Each time that scarlet bloom we see,
The rich aroma and the feather-like softness
Which, displayed in your plastic palace eternally,
Inspire us to dedicate ourselves to some unknown future
And, at the same time, challenge life with zest...
With a spirit which continues blooming
more and more each year
As we pursue the fulfillment of each and every quest.

Craig E. Burgess
Cherry Hill, NJ

[Hometown] *Audubon, NJ* [Ed] *master's degree in education* [Occ] *Spanish instructor* [Hobbies] *town and church historian, photography, travel, poetry* [GA] *civilian humanitarian award from Chapel of Four Chaplains A career Spanish instructor, I served as faculty advisor to an adopt-a-grandparent program at a local nursing home and advisor to an international language club: young students who received international recognition for a literary magazine,* Passport. *After retirement, I served as a liaison to the US Navy for twenty-five years from Audubon, NJ, home to three of the nation's Medal of Honor recipients and known as "The Most Patriotic Small Town in America." My poem was inspired by the work of a sculptor who carved a red rose in plastic.*

Let Not His Dream Be Forgotten

Let not His dream be forgotten... Let's give His dream new life!
For that mountain top still awaits us,
To stand united; to conquer; to engage in the ultimate dreams together.
to see the other side.

Let not His dream be forgotten... Let's give His dream new life!
Let not the wars and prejudice, nor our divided government,
disillusion us reach out, we will overcome, and reach many mountaintops.

Let not His dream be forgotten... Let's give His dream new life!
Non-violence was His challenge, economic equality was His concern,
doing God's will was His goal, passing the torch to us came from His soul,
so let our moral conscience be awakened.

Let not His dream be forgotten... Let's give His dream new life!

Judy A. Johnson
Indianapolis, IN

[Hometown] *Indiana* [Occ] *retired administrator* [Hobbies] *reading and writing poetry, crocheting prayer shawls for the sick and shut-in* [GA] *being able to enjoy my mother who is 101 and sharing life with my 33 grandkids and 33 great-grands*
I love reading and writing inspirational poetry in hope of helping others as they journey through life. As a child, reading poems assisted me through many areas and continues to do so today.

The Paddies

It is an early summer's eve, and the rice fields
have been flooded with cool, crisp waters.
Nightfall, lanterns swaying in the delicate breeze
while casting tiny rainbows through the dew
upon the grasses.
The sound of crickets and rain frogs' serenade
in the darkness as peaceful beauty descends
upon the planting of a new crop.
One by one the prepared seedlings are
pressed into the wet ground, mindful of
the space between as repetition has taught.
So many times, this ballet has been repeated,
each step perfectly balanced, for some,
no longer can they rise to greet the morning sun.
One hundred and twenty moons will pass
until harvest, as hours turn into days.
This graceful dance continues as hundreds of
fireflies bring the passing of another year's
tradition in the rice paddies.

Joann C. Martinez
Waco, TX

[Hometown] *Tachikawa AFB, Tokyo Japan* [Occ] *caregiver* [Hobbies] *fishing, tying flies, camping, cooking* [GA] *taking care of my mother*

The Eternal Moment

There is no time.
No past
No Present
No Future
There is only now, the eternal moment
Everything that has ever happened or will happen is occurring *now*!
In order to be fully alive and fully awake, you must live in the *now*.
There is no other reality.
Everything else is just smoke and mirrors.

Jane Matti
Moriches, NY

[Hometown] *Moriches, NY* [Ed] *master's in education* [Occ] *teacher, author, professional lecturer* [Hobbies] *ballroom dancing* [GA] *giving to perfect strangers and rescuing dogs who rescue you right back!*

Our Dog

He gives love to all
  love comes from his eyes
    from his voice
His touch is happiness
  for all to touch
To look his way is special
When we look his way
  we see love, joy, happiness
Each day has joy with
  with his presence
The only time of sadness is when
  he can't bring you feelings
    of joy, love, and special life
While we see him
  each moment
    each day
All we learn is love
  Our dog
    but look closely and
      reverse the word dog—what is life about?

Donald R. Taylor
Mesquite, TX

[Hometown] *Mesquite, TX* [Ed] *veteran, English teacher, writer* [Occ] *English teacher/retired* [Hobbies] *woodworking projects, writing* [GA] *veteran 27 years, teacher 38 years, married for 62 years—same beautiful woman, Shirley*
The poem "Our Dog" is a reflection and life with our special dog—Sparky T. King. Sparky T has left us—died November 21, 2021. He has returned to Heaven and we miss him with all our hearts. This poem is him and his love. I have written a children's series about the Adventures of King Sparky T. *"Our Dog" is a reflection of both our sweet dogs. As you read the poem and finish reading—reverse the letters of dog and you see another picture!*

A Sonnet for Romance

Many of Mozart's marriages were dreams,
Beethoven's, also. Make notes about that!
But likely, the two men never quantified
How our jaws build up and tear apart in the dead of night.

It simply is, as if life's ebb and flow or kisses differ,
Still barely at all from Hamlet's encounters.
The Danish Prince knew loyalty and love—loss, too—
And well before the Lord Chamberlain's daughter

Sorted his sonnets from among her treasures—
Only to give them all back! Oh, neither the strings
Of woe, nor leaps of faith can halt the flood of stories
By Time's great telling! So, each of us must be ready:

While wasted time chronicles desire and prefiguring,
The heart clocks the stopwatch of living and loving.

Jeffery Moser
Aurora, CO

[Hometown] *Aurora, CO* [Ed] *PhD/ABD in English literary studies* [Occ] *college, English faculty since 2011; lifelong democratic party activist* [Hobbies] *painting, drawing, stamp and coin collecting, family history, amateur entomology and geology* [GA] *served four years as deputy state treasurer for the state of South Dakota, 1995–1999*
In poetry we discover ourself, and we communicate our concerns. The poet shares themself with the reader and the page, and for all time. This poem is inspired by my interest in history, great occasions, and experiences. I am most interested in poetics, especially meter and form. The sonnet form has not been exhausted! Nor has love!

Love...Has Many Colors

My darling mother died when she was 45
A peaceful time till death arrived
We talked, laughed and cried...
She wrote a note: thanks, it is my life!

This is her life...
Her hair was long and flaming red
Her lips and nails, her body was perfect
Red roses filled her room...

A perfect secret no one knew
A business that she dearly loved...
Love...has many colors...
Red roses filled her room!

I could not do what she did well
I worked from 9 to 5 when I came home,
She was alive and beautiful,
Red roses filled her room...

Celebrating love...
They all came to sing the last song
Who am I to judge... after all...
it was her life...
Red roses filled her grave!

Helga F. Gross
Amargosa Vly, NV

Depression: Blizzards and Blue Sky

Emotional snowflakes swirling all around
Soul and spirit, snow globe bound

Pressure lifts, off lung and heart
Through prayer and thought, chains fall apart

Slowly rise from Hell's despair
Enough to know that friends do care

Try as they may, the veil never changes
Life's quirky gift, fate pre-arranges

Ours in not to reason why
But to know that through each blizzard there is blue sky

Lori Lassetter Robinson
Livermore, CA

[Hometown] *Livermore, CA* [Ed] *consulting/education and training* [Occ] *retired software consultant* [Hobbies] *archery, wood carving* [GA] *giving my kidney to my son—organ donor*
When emotions are high or low and the moment strikes, I am compelled to write.

Fleur

Have you met the poodle
with such flare?
She jumps and spins and dances
leaping high in the air.
Just as fast she changes directions
and looks at you boldly
with a serious stare.
On a walk one day this happy poodle
happened to run into a chocolate doodle
who instantly loved Fleur
the poodle.
Hours of friendship came from that meeting
along with the happy, hilarious greeting!

Linda Marie Coppola
Seminole, FL

[Hometown] *Seminole, FL* [Ed] *business and fitness* [Occ] *retired* [Hobbies] *poetry, yoga, senior fitness* [GA] *raising three beautiful daughters*
I wrote this poem as a tribute. This amazing creature touched my heart and has since passed away but will always be remembered.

God Cares for Mothers with Unborn Babies

Scared, pregnant, not knowing what to do,
God cares for you!
God's heart breaks for you,
Hearing your cries,
Loving you so much,
Giving you strength to get through!
No matter what has happened,
In your life,
You have forgiveness,
All because of Jesus' love!
God loves unborn babies, too,
Even before you were born,
God has special plans for all of you!
Healthy, sick, disabled,
Adopted, foster babies, too,
God is able to work through you,
Bringing joy to lives,
Touching many hearts,
Lighting up the room with love!
Your life may be
Long, hard, or very short,
Still people's lives
Will never be the same
All because you were in it!
God cares for you!

Angela Christine Michael
Mesa, AZ

[Hometown] *Mesa, AZ* [Ed] *high school, some correspondence courses* [Occ] *house keeping Christian care home* [Hobbies] *writing, reading, listening to music, arts, and crafts* [GA] *sharing God's love with others I have a learning disability. Still by God's grace I worked as an assistant childcare teacher mostly with infants and toddlers and two's and three's for fifteen years. I was also able to volunteer through a school program at a summer camp a couple years with special needs kids; they are all very dear to my heart!*

Before I Go

With lots of love
And gratitude in my heart
I want to thank you God for my sister Julieta
For all her love and support over the years.

When she was three years old and I was five
We lost our mother, and
Until we became moms ourselves
Mother's Day was the saddest day of our lives.

We were four sisters
Loved and took care of each other growing up
Since we lost the two elder ones at the age of 81.
My only living sister is my best friend and
sometimes mom.

She is now 85 and I am 87.
We remember traveling with our children,
Enjoying their sing-along all the way.
We all had good times together, and
Nowadays we enjoy playing cards.

I love my sister Julieta with all my heart.
Before I go I want to thank you God
For being so good to us.

Esthela Maria Egeler
Oak Park, CA

[Hometown] *Oak Park, CA* [Ed] *secretary/book keeper* [Occ] *banker/retired* [Hobbies] *gardening, crafts, playing bridge, painting by number* [GA] *my paintings by number and needle cross stitch*
I am an eighty-seven-year-old lady, living in Oak Park, CA. Since 1973, married to my husband, Walter, for fifty-eight years, mother of one son and two daughters with four grandchildren. My thanks to Eber & Wein for publishing my poems over the years. My favorite one I wrote is "God's Little Garden." My poem was inspired by my younger sister, Julieta.

Two Four-letter Verbs

Two four-letter verbs have the world at war,
The polarization of love and hate.
All humanity must demand rapport.

Hate. A foul emotion innate in evil's corps.
Rapacious mortals await fiery fates.
Two four-letter verbs have the world at war.

Love. Fealty. Ardency. Cherished ardor.
Such emotions to heal.....the earth awaits.
All humanity must demand rapport.

Hate guides the mind to evil's wretched core.
The color of hate is black.....light abates.
Two four-letter verbs have the world at war.

The color of love.....the rainbow's decor
Sunlight, the earth's disinfectant state.
All humanity must demand rapport.

Truth was esteemed in bygone days of yore.
Fiend despotics our laws drub and ablate.
Yes, two four-letter verbs have the world at war.
All humanity must demand rapport.

Jan Brock Hetherly
Scroggins, TX

[Hometown] *Mount Pleasant, TX* [Ed] *BA in fashion design/merchandising, Texas Christian University, Ft. Worth, TX* [Occ] *creator of WombBooks, children's audio, video, and hardcovers, writer, illustrator, and voice-overs* [Hobbies] *silk art, card games, life and friends* [GA] *awarded poet fellow by Noble House, London, England, 2006*
This poem is written in the form of a villanelle, introduced to Jean Passerat, a seventeenth-century French poet. Why do I continue writing villanelles? Because this form is short, playful, challenging and perfect for repetitive subjects, war, love, and echoing life's stories. Try writing your next poem in the villanelle form. Have fun!

The Long Road Back

The long road back
Is a weary road
When you have carried
A heavy load.
But don't lose sight of your utmost dream
Though now hopeless
It may seem.
God lights the way
And clears the path
Of such obstacles
As fear and worth.
You can trust His love
And heavenly grace
And lead you to
A tranquil place.
And when you find
Such peace of mind
Never wander to
That path behind.

Alma M. Gaines
New Rochelle, NY

[Hometown] *New York* [Occ] *hospital cafeteria supervisor* [Hobbies] *from a little girl, always writing and reading* [GA] *working with NAACP eastian stars corp Red Hat Society*

Lake Michigan, My Friend Again

How like the lake I am:
At times, numb, sleek and cold,
With frigid precision, so I've been told.
But wait until the spring melts my ice
And waves within my soul rise twice,
And fall and rise and fall and rise
To heights of passion,
Reaching to the skies.
Or if my gentle self begins to show,
I ripple rhythmically and softly catch
The breeze that blows.
Moved by winds to waves that shake,
I dream that I'm as mighty
As this noble lake!

Paulette Jean Davis
Janesville, WI

[Hometown] *Racine, WI* [Ed] *BS secondary education* [Occ] *retired teacher* [Hobbies] *poetry, song writing, yoga, puzzles* [GA] *inspirational grandmother*

Autumn

Falling of yellow leaves
Fluttering to the ground
Breeze gently tickling at your ears
Fresh crackling fire smoke dancing to your nose
Colder and crisp air crawling in every day
Making bearable and unbearable to be outside
Hot chocolate steaming from a cup
Melting marshmallows mixing in with cocoa
Goblins and ghouls asking for chocolate
Pumpkin pie with rich whipped cream
Faint Christmas music singing in the air
The holidays are upon us
Waiting for us to join

Jamie Fernandez
Victorville, CA

[Hometown] *Garden Grove, CA* [Ed] *MA in special ed (soon to be)* [Occ] *speech language pathologist asst.* [Hobbies] *reading, walking/hiking, crochet* [GA] *silver & gold award in Girl Scouts*
I attended Cal. State Fullerton with a major in communitive disorders. I work with children who have autism, Asperger's, stuttering, articulation, and cerebral palsy. I enjoy crocheting. My grandmother taught me when I was in grade school and I haven't stopped.

School

Study is a friend of mine with an urge to make me Smarter.
Controls my pen to write with a style that is Clever:
Handing me knowledge and self-pride. This Helps
One to exercise self-management. Every page of life Offers
Options, with many visions to create and paste ideas Online,
Letting the essence of words be inspiring to last a Lifetime.

Students are the voices of tomorrow's songs and Statements
Concerning the custom and culture of all Islands and Countries:
Harboring an AIM (Ambition In Mind) to be good and Honest,
Overstating actions from all to promote vacations in Orbit,
Obeying law and order to defeat evil and the corrupt Ones
Living with schemes and lies to support their Leaders.

School teachers are vital in educating Students:
Creating daily subjects to make us all savvy Competitors.
Hope (Has Outstanding Personal Expectations) to do Homework
Operating with assignments, complying with Obligations,
One day after another, to turn the light of success On
Life style jockeying to be winners with lessons Learned.

SCHOOL can also be interpreted in a sensible way:
School Children Have One Obligation: Learn.

Hugh Thorne
Hartsdale, NY

[Hometown] *Hartsdale, NY* [Ed] *communication analyst* [Occ] *retiree* [Hobbies] *soccer and bike riding* [GA] *two beautiful daughters*
I was born in Trinidad, WI. I dropped out of high school due to circumstances: I came from a poor family. I later served in the US Army as an MP. A few years ago, an idea came to me during meditation to write a new form of poetry known as ACROTRION. The extraction of letters from three words: Acrostic, poetry, and vision. I added form and fitness to highlight the sprinklings of aphorism, didacticism, and a touch of beauty to enhance a POEM with (Personal Observation Every Moment) and alphabetic vistas in acrotrion poetry.

Rhythm and Rain

the night was very dark and gray
the lightning flashed the light of day

the thunder echoed loud and clear
its presence drawing ever near

the raindrops fell enclosed in ice
and danced to a tempo that was nice

the grass, the flowers, the shrubs and trees
swayed gently in the musical breeze

the soothing melody of the falling rain
hypnotized the window panes

the rhythm, and the steady pouring of the rain,
muffled fears with a sweet refrain

Florace G. Hensley
Titusville, FL

[Hometown] *Titusville, FL* [Ed] *West Virginia and Florida* [Occ] *retired, 15 years Jess Parrish Hospital, 10 years in my own catering bus.* [Hobbies] *cake decorating, floral arrangements, photography, sewing, short stories and poetry* [GA] *caregiver for family members and friends, so thankful*

Shadows

Oh the shadows
Of the sun
What has the world
Now become?

And it seems, we're
Not talking, so our duo
Is now a group of one

As we see the anger
And feel the rage
These actions are getting
Violent, even though
We try to turn the page

Always searching for the answer
Some doubters say they're none
Now back again to the beginning
In the shadow of the sun

And yes, we're still wishing
For that miracle, to excite
Both the old and the young!

Willie Flud
Far Rockaway, NY

[Hometown] *Far Rockaway, NY* [Occ] *retired soldier* [Hobbies] *poetry, puzzles, and music* [GA] *serving my fellow veterans*
I am a retired OEF vet, who enjoys poetry as a way to reach people and hope one day to publish a volume of poems from the heart.

Who Are You?

You are there, you are here
What have I done to deserve such attention?
Who are you—everywhere I turn you are there?
Should I be afraid—for my life all the time - no?
But who are you—someone dark?
You come into my life and destroy things I have
That do not belong to you, but to me
Maybe someone is confused about their life
So, you involve me—why are you so mean?
You seem confused about your life to draw me into it
You lied to get yourself out of trouble
Who are you anyway?
This will not help you—
For there is a power stronger than all of this
Why put people through this
So, you can escape your bonds—
One day you will answer to the almighty
As it is written 'Vengeance is mine,' said the Lord.

Shirlene D. Williams
Las Vegas, NV

[Hometown] *Prior: California/Nevada* [Ed] *several degrees* [Occ] *retired management analyst/pharmacy tech* [Hobbies] *piano, art, going to estate sales* [GA] *living and having fun and succeeding in medical school Dedicated to my God and Jesus Christ, to my children—Darnel M. Mitchell, Tracy L. House, Karen S. Mitchell, and my best friend Rosalyn Hall-Jones.*

Look for the Light

Look for the light
my brothers and sisters.
Look for the light
and do not delay.
Look for the light
my brothers and sisters.
It will guide you when you pray.
Follow the light.
My brothers and sisters.
It will surely show you the way.
Follow the light
my brothers and sisters.
It will guide you when you pray.
Follow the Lord,
my brothers and sisters.
Jesus will never lead you astray.
Follow His light
my brothers and sisters.
Let Him shine for you each day.
Stay on His path
my brothers and sisters.
Follow His light.
You are not alone.
Stay on His path,
my brothers and sisters.
He will take you safely home.

Charlene Anderson Newell
Draper, UT

[Hometown] *Draper, UT* [Ed] BA *music education composer, teacher* [Occ] *vocal/piano teacher, mother of 12 children, 42 grandchildren and 6 great-grandchildren* [Hobbies] *write poetry, dancing in younger years* [GA] *family, life long goal achieved - music composer - staying optimistic through challenge, being married for 62 years to Robert R. Newell*
This poem was written in song form to match the melody.

One Nation

One country without a safety zone;
Bullets sprayed over the streets and
into homes.

Nowhere to run, nowhere to hide, nowhere
to find protection
from this vigilant epidemic insurrection.

Innocent people dying, circle chalk outlines
spense shells casing on sidewalks and
city streets;
law officers and first responders cannot
compete.

How can one nation come together and
begin to heal;
all these mixed emotions that one feel.

One country in a war zone, without
self defense or representation;
how can one control the guns that
now plague one nation.

John W. Johnson
West Berlin, NJ

[Hometown] *West Berlin, NJ* [Ed] *high school graduate* [Occ] *technician/retired* [Hobbies] *music, draw, write, gardening, landscape, decorating* [GA] *saving lives, military, helping people*
I am a senior. I worked several jobs; started at the bottom, promoted to a top position. I received an award by Camden Bureau of Police for rendering aid to an injured detective. I live a very quiet life, what I call my little oasis. It gives me great pleasure to know my writings and arts continue to inspire society as a whole. My poetry brings to life the world as we live.

Hounds Two-eth

The heart eye glimpsed similarity
Between my old grouch dog and the old grouch me

We latch onto the thing that moves
With focus that has spiraled grooves

Like hard locked lasers we watch 'til blink
That which makes our grouch hearts sink

His voice is stilled as he is poised
He'll lose his edge if he makes noise

And I speak not for much the same
But mostly since I cannot name

There is no word no thing to say
For what we see that's on its way

Some think we fear and tell us so

But true it's not
We simply know

Pamela Lynn Stiles
Baltimore, MD

Think of poems as paving stones as we lay a path toward peace. Each stone brings us closer to a world in which every living being is respected and valued. Keep writing. Keep laying stepping stones down with thought and care, and we will find peace. We will get there.

A Message in a Bottle

A message in a bottle cast
into the sea,
it will float upon the waves
for what seems like eternity.
Some day the bottle will land
on a distant shore,
and someone will find a message
from a long time before.
A message from a distant
past that is no more,
a bottle containing memories
long ago that open closed
doors.

Robert A. Calhoun
Philadelphia, PA

[Hometown] *Philadelphia, PA* [Ed] *high school/some college* [Occ] *municipal guard/retired* [Hobbies] *reading, writing poetry, art* [GA] *being published in poetry books*
I enjoy the creative process of writing poetry. My ideas come from many diverse sources. I just have to look around me at the natural world, human condition to find my inspiration for writing poetry. Poetry is a wonderful way to express your true feelings. And you find you're always seeing the world around you with new insights. My poetry inspired to new heights of awareness.

Doing Me

Can you believe this
  I am just doing me?
Symbolic lady with branches
  Who else could I be?
    Not anyone else but me.
      I am just doing me?
Twigs intersecting systems now amiss
  I am just doing me?
Feminine but not weak conducting business
  Who else could I be?
    Not anyone else but me.
Societal bias malaise void of justice
  Nemesis plaguing equality begging mercy
A feminist I am whose work is endless
  Who else could I be?
    Not anyone else but me.
Hate urinated on peace because hate is a disservice
  Relentlessly my stories will fight for true liberty
Protesting sweetly prejudice in America to be dismiss
  Who else could I be?
    Not anyone else but me.

Bozana Belokosa
Pasadena, CA

[Hometown] *Detroit, MI* [Occ] *writer* [GA] *being around gifted writers*

The Poet

Long before a written word
Many poets have been heard
Sublime were as they spoke
Taken in by people's hope

Words may ramble in their head
Must get out or die in bed
Phrasing thoughts may come hard
But it would please a budding bard

Many poets have passed aft away
Dylan Thomas, Longfellow to say
Frost, Whitman, and Sandburg some
Many more oft unknown will come

With words a many to have a say
Always hoping that then they stay
I must have struggled when young
Was old before I could sing my song

Long to lie upon mostly aging back
To look up at the stars in actual fact
The universe knows where it's from
What it needs, from where it comes

I will not linger on the spoken word
Others will want to oft be heard
Suffice to say important is the day
When The Poet has nothing else to say

R. Christopher Eng
Grand Marais, MN

[Hometown] *Hopkins, MN* [Ed] *teacher/psychologist* [Hobbies] *writing, models, stamp and coin collecting* [GA] *first poetry book*

My Precious Tom

When I met you I knew you were the "one"
We got along so well and had so much fun
I'll never forget you

You loved the Lord and treated me so well
We planned our life together and knew it would be swell

We were so in love and knew right from the start
We spent time together and gave each other our heart
I'll never forget you

We were blessed with two beautiful children
Then the joy of our lives four sweet grandchildren

Now you've gone to be with the Lord
I am so lonely, life seems to be a bore

I long for the day we'll never have to part
You will always have all my love and all my heart
I'll never forget you

Marshelle Carberry
Fresno, CA

Awe-west Texas

A storm is brewing
in the unpredictable desert skies of West Texas.
Drilling Rigs, pumping jacks, towers of light,
provide a backdrop to the hardworking way of life.
Jack rabbits, lizards, snakes, and cactus fill
the open prairies—exploding with mesquite trees
that abide side by side.
It is a place with and without expectation,
vast and indescribable, bound in a pure
atmosphere, the kind that clears the pesky
voice inside your head.
It is a place of human silence.
There, you can look beyond yourself,
for there is no-one else!

Alisha Beauchamp Boettger
Conroe, TX

[Hometown] *Midland, TX* [Ed] *community college business* [Occ] *human resource manager* [Hobbies] *writing poetry, crafts, women's ministries* [GA] *Having a great family that loves Jesus!*
I was born in West Texas and grew up with five sisters and one brother. My dad was a genuine cowboy/oilfield worker. He traveled around Texas and New Mexico judging rodeos, working on ranches, and in the oilfields. My mother was a waitress and bartender and a great short order cook. Growing up in the baron lands of West Texas gives a person a different perspective about life. Texans have a code all of their own—be friendly, do what you say, your good name says everything a person needs to know about you, lots of kidding around makes one tough, and if you dish out BS, you better be able to take it. I love America, I love being a Texan, I love Jesus and Jesus loves you!

My Magic Soup

Eight cups of chicken broth, two cups of dried peas. Two round onions, diced, if you please.
One large ham bone, one dash of salt.
    My soup is magic I stir it in the pot. My soup is magic I stir it in the pot.
My three little children patiently wait, as I stir the soup so hot.
    My soup is magic, I stir it in the pot.
    I stir a dash of love, I stir a dash of hope, I stir a dash of wisdom.
I stir a dash of spring. I stir a dash of summer. I stir a dash of winter and fall.
    My soup is magic as I stir it in the pot, and it tastes good, too!

Virginia Degner
Castro Valley, CA

I enjoy making soup. It was fun to see if I could write about soup. I live in Castro Valley, CA with my husband of sixty-two years, Duane. I am the mother of three children and the grandmother of four. I am full of wonder at the passage of years. So fast the years have gone. I am working on my tenth book. Contact me at Virginiadegner.com I would love to hear from you. I am eighty years old. P.S. The magic is that the recipe is in the poem. Tweak and add your own stamp to my soup.

Mind over Matter

I recently saw a specialist
who suggested I use a cane.
Instead I tried the holistic approach
now I'm walking without pain.
Don't buy that sad story—
we've got to get old and lose our health and dignity.
It's mind over matter.
We won't lose control.
We don't have to get weak and rickety.
If we start when we're young,
taking care of ourselves,
eating right, exercise, and plenty of rest
we can visit those folks in nursing homes
but not enter the place as a guest.

Lawanda Gray
Pineville, LA

[Hometown] *Pineville, LA* [Ed] *10th grade* [Occ] *homemaker 85 years old* [Hobbies] *art, painting on canvas and porcelain, writing songs and poems* [GA] *raising 5 children who gave me 10 grandchildren and 14 great-grandchildren*

Thank You, Mr. Marzetta

In 1960s, I sat in Mr. Marzetta's 5th grade class
At Lincoln School, on east side of Spring Valley.
As us students listened to Mr. Marzetta at blackboard,
While he was diligently teaching us long division,
As some of my classmates found math very easy,
But unfortunately, I found it quite difficult.
I asked questions; Mr. Marzetta patiently explained.
I listened—attentive, worked hard, very thankful.
Mr. Marzetta is a great teacher, person, friend.
As my friends and I remember all of his pep talks
On growing up as adults, right from wrong, hard work,
The world, good friends, keeping our word, and faith.
He also helped me out with math after school—at home.
My grades, attitude improved; I felt good with myself,
and Mr. Marzetta was my favorite teacher, who was,
Very serious, strict, yet caring, understanding,
Who always took the time to help his students out.
My classmates and I looked up to him with respect.
Besides math, he helped us out with many things.
I'll always cherish his great advice, sense of humor,
As he smiled from the blackboard behind his desk,
In his friendly 5th grade classroom many years ago.

William D. Irwin
Princeton, IL

[Hometown] *Spring Valley, IL* [Ed] *associates degree at Illinois Valley Community College, Oglesby, IL* [Occ] *restaurant worker* [Hobbies] *locally know published author (science fiction/fantasy) and poet (nature, spiritual/religious, childhood memories)* [GA] *served in the United States Navy in middle 70s over in Guam*
I also dedicate my poem to all my friends I've lost contact with (including Ruth, Pearl, Tom, Paul, Lynne, Geri, Brian, Landlord Bob, songwriter Wren, Dave, job coach Ralph, work partners Cathie, Chris, Vikki, Judy, Michelle, Grandma Goodrum, Owen, Jana, Kentuckian Shirley and family, Martha, Larry, John, Pastor Harper, all church and writing groups, school and navy friends, etc.) who enriched my life.

Prehistoric Dream

I dreamed I met a dinosaur who began to talk to me
I was surprised I could understand his speech arousing my curiosity
I climbed up on the back of this gigantic brontosaurus
and whispered in his ear we should share what we know about us
I asked him about Charles Darwin and evolutionists of the like
But he told me, they must think they're smart and ought to take a hike
He said to check the Bible and believe what God said;
I felt so embarrassed that my face just turned red
I said I thought he walked the earth 65 million years ago
but he said he was in the garden when God created people and when God ordered them to go
He said that couple really blew it when they disobeyed the Lord
Now with their foolish descendants on whom God's wrath is certain to be poured
He said his worst fear is bloodthirsty Tyrannosaurus Rex
While you modern dudes everywhere have violence, drugs, and perverted sex
Suddenly I felt a soggy, dripping tongue slob on over my face
Awakened to find my dog wagging his tail all over the place.

William H. Shuttleworth
Jacksonville, FL

In my younger years, I've enjoyed preaching the gospel in inner-city rescue missions, also playing on a church softball team many seasons after working my job at furniture restoration. In Florida, I became an exhibiting artist, enjoyed a couple cruises to exotic islands, plus a sacred tour of the Holyland. A poetry contest turned me into a poet, having authored a few titles of my own eventually. I've enjoyed seeing my poetry effort displayed in a beautiful anthology like this, along with the poetic work of many others. I've had my share of bumps in the road, but all in all, I've had a blessed life indeed!

What I Know for Sure

Life is fine at eighty-nine
With a lotta twists and turns
Walkin' through the rough times
Yet, many lessons to be learned
For sure.

I've kicked and screamed along the way
Wanting things to go my way
Trying every way to save
What I considered mine
My plans changed like the wind
From time to time to time.

I gave up absolutely
March 3rd of seventy-three
I never felt alone again
A miracle for me.

My life was on a roll for years
Through the smiles and the tears
My family's needs always, front in mind
I'm more grateful each given day
For the many choices made
From time...to time...to time.

Jo'Ann Boggs Cordova
Hesperia, CA

"Man plans," "God Laughs." These words are planted indelible in my mind. Peace of mind doesn't come easy. Born and raised in Kansas, moving to California (1955). Memories of yesterday are one of my greatest gifts, treasured in every way. Through all the twists and turns along the way, love of people, places, and things have got me up to present time. Truly understanding, "Yesterday is history, (for sure), tomorrow a mystery." Each day is a true gift, knowing without question, "This is not a dress rehearsal."

Look to See Him

Take a look in your eyes,
and look up at the sky, look to see
Him. And see in your eyes to see
His eyes of heaven.

  Look beyond the ocean, to see
the glory of God within the ocean.
See a smile within us, and see
God beyond the ocean.

  For we are here because of His
love. For we see things beyond the
ocean. We look to see Him
For we are God's children beyond the ocean.

Dianne Hill
Morris, IL

[Hometown] *Morris, IL* [Ed] *Naperville Central* [Occ] *Housewife* [Hobbies] *Writing, baking, reading* [GA] *Having my own books published*
Writing is a feeling of hope, love, joy and sadness all in one. Sometimes people forget that. The one true thing is love and loving everyone around us. Hearts, Dianne

A Prayer upon Reaching My Sixty-Fifth Birthday

Lord, in all I say or do,
May I ever walk with You.
Fix my heart on things above,
Guide me, fill me with Your love.
For I have naught that I can give,
Only by Your grace, I live.
Jesus, Savior, I adore,
Help me love You more and more.
You alone my All in all,
And when I stumble, when I fall,
You, my dearest Lord, are there,
Keeping me within Your care.
Forgive me when I go astray;
Surround me with Your love and grace.
MARANTHA! Jesus, come,
I'm filled with joy, to look to Home.
Your coming's near, Your coming's sure,
For even now, You're at the door!
My faith will change to blessed sight,
Fair Jesus, You my great delight!
And safe in You, my spirit blaze
To bring You worship, joy and praise!
These sixty-five years that You have given,
My prelude to my life in Heaven.
I thrill to bring You glory, Lord,
And be Your child forevermore.

Joyce Keedy
Towson, MD

[Hometown] *Towson, MD* [Ed] *BA in music (theory and composition)* [Occ] *church organist/choir director; music teacher* [Hobbies] *music, writing, drawing, painting, walking, history, geography* [GA] *trusting in Jesus Christ as my Lord and Savior*

This poem was written on my sixty-fifth birthday, July 23, 2022. I first trusted in Jesus as my Lord and Savior as a young child, and have had the joy of loving Him and serving Him throughout my life. Have taught over 900 children and adults to play musical instruments, been organist of one church twenty-nine years; organist/choir director of another church six years—and still counting! All to the glory of God! Jesus is my eternal joy; without Him, I am nothing. I delight to be His child forever, and joyfully anticipate His promised, soon return.

Raining

Rain and shine
is on my mind
it's raining, some
other time from
the behind, it's
scare my mind
it's raining, the
clouds are dark
I am pepair out
it's wet about
so quick, shout
the thunder loud
so keep it down
it's raining.

Beverly A. Foster
Pitcairn, PA

What More?

In the west wildfires burn
In the east flood waters churn
Temperatures worldwide rising
The human race slowly dying
Lakes and rivers running dry
Crops on the vine wither and die
Death, pestilence, disease...what more
Does our current future hold in store?
As our world spins out of control
What now will be the politicians' goals?
The time long gone to cover their rears
Bowing down to their collective peers
Time now our world to save
Before the last of us is in the grave
Race against race, nation against nation
Food shortages and runaway inflation...
We must together work in a race against time
To save humankind or commit the ultimate crime

B. J. McKee
Mint Hill, NC

Do You Remember 2nd Poem

This poem has no rhyme or reason,
but memories don't, do they? Hi Sis;
Do you remember the porcupine?
Do you remember the polly-wogs and tadpoles
at the pond? Or the tiny toads under
the street light? Do you remember
Auntie Ruth and her yellow twin sweater
set? Or Aunt Emma, waving from the
ambulance whisking her away?
(Never to return.) Do you remember Doc
Welch and his retired racehorse? Or
Albert Parks with his crippled foot
and wild ducks? Do you remember peg-leg Louie?
Or the new guy in town with his team and wagon
who let us ride along? Do you remember
our Swedish grandma only allowed us 1/2 a
potato or 1/2 slice of bread with dinner,
saying "that's all small girls need." Do you remember
two white mate swans that hissed at us and
scared us? Have you "some remembers"
for me? Love, Sis.

Constance A. Warren
Detroit, MI

[Hometown] *Detroit, MI* [Ed] *some college Wayne University* [Occ] *retired LPN* [Hobbies] *writing* [GA] *3 years served in USMC*
My sister, eighty-six, and I, eighty-nine, don't use the phone; we write letters with a theme "Do you remember?" It's a surprise how we saw the same thing so differently, or rarely exactly the same. Only of interest because she moved out of state.

Little Friend of Chaos in '44

Red thunder over US prey
Bomber from Hell missed a kitten today
Now through snowy night
Orange ball of fluff
Lonely little thing
Winter kitty
Seeking balls of yarn
Then mice
In bombed-out barn
"O you sweet thing," I said
Grabbing blanket
And milk instead
After little midnight snack
On floor I rub arching back
"Mew mew," he calls
As snow again begins to fall
Old sleepyhead
With blinking nod
Into basket
And I to bed
But not to sleep
The sky to watch
A special vengeance still to keep.

David M. Schmidt
Panama City, FL

[Hometown] *Oklahoma City, OK* [Ed] *BA Northwestern University—1961* [Occ] *retired* [Hobbies] *model car collecting, collages; intelligence research* [GA] *caregiving*

Go West!

You've heard it said, "Go west, young man, go west!"
Your spirit, soul, and body are in stress!
Go where the mighty buffalo roam,
Go far, far away from home,
Where the sunsets are the brilliance of God,
Where men found gold and wild beasts trod.
The Grand Canyon rules with its mighty wonder.
Give God the glory, kneel in prayer and ponder.
Glistening cold streams of water flow,
Fish to catch, the pace of life is slow.
The campfire snaps and cracks with glee,
The gift of morning, much more to see.
God's gift to you, life is the best,
You've heard it said, "Go west, young man, go west!"

Sylvia Weakley
Etlan, VA

[Hometown] *Etlan, VA* [Ed] *nursing assistant* [Occ] *caregiver for young and old* [Hobbies] *singing and gardening* [GA] *giving my heart to the Lord Jesus Christ*
I have had the blessing to be able to take care of my young baby grandson, Wes. His father, Jerdian Nickolson, has enjoyed going west of the USA, to hunt. I hope and pray Wes will grow strong in body and soul, in the Lord Jesus Christ, but are able to go west and enjoy hunting and fishing and be able to gleam from the nature of God! Genesis, chapter one—The Story of Creation.

The End

Sky pale white shadow
of blue patches swallow
gray hallow sliding through
everlasting days.

Clouds of mountain crystals
that hide sunlight that float
in a roomy mist of maze.

The beauty that goes on with
time in this world you will
never find.
The heaven is forever and
a day, chamber bittersweet love
will never fade away.
Tears of rain flowing from the
clouds, slumbering thunder the
round sound "it's very loud"!
Sounds that wake the dead with
winds of angels passing by, clouds
of sorrow, doves no longer fly.

The end of days for you and I
In God's hands to subside.

Patricia Ann Allen
Baltimore, MD

A beautiful mother who loves to write poetry.

Frenzied Romance

My Tara and I were playing like children, careless, joyful and sweet. They judged us both to be absolutely mad, and pulled us right off the street. My Tara is a wonderful person, an absolutely beautiful girl, though we're both withdrawn from reality, living in our own personal world. We are not like a couple of kids who must be watched constantly to keep us from behaving badly. Tara and I are both deeply, wildly, in love with each other. Crazily, even madly. We're totally oblivious to the attention of doctors and nurses, and during therapy sessions we don't listen that much. We listen only to each others voices, and looking dreamily in each other's eyes. And each other's faces we like to touch. Perhaps we're both irresponsible and quite immature, but we don't care, our romance will last. Our love will eternally endure. Restoring us to some degree of normalcy may be futile and quite vain, we're both happy being out of our minds, happy being quite insane.

Alan Knight
Champaign, IL

[Hometown] *Champaign, IL* [Ed] *high school* [Occ] *hospital kitchen worker* [Hobbies] *reading, poetry, watching trains, and old time movies.* [GA] *having a poem published overseas*
I think writing poetry is a wonderful way to express one's feelings and inner most thoughts in a personal way, without feeling embarrassed or ashamed. I am grateful for the privilege and opportunity to do just that. Thank you.

Break-Through

Day still in morns
Grey clouds
Waits for nights
Covering shadows,
Suddenly, light pierces
Through the heavens,
Filling my heart
With fog and blessings.

Jo Worthington
Lakeland, FL

[Hometown] *Baltimore, Maryland* [Ed] *Master of Divinity/Minister* [Occ] *Bread of Life Ministries*
[Hobbies] *Playing cards and games with family*
Dark and grey clouds with storms have filled each day, as I waited for my insurance to cover the damage in my house from a clog pipe. Joy in my heart left with the sunlight. I was placing my dishes on the shelf when suddenly light broke through the clouds. I began to laugh.
This poem came forth when God filled me with His joy.

Brittany

My great-granddaughter Brittany
Is sweet as can be;
She hoped to find a pen pal
And decided to pick me.

It made me very happy;
I thought, what would I say.
There's lots of years between us
And miles in all our ways.

I found out really quickly
That, that was what was fun
To see the difference in our thoughts
and all the things that we had done.

So, my origami creature
Is now in its new home.
While I read my latest letter
With Twinkle Toes, my little gnome.

So, keep the letters coming
And I will do the same;
It brings the family closer
In heart as well as name.

Freda Sigfridson
Roseburg, OR

Clickity-Clack

Clickity-Clack - Clickity-Clack
Don't look back don't look back
Look ahead, see what's there.
Look around so you can share.

The train is moving down the track.
Clickity-clack don't look back.
Your future lies ahead it's true.
So much to see. So much to do.

As you look ahead you'll see
God is there waiting for thee.
He's always watching, caring for you.
He guides your steps each day
Through and through.

Your life as a train is right on track.
Clickity-clack don't look back.
Just say a prayer to our Father above
And He will surround you
With His unfailing love.

Ruth Freeman
Pacheco, CA

[Hometown] *Pacheco, CA* [Ed] *bachelors degree* [Occ] *retired food service trainer* [Hobbies] *make little boxes out of plastic forms* [GA] *Louise Subblet Award 1994, training achievement*
My inspiration came from a train trip. Seeing God's beauty and trusting Him for safety.

Pup

She looks so beautiful, as she saunters past.
The air behind her emanates an ambrosial scent.
Her movement accentuated gracefully without intent,
never aware of the elegance she presents.

When comparing this beautiful sight,
what comes to mind is a butterfly as it ascends.
Her grace and flow, her lighted footed steps,
humble eyes her beauty she does not comprehend.

Dolores A. Kutzer
Kill Devil Hills, NC

[Hometown] *Outer Banks, NC* [Ed] *BS, MS, PharmD. Univ. of Pittsburgh* [Occ] *retired professor of pharmacology* [Hobbies] *painting, stained glass, mosaics, and writing* [GA] *to run marathons and sell my artwork*
I am a mom to one daughter and one dog, a wife, and a friend to many.

"2036"

Amidst the earth an unbridled followings arise
As on world leadership when evil is uncalled for
All for some in one corner one for some at one side
They lure both the bad and the innocents with disgust
Violence be their anticipation, good wishes are mine
Their proud heart and mind look glittered on their eyes
But all their labors are but destructive and vain
And by their hands and minds their hearts bleed
Darkness looms as it carries life no more
In the streets and at homes and at work on countdown
There's no God. It's only a title, not the Creator
Not a particle which the LHC at CERN is looking for:
Not the Rats, the predators or the conspirators.
Jesus is not a creator nor the beasts we have known
But Christ is above all names and everything.
Born in 3 BC, before Him and after are destroyers
Preying the people with abortion, beheading, injection,
Paralysis, crucifixion, war, nuclear, Second Amendment,
Drug addicts, illegal immigrants, re-ligion,
Gender bestiality whatever they can uprise in lands
And in seas to harm, kill and beyond for weapons and
Crucifix as symbols of death shall be erased
From the sign, the 666 and the beast
(When the West, Muhammad and China the Dragon)
Collide, the end of the world begins but I dare
The killings and Second Death shall be left behind.

Diomedes Despues Dalde
Brooklyn, NY

[Hometown] *Astoria and Brooklyn NY* [GA] *to save humanity from since we were unborn babies and beyond, the plants, domestic animals are yet to come*

Conversation with Dios, Jesus, and angel and the Great Lady in amazing visions inspired me to compose "2036." The first three happened in Tondo, Manila. The Great Lady said, "Two-thousand-thirty-six," when I asked her when will all she shared occur, happened a few years ago in apartment where I live. We only need plants and domestic animals to survive. We should end abortion to gender equality to fight climate change. If humans become extinct first who will tend the soil? Groups of humanity are dangerous for the survival of the fittest. Breathe Catholic. Church state unification.

Memories

Memories
of many years
past frozen
hold together
even with
a broken
windowpane.

Kathy Cullen Langen
Batavia, NY

[Hometown] *Hamburg, NY* [Ed] *BA in English from SUNY at Buffalo; associate's degree in commercial art from Genesee Community College* [Occ] *retired* [Hobbies] *sewing, reading, writing* [GA] *being employed at the Central Library of Rochester and Monroe County business and social sciences division for 14 years*
I was born in Buffalo, NY to Elanor and Matthew Cullen on August 2, 1946. I earned a degree in English from the State University of New York at Buffalo in 1969. I won a regents scholarship which allowed me to attend. Currently I live in Batavia, NY and am retired from the Central Library of Rochester and Monroe County business and social sciences division. I started writing poems in 1988.

My Marine

My son you joined the marines
you were just eighteen
you were just an average teen
who thought the world
owed you something special
so you left with a chip on your shoulder

From basic training you graduated
then to motor transport school
to emerge a truck driving marine
then home you came
while on leave you married
your high school sweetheart

But again duty called
and off to California you went
then across the sea of blue
to arrive at your base in Vietnam
now stationed in that war-torn land
I think a hard lesson you are learning

In just one short year
from boy to man you have grown
and from your shoulder the chip has fallen
so I pray that God in His mercy
will give you a future long
so you may reap the good
of the lessons you have learned

Evelyn Stonesifer
Lecanto, FL

I've just turned ninety-seven years old—a long life—and have seen a lot of good and bad. So far I've had a good life spent with family and friends. I thank God for giving me a good life.

Wordplay

Sometimes words jingle and jive,
making me feel glad to be alive.
Sometimes they dance all over the page,
other times storm out in a mighty rage.
Some words laugh, making me happy,
others ooze out awfully sappy.

Words love to play and sing a song,
no one can say their rhythmic beat's wrong,
for the pen, takin up whether day or night,
has the only power to determine what's right.
And if words desire to be stately and strong,
reflecting a time when right knew what was wrong,
so be it, I say, let the words march free
for they know how to behave in good company.

Sometimes words hurt, as they pull and twist apart,
you may even cry as they pierce your heart,
or words may join hands and skip on their way,
bringing out the child within who wants to play!
If you're lucky, you may read words so fine,
you understand how truth and beauty combine,
for the writer, the poet, can only reveal
what you, the reader, experience and feel.
If an author phrases ideas in words that sing true,
she shares her beliefs, her life's meaning with you.

Susanna Mason Defever
Anchorville, MI

[Hometown] *Manistee, MI* [Ed] *Manistee public schools: Washington Elementary, MHS Central Michigan University, Wayne State University* [Occ] *retired professor of English at St. Clair County Community College* [Hobbies] *traveling, reading, writing, collecting books and art, making scrapebooks of travels, attending concerts and plays, being a member of "SC4 Retirees," enjoying family, serving on the local library committee*
In childhood, nursery rhymes seemed to sing stories. This fascination led me into poetry so when the fifth-grade teacher introduced Robert Frost, I fell in love with "Two roads diverged in a yellow wood..." and have followed those paths through life, writing my first poem for her. Later Shakespeare expanded that love into a wider appreciation of language and imagination, but it was Thornton Wilder's question, "Do people ever realize life...?" that led me to become an English teacher, helping others discover the power and beauty of words. Retired, I indulge in poetry.

The Summer of 2022

Hearing the tremolo of three-toed tree frogs
Inhaling fragrant scents of lilies and apple blossoms
Imagining a fantasy of vacations, are all for
amusing frolics of the summer of 2022
Our eyes met and locked into place as nothing shifted
your gaze from that moment of wonderment. Slowly
step by step you approached pleading for me to not go
away, please stay. You, mewed, purred, hugged my sock
yearning to be patted. It is your way to say "feed me"
Who left you here, a cat with no claws? What can I do?
Be a friend, of course. You can defend yourself in the
summer of 2022. The summer of 2022 springs forth
beautiful audible music concerts featuring tambourines,
cymbals, flutes and strings, leaving cares behind to
enjoy spirited sounds carried on currents of fresh air
blue skies, Fourth of July observing needed freedom
in the USA. Freedom to enjoy what God has given us.
Calling the blessings of safety, love and protections
as we press on to the highest calling with help from
God, Jesus and Holy Spirit at all times. Peace and
reconciliations for giving thanks through summer of 2022.
Expect miracles like Tommy Tom Tom as he is called
making his way to survive, pushing to the not elusive
illusions striving relentlessly reaching the marvelous
age of one hundred twenty-two in the summer of 2022.
It is not too late to begin again in the summer of 2022.

Joan Mays
West Brooklyn, IL

[Hometown] *West Brooklyn, IL* [Ed] *art/agriculture/music* [Occ] *horticulture* [Hobbies] *songwriting, gospel music jams, writing stories, poetry* [GA] *a friendly family*

Summer of 2022 has great significance because my family is one of those that migrated to the USA over 100 years ago. It was the time when America was young and needed new people to work on education, publishing, sports, music, mining, and travel industries which keeps the USA sustaining and supporting itself for survival today. Refresh 2022 with the Pledge of Allegiance, reading the Ten Commandments, the Bill of Rights, and being acquainted with the Constitution.

For God My Heavenly Father So Loved Even Me

For God my Heavenly Father so loved even me
He sent His only begotten Son, Jesus Christ to
Die for me on Calvary's cross! Just so He could
Seek me and save me when I was totally lost
From all of my numerous and habitual sins!
Jesus Christ, willingly sacrificed Himself, in order
To set me free from death, hell and the grave
And now I can praise my Lord Jesus Christ all
Because I have been redeemed by the spotless
Life saving atoning blood of the Lamb of God!
Jesus Christ, died was buried and rose again
From His grave on third day in order to save
My soul and my spirit from the bondages
And the heavy chains of endless shame and
Everlasting miseries—He has liberated me!
Throughout all of my never-ending eternity
Because the Son of Man has set me finally
Free; now I am truly freeborn indeed! And
I am a beloved daughter of the Son of God
And I am a heir to His kingdom of eternal life!

Roxanne Lea Dubarry
Everett, WA

[Hometown] *Everett, WA* [Ed] *associate of general studies Everett Community College 2001* [Occ] *disabled/senior* [Hobbies] *watching primarily religious television, writing, reading the bible and other Christian literature* [GA] *being able to volunteer in my local community*
I am a self-taught Christian and inspirational poet and writer who has had poems published in numerous poetry anthologies including Eber & Wein and All Poetry. Also I am an internet poet and writer who is on various websites and have written on various topics including religion and politics. Currently I am an inactive member of Faith Lutheran Church. Along with my deceased mother, Eleanor May Dubarry, and a couple of friends, we published poetry booklets for former church bazaars to benefit non-profit organizations sponsored by Faith Lutheran Church. I live in an independent 55+ disabled/senior housing apartment complex. I am single, have never married nor have I had any children. I have sang in several church choirs in the past, and I worked in the church library of my former church, Calvary Baptist. I now reside in South Everett, Washington. I consider it to be both an honor and a privilege to be able to submit my poetry to Eber & Wein and to be part of their poetic community.

Timeless Passage

As being
    irrevocably slips
    towards nonbeing

Life's essence
        gently reassembles
        upon the Buddha's
        contemplative touch

Ron Matros
Mesilla, NM

Life—like surfing an irresolute wave.

Beneath That Tree

The owl stays perched high in the ancient tree,
Watching, listening while each century
Parades below: each carves its songs in stone
Each raises trumpets for the true: every
Songbird trills those same tunes precise in tone
To its own century. In every place
Through an age whirl the storms of auguries
And always there appears that leaden face,
Slyly leering with mad depravities:
Man is low-bent toward such proclivities
And strutting with force then consolidates
Power: never enough that satiates.

Beneath that tree still yelps our ignorance
While the ancient owl keeps its elegance.

Carmen Marie Ruestow
Boulder, CO

Luca

Little angel of the universe, you have surrounded my heart
With the most wonderful sentiment ever experienced ...
Be a Babushka! A Granny! Abu! Oma! Nona!
Or simply ... your Lorito!

Life meaning has too many interpretations,
but being my first grandson
is unique, is tenderness to the top.
Feels like I am in the Seventh Cloud!

When having you in my arms,
I can feel the peace that you give me.
The clock stops ...
and I just want to be close to you ...

I kept thinking now ... your smile, your sweet eyes,
when you are going to say your first words,
when you are going to show your first steps,
when you are going to call me Babu!

Oh! my sweet Luca,
you are so little now but I am already imagining
when you are going to get lost with Babushka!
To go places, to go shopping, to play hide and seek!

Love you my little angel,
Loving you with all my heart.
Loving you ... to the moon and back!

Lorena M. Conrad
Reynoldsburg, OH

[Hometown] *Reynoldsburg, OH* [Ed] *business administration, marketing, accounting, interpreter of 5 different languages* [Occ] *accountant, interpreter* [Hobbies] *poetry* [GA] *working with different communities because I am proficient in five different languages*

A Creator's Plan

Talk of the world life that's evolved,
Thought in the problems nature solved.
Life has become the making of a human thought,
The Maker started with the basics for one taught.
That being educated for a sight and place to train,
God made a life like Himself to create that to remain
He wasn't making something to just take and achieve,
The thought in 'His' plan was to grow and believe?
This thought from 'His' knowledge starts with US!
Maybe most or maybe less will see past whatever must?
That's a life with knowledge to create more without lust.
A sight to see growth for all life with purpose to evolve,
Each with a function and reason to work, and then solve.
No one life is here for its self to gain function on Earth.
What was made by God serves a purpose from birth.
Growth and function is in purpose for reason;
Solving God's function is for His pleasing.
Plans can change but destination will not.
Sight for eternity is of Him that's sought?
For the Makers' conclusion is of destiny,
Even sight in time is known by thee.
The function of life is of His will and plan,
For sights and reason are of demand.
For continuance!

Gerald Anthony Piche
West Chazy, NY

[Hometown] *West Chazy, NY* [Ed] *EJHS Essex Jct, Vermont* [Occ] *retired, drafting, builder* [Hobbies] *writing, auto work, nature* [GA] *writing my book*—Perception of the Imagination—Sight in the Window of Life, *2 books in 1*

I wish we the people took care of this beautiful earth; it's our home. Each country is like our room; parents teach the young to keep their rooms clean, so we the people should keep this earth clean. Nature lived here millions of years; humans are polluting it in a very short time just to please ourselves. 'God made us the caretakers.' Be responsible to life—help life live.

Spirit's Intuition

My optics aren't myopic,
more methodically exotic
on controversial topics.
My thoughts aren't microscopic.
My ears aren't inexorable;
they're exploratory, foraging
through forests for the oracle.
My fears are still deformable.

I try to ameliorate,
when others are ambivalent,
so when I deteriorate
I'll receive the equivalent.
See, if I experience pain,
how come I would give it then?
For an inferior gain,
or to feel some significance?

However, there are still those conditioned
to a coat of amaranth,
only seeking fruition
in issuing banishment.
Instead of soul nutrition
they gained riches in the inanimate,
so my Spirit's Intuition
hid me from intangible intransigence.

Josiah T. Gingras
North Oxford, MA

[Hometown] *North Oxford, MA* [Hobbies] *writing poetry, writing rap songs and short stories, drawing, and acting in plays, climbing trees, street poles, roofs or anything that can be climbed*
The day I can condense the omnium-gatherum of words, thoughts, and actions throughout all of space time into a single piece of literature is the day my writing prowess will prove to be axiomatic. Until then, I'll keep progressing and manifest my prosperous destiny. Even when troubled with adversities, I'll transform them to be my adventures; even when I'm lifeless, I'll shine an infinite light! My time on this earth may be ephemeral, but that only pushes me harder to make an impact that is eternal.

Architect of Angels

Divine shadow of darkness
graced by a heavenly glow
echo of the breath of
a loved one far away long ago

Passing fancies of pleasure
still precious as they may be
promise of treasures yet to be

All cut from the same cloth
pattern is well-designed
circles triangles or squares
we're all one of a kind

Only as free as the cloth
free to be cut again
when we all become one
God will adorn Himself
with us
as we adorn ourselves
with Him

Roy A. Smith
West Columbia, SC

[Ed] *high school, United States Navy* [Occ] *food service* [Hobbies] *reading, writing movies* [GA] *retire life achievement award*
Roy Acuff Wabash Cannonball country music fan. I learned about life in the navy. Tie that marital knot drop anchor. Learned a lot in the movies. Here's looking at you kid. R & B music Earth, Wind and Fire. Dave Brubeck Take 5, Dr. Zhivago, KYU Sakamoto Sukiyaki

My Lord

Thank You, Jesus, for loving me
Thank You, Lord, for Calvary

I praise You Jesus, lift Your name on high
It is Your name Lord that I cry, Jesus!

Thank You, Jesus, ever true
Thank You, Lord, for all You do.

Thank You, Jesus, for loving me
Thank You, Lord, for eternity

Oh! Mighty Jesus, worshipful king
Thank You, Lord, for everything!

I praise You Jesus, Holy Spirit, too
Bless me and keep my heart true.

Thank You, Jesus, for loving me
Thank You, Lord, for Calvary

I worship You Jesus, Your praises to sing
Forever and always Christ my king!

Shelley R. Bendele
Somerset, TX

[Hometown] *Somerset, TX* [Ed] *Somerset High School* [Occ] *secretary* [Hobbies] *reading, writing, bird watching* [GA] *accepting Jesus as my Savior*
I just wanted to give God the praise and honor He is so worthy of. I shudder to think what He brought me from and where He has led me. He is everything. My poem was inspired by my awesome God, Jesus!

Beautiful Abundance

Thank you, Dear Creator God, for the beauty bestowed
upon Planet Earth with all of nature's embellishments
displayed in such a grand array with lakes and seas,
across the star-filled skies and plenteous land,
the beauty of trees with birds nestled in their boughs
to sing their songs and greet each day in peace
and purpose in Your plan, without the ills of man.

Thank you for the mountains grand
and for the floating clouds that bring the rain
to bless the waiting, thirsty land;
for wildlife that lives within the forests deep,
in the meadows, in the seas, and on the sand.
Thank you for the open fields
that yield the crops to care for all,
thank you for the grandeur of the waterfalls.

Thank you for the love that still abides
within our hearts, within our homes,
within the hands of those who serve.
Bless this world with Your great love
and bring us acumen to share and learn
that all we need is here at hand
to live in peace in this great land.

God bless America.

Vesper L. McDonald
Omaha, NE

[Hometown] *Omaha* [Ed] *Bachelor of Art, Master of Business Administration* [Occ] *retired* [Hobbies] *writing, crocheting, rescued pets, gardening* [GA] *writing: diary of over 400 poems & book re solo business trip to Nigeria, West Africa*

A full life with a soul-mate husband and four children, combined with an extensive business career to help care for and educate them, while completing my educational degrees along the way has provided many experiences and learning situations. It has taught me to look for and see the many little miracles that happen daily in all our lives—and which continue into retirement. My diary, written in classical-style poetry, chronicles the lessons of my lifetime and constitutes my legacy.

FRB Chief Jerome Powell

It began with people complaining about high prices.
Such as, high gas, food, and drug prices.
President was blamed for his $1.9 trillion stimulus.
Was our high inflation due to Russian-Ukraine war?
COVID-19, labor shortages, congestion at our ports?
So FRB Chief Powell raised interest 75 basis points!
America, let us pray for a healthy economy!
Let us work together!
Whites, blacks, Asians, and Hispanics!
Think positive. Be Patient. Share!
Please support America!

Tulane Emiko Ebisu
Honolulu, HI

[Hometown] *Honolulu, HI* [Ed] *BBA business economics & statistics, University of Hawaii* [Occ] *retired* [Hobbies] *playing on my keyboard 1-2 times a week* [GA] *mathematical ability, trends, love for music and poetry*
I have always loved writing poetry. You see, I have played the piano since age twelve. There are musical waves in my thinking and writing. I enjoy all kinds: patriotic, rock and roll, Christmas, Hawaiian, religious, and popular.

His Gift to All of Us

The world is such a sad, sad place
It is hard to find real peace
Unless we look deep inside ourselves
And ask God to help us see
The path He has chosen for us
To help find the peace we seek
If we only open our hearts to reveal
That faith and love are all around
And goodness can prevail
With His help it's easy
Now we are able to see!
So let those feeling flow freely
Once we accept the person
That God has meant us to be
We can endure what the future brings

Judy Ann Hyland
Surprise, AZ

[Hometown] *Chicago, IL* [Ed] *associate's degree in business* [Occ] *retired* [Hobbies] *poetry, painting, crocheting, writing stories* [GA] *Besides being a mom, I wrote a children's book that was special to me. I love writing poetry and painting. The best job I ever held besides being a mom was working with special needs children. Arizona is my home now and I really love living here.*

I Know You

I know you, I know you,
I know you, I do!
You look so familiar
Like someone I knew

A long time ago
In a far distant past.
My memory now fails me
It's not very fast.

A spark or a glimmer
A song or dance
Will bring back your name.
It's a matter of chance.

Maureen McLaughlin
Houlton, ME

[Hometown] *Houlton, ME* [Ed] *high school, 3 years college* [Occ] *domestic engineer, grandmother* [Hobbies] *designing, crafts, poetry, and writing* [GA] *my children and family*
Poetry, like music, has a rhythm. When I write poetry, I get a subject and then choose words that form a rhythm. And sometimes the poem turns into a song.

Oh Turn

Oh turn, love, oh turn me on.
Oh love, love, on every lip! Tell me a story,
give me a show of lust and glory.
Give me spring and the spring bird's song,
Take me to the heights, and the depths,
Lower me and raise me, shudder and break me,
make me believe love can truly be!
Tell me you adore me, but don't bore me,
I can't take rejections. As Emily said, one can't
fake an orgasm! Cage a burning, yearning!
Oh turn, love, day into night—be a phantom of delight,
and turn low that light—love can see into the night.
Make it last, make it quick, love, or slow,
All night long as your spell binds us tight, we glow.
Oh turn, love, that TV on, find that channel bright
Where all things turn out right.
Oh love, be coy or rough, sulky, or tough,
On the screen or off, shot from real life,
Give your fans, love laughs, tears, and spills,
Saying love, love where have you been?
Oh turn, love, oh turn me on!
Spin me like a top! Give me sighs and moans;
make him tall and handsome, her slim and beautiful.
Love, passions, always burning into the night!
Send me to the moon, give bliss and eternal delight!
A soap never ending, oh love, love, turn me on! Everlasting!

Lonnie Bailey
Pineville, WV

[Hometown] *Pineville, WV* [Ed] *Regents BA degree/poetry* [Occ] *writing* [Hobbies] *running/walking competitions: 143 awards to-date* [GA] *22 published books, poetry in 133 anthologies, army veteran*

Three Days and Three Nights!

God has used many individuals as prophets over the years; however, these persons are still subject to their own will, to choose their own path. When one sorrowfully believed that God was not fair and chose to buy a one-way ticket in the opposite direction to the one that God directed, he found himself in the middle of a gigantic bath! When Jonah was tossed overboard to save the ship from being destroyed he found himself in the belly of a great fish! There was no greater misery or torment than this, that he had ever found! He prayed and promised, lamented and then he got his wish!

He got up, brushed himself off, and hurried in the right direction afraid that God might change His mind! He spent long hours up one street and down another, warning the people of that wicked city! The news reached the king of Ninevah and then spread throughout. They knew they were doomed if they didn't repent! The entire populace got down on their knees, king and all received God's pity! This should have been great news, and was the Lord's intent! No, Jonah ranted and raved with selfish pride. Instead of relying on His Lord he relied on a gourd! The inconsistencies of a carnal mind, so soon he forgot the crazy three days and nights!

Royce W. Sappenfield
Ceres, CA

[Hometown] *Stockton, CA* [Ed] BA *teaching credential* [Occ] *elementary school teacher 32 years* [Hobbies] *body building, bowling, senior softball* [GA] *baptism 1971, donated 33 gals—6 pints of blood since 1955 and therefore have saved 798 lives*
Prophecy has been used by God to all and sundry to prove his word! "I tell you what's going to happen before it happens so that you will see, and believe, and know that I am God!" Prophets and prophetesses appeared throughout biblical ages and beyond. While there are many professing seers and on the surface seem real there are unequivocal characteristics that regulate the truth of the statements and therefore cause them to be valid! A prophet has to be 100% accurate. God is immutable so He never makes mistakes! A prophet will never contradict the bible! Amen!

Silent Sentinels

We walk among you
we rarely speak, unless asked
you rarely ask, we accept it

we took an oath to defend you
hidden scars speak to our devotion
under one flag we go forward

only our mothers know the agony of our death
we know the ecstasy of survival and life
we are your sons and daughters

we are the veterans of America
we walk proudly among you
in war and peace, we are the silent sentinels

David Richard Huff
Auburndale, FL

[Hometown] *Auburndale* [Ed] *AA degree in math, BS AE degree in aeronautics, teacher's certificate in foreign education* [Occ] *retired intelligence analyst, United States Navy* [Hobbies] *photography, growing organic food* [GA] *publishing of my second book,* Farpoint Mindstation II
I am a fourth generation Florida native. I served in the US Air Force from 1970 to 1975. I have traveled to forty-two countries and twenty-five states and most recently a river cruise through the Rhine River valley.

Desperate Situations

It's very hard to believe all the changes that have come about
so suddenly for me and my family.
Two weeks of continuous prayer night and day, about
situations I thought were almost hopeless.
I was in this sad state of mind about a year ago and no one to
help me.
I'll never forget September last year because not much was
going right for me and I was speechless.
I continued praying for me and my family because I lost my job
and had so many bills to pay. And I was several months behind
on my mortgage.
I was beginning to give up on life, on my family, on myself,
then suddenly the Lord brought me a wonderful blessing.
Until this time I had no success in finding a job, soon could be
out the door with all of our luggage.
Out the clear blue sky, I received a call for refinancing.
My two weeks of prayer had not ended, but already new doors
were being opened for me and my family.
There was more good news and more to come.
I got through with the refinance for my house and we
celebrated with so much company.
I got a job with a promotion shortly after. Everyone was
excited, and there was peace once again in my happy home.
Everything was solved, back to normal, and my "desperate
situation" was now long gone.

Dalston Harrison Jr.
Brooklyn, NY

[Hometown] *Brooklyn, NY* [Ed] *high school* [Occ] *licensed lead 1 security supervisor* [Hobbies] *writing, sports, music, photography, writing poetry* [GA] *four published books, licensed security officer, public notary*
I am an accomplished poet, author, editor who has been writing all my life and I excelled at it in high school at Tilden High School in Flatbush and that inspired me to write my first published book called Collection of Poetry *published by Dorrance Publishing. I also have sixteen other compilations with other poets. I am currently working on three new projects which I plan to publish by the end of this year. My family is my true motivation as I continue to write my inspirational words of poetry which I share with others constantly. I am thankful to God for all of my above accomplishments and I am also working on a gospel book called* Spiritual Reflections!

A Mother's Gift

A mother's pride pearl jewelry
        shine and glow of embellishing
display to see
on the wearing neck
to bring in a radiant look
        from a hand custom made
passing on from generation
        with a priceless and valuable possession
As a sovereign gift
for a special occasion
        on a wedding day
As a symbol sign of love
        Far beyond my description
that is filled with gracious kindness
        with the share of bonding
of a witnessing motherhood
        as a reminder
for one to carry on the legacy
        from the family tradition
to leave with a cherish
        of a lasting memory

Hanh N. Chau
San Jose, CA

God's Unique Rose Garden

I believe there's a unique rose garden
Where a sturdy rose bush grows,
Among the twigs and branches,
There sits a beautiful rose.
Though the stocks are strong and
Thorn-less, the stems are never bare;
Here grows a large enchanting rose,
Her beauty so elegantly rare.
Standing out among the others,
Her uniqueness is heavenly fine,
A rainbow of many colors,
Throughout her petals are entwined.
In God's unique rose garden,
The rose will never wilt away.
Her blossoms will bloom again and again
And the rose will never fade.
In God's unique rose garden,
It's a wondrous sight to behold
To see the birth of eternal growth
Where the rose will forever grow.

Judy Ann Campbell
Escalon, CA

[Hometown] *Escalon, CA* [Ed] *AA in psychology* [Occ] *perametic, chiropractic philosophy asst.* [Hobbies] *writing poetry, reading, sewing, gardening, biking, teaching autistic children* [GA] *getting my first poem published*

I am a writer by heart and soul. I read, grow dahlias, enjoy arts and crafts, sew, cook, write poetry and stories. I am retired and enjoy my husband and grandchildren as much as I can. I live in the central California valley surrounded by dairies, almonds, walnuts, and just about any fruit or vegetables you could wish for. I was inspired to write this poem while I was sitting on my patio looking at my flowers and wondering about God's flowers in Heaven.

Where I'm at Is Not Where I'm Going

Numb
Confused
Despair
Misunderstood
Withdrawn
Are emotions that I wear
Torn between F*ck this job and let me do
a great job, so I can have upward mobility
but management doesn't care
My soul screams, "Time's up"
Put in two weeks and go elsewhere
Simply trying to get by, no such thing as
"me time" or "self-care"
Being a mom 24/7; 365 consumes my time
Lost identity
waking up each day confused
telling myself as long as I stay true to myself
contentment is what I'll find
because wherever life take me
I know, that I'll be fine
Reminded daily that God is paving a better way for me,
so, why hurry?
When God's making room for longevity
and not temporary sustainability

Jessica M. Charest
Worcester, MA

[Hometown] *Worcester, MA* [Ed] *associate's degree in criminal justice in science; currently earning my master's in criminal justice with a minor in psychology* [Occ] *residential counselor*
My poems about being in the process of overcoming postpartum; while being stuck for a while unhappy in a vicious cycle called life. To finally taking the necessary baby steps to making progress in feeling like myself again.

America the Beautiful

We live and work in America
We design and build in America
The land of the free
Don't seem like that anymore
Politics are intermingled with privacy
Economy is rising more and more
A search for the basics is to implore
The constitution was meant to guide
But it gets twisted and turned out of sight.
America welcomes the immigrants
For work, trade and relations
Each home has its family culture
But in public adapt to local customs.
It will all work just fine
If we all join together in time.

Margarete Lisa Flatebo
Ophir, OR

[Hometown] *Ophir, OR* [Occ] *retired* [Hobbies] *painting, golf, travel, writing* [GA] *immigrating to the USA*
Born in Eastern Germany, now Poland. Father was an artist, mother owned a grocery store. Poetry was in school curriculum, an imaginative literature in verse, a form of art, versatile to many artistic ventures. Composers translate poetry into music, painters into great masterpieces. I studied in England and France, took a hotelier's course in Berlin. As a stewardess for Pan Am I was inspired to immigrate to the USA. Writing and reading poetry is like taking a rest from daily activities—a spiritual relaxation. I oil paint in the 'old masters' style and hope to finish my memoirs one day.

Lyndon B. Johnson—Political Genius and Political Animal

Lyndon Johnson was a mover and shaker
who had more moves than the LA Lakers.
His legislative magic produced civil rights,
yes the black community loved his fight.
When it came to wheeling and dealing
that is when LBJ was most appealing.
Lyndon, the congressional miracle worker
but as president he was no shirker.
LBJ knew all the political tricks;
his enemies knew that they were licked.
Shakespeare would have admired LBJ,
just as Othello, Macbeth from his plays.
Lyndon was a king maker and power broker.
And, so I must end my story
of a master politician and all his glory.

Larry Calhoun
Capitol Heights, MD

[Hometown] *Capitol Heights, MD* [Hobbies] *crossword puzzles, reading about politics and journalism* [GA] *solving crossword puzzles for money*

Bumblebees

In spring, when my Linden tree flowers,
they cover the delicate clusters of blooms
like a blanket—fat, one-inch-long critters
of buzzing intensity, hanging it seems
from virtually every source of nectar
and draining its microscopic sweetness
before hum-buzzing on to the next cluster.
As a boy, those big black buggers
terrified me. They still do, raising
the hackles on back of my neck.
Hornets do, too, having been stung
rapid-fire as a young'un by a squadron
of enraged inhabitants of a nest
I was foolishly bombarding with rocks.
But back to the bumblebees—
or rather, for a moment, the honeybees.
Whatever happened to those kindly critters
you'd kick up from clover blossoms
when racing across fields as a kid?
They're outnumbered at least ten-to-one
by big bumblebees on my Linden tree!
Are weed killers decimating the clover?
Or is it simply that, in today's world,
the bigger and stronger must always win out?
I hope not, because I still dislike bumblebees.
And hornets.

Joseph Henry Kempf
Indianapolis, IN

[Hometown] *Indianapolis, IN* [Ed] *MA in creative writing* [Occ] *retired* [Hobbies] *coin collecting, fishing* [GA] *5 children and 13 grandchildren*
Eighty-one years old and still kicking and still writing! But no great-grandkids yet! Drat!

The Roller Coaster Ride of Life

My life was a life of uncertainties
tears covered my eyes. So many struggles
so many fears. Life has its ups and downs
like a roller coaster. I fall. I rise. The lows,
the highs, round and round I go.
I can't breathe scared so I scream
slow down stop. I want off this roller coaster
ride of life. I thought life was a thrill and
a fun ride. But I am caught up in this
spin of life. My mind like the ocean roaring
to and fro but where can I go?
The track of life is uncertain.
We have our highs in the mountaintop
then we have our quick drop in the
valley,
Ride has stopped lights are out.
It's daylight the start of a new day.
Lord let the worries of the day fade away.
Lord take my heart and give it ease
would you please. Life isn't easy
but I will rise if you hold my hand
and take this ride of life with me.
Now at peace start the ride let's fly
high and soar like the eagle, my Lord and I.

Margo Pennella
Jackson, NJ

[Hometown] *Jackson, NJ* [Ed] *college* [Occ] *chef* [Hobbies] *shooting pool, volleyball* [GA] *received humanitarian award working in mission feeding the poor*
I wrote this poem because all of us in the world are going through something and I want to encourage everyone; we can rise above everything with God's help.

In the Land Where the Bears and Tigers Sleep

(In loving memory of Andrew Thomas Koronkiewicz)

In the land where the bears and tigers sleep
Rests the man whom I had once called brother,
And he climbed over his mountains so steep.

We snuck under the warm blankets so deep
To hear bedtime stories from our mother
In the land where the bears and tigers sleep.

The boy grew into a man with a leap—
He knew there were new grounds to discover,
And he climbed over his mountains so steep.

The profits of his labors he did reap,
To support his significant other,
In the land where the bears and tigers sleep.

In his life, changes continued to sweep,
Facing one challenge after another,
And he climbed over his mountains so steep.

The pains of life have taught us all to weep,
But from worldly wounds he will recover,
In the land where the bears and tigers sleep,
And he climbed over his mountains so steep.

Thomas Koron
DeKalb, IL

[Hometown] *DeKalb, IL* [Ed] *AA, BA, MM, DMA* [Occ] *writer* [Hobbies] *poetry, music, movies, literature, and history* [GA] *my daughter Rayana*

I have always had a strong passion for poetry. I believe that it is more than just words on a page, and it ultimately has the power to change our lives. I am particularly fond of the works of Edgar Allan Poe, William Shakespeare, John Keats, Robert Browning, Christina Rossetti, William Wordsworth, Samuel Taylor Coleridge, Percy Bysshe Shelley, and Lord Byron. All of their poetry is powerfully written in their own unique voices. Reading their work has definitely had a profound impact on me as a writer. My favorite poetic forms include the sonnet, the villanelle, and the dramatic monologue.

women's bane

an open grave prays
to headless angels
and cradles dead birds

a bright will o' wisp
sweeps me up and takes
my breath with a kiss

a mattress bleeds rust
like a fence that hugs
my neck with black barbs

a body made of
china draws patterns
and calls them tattoos

an "X" on the tree
and the woodsman kills
what looks up at him

a wire pulls my guts
through me like a wet
bag of groceries

in the cracks each time,
a purple flower

Juno von Palko
Clarksville, TN

[Hometown] *Clarksville, TN* [Ed] *College Graduate* [Occ] *Writer* [Hobbies] *Writing, reading, surfing the web* [GA] *Winning 4th in the SEJC*
My poem is inspired by The Path. It's a video game about six different Little Red Riding Hoods facing their wolves. Ultimately, it's a story about accepting trauma. One of the most traumatic things a woman must accept is the ugliness of femininity and all of its implications. But in every aspect of it, there still lies flowers.

A Life

At birth, I did not know my father or mother
I started out very small
Being knitted together by my heavenly Father—
He gave me a family, too! I became the sister number three
God had so many plans for me
Since my father passed away when I was four
I don't remember him at all
Memories of family are special
My close bond to my middle sister shaped my life in many ways
We learned to trust in Jesus! Then my sister moved away
I started college for a nursing degree there were many busy days
Waiting tables to pay my way—expenses
A marriage, and a new home—many changes
Several homes, several states
Combining a nursing career and a family
Five children make lots of memories
My fifty-one years of nursing was ended
On the way to work—A head on collision
Then a skull fracture, broken neck, and concussion!
God brought me through, but lots of decisions!
Now the children are especially dear
Despite living alone, some are near
Cancer likes to poke a nasty head but God tells me not to fear
And it too will be an old memory
So now: A quilting hobby brings me cheer
And it's been eighty six-years since
God brought me here!

Martha Kephart
Albuquerque, NM

[Hometown] *Albuquerque, NM* [Ed] *BS nursing* [Occ] *registered nurse* [Hobbies] *fishing, sewing, doll collection, planning quilts to sew, being Grandma* [GA] *several, but 1989 I was special duty nurse to NM governor* *

I have always liked to write poetry in my spare time. I love to draw but now that has turned into creating quilt tops for sixteen grandchildren and seventeen great-grandchildren. My poem is kind of a picture of my life. God has allowed me to also experience some of the problems my patients had!

Don't Blame Your Children?

Don't blame your children, when they're found
Drinking, gambling, and running around.
If I was the kind to bring you to shame,
Is it the children or parents to blame?
Where's your children—your pride and joy?
Where is your son and daughter?

We read in the papers here and there of
Killing, stealing, and man crying everywhere.
How we sound, when we know it's a trend.
This younger generation—where will it end?
But can we be sure with self alone?

Too much money to spend, and too much idol time.
Too many movies, passion, and crimes.
Too many books not fit to read.
Too many parents running the streets.
Too much evil, and too many children
Are encouraged to do wrong.

Kids don't make the liquor.
They don't run the bars;
They don't make the laws;
They don't buy the cars;
They don't sell the drugs;
It's all done by this older generation—greedy for gain.

The sins of the nation blame it on them.
By the rule of the blameless—the Bible makes known;
Who's there among us to cast the first stone?

Fred Cato Jr.
Casa Grande, AZ

Pictures in the Sky

Sit on the porch
look out as far
as the eyes can see.

Something is floating
across the sky
with incredible, effortless ease.

Clouds take on
all kinds of shapes
that are sure to please,
explorers of the sky like
you and me.

So, sit back, relax, set
your spirit free.

Take time to find
pictures in the sky.
It's a lot of fun!
Guaranteed!

Julie K. Brincks
Johnson, KS

[Hometown] *Johnson, KS* [Ed] *master's in early childhood education* [Occ] *educator* [Hobbies] *bible study, hiking, drawing, spending time with family, writing poetry, travel* [GA] *living life*
I'm a stay-at-home grandma who enjoys spending time with family. I have picked up a new favorite hobby in the past year. That hobby is hiking in the Colorado Rockies with my sister, niece, and granddaughter. I still enjoy writing poetry and drawing when time allows.

Tony's Grill

Oh what a thrill, oh what a thrill
Was the historic celebration at Tony's Grill
For me, time stood still
It placed me back on blue berry hill
Then the mariachi's started playing
Igniting the crowd to cheers
They played La Ley del Monte
Whose message brought back some tears
Public speaking is not my forte
But give me the mike
And I'll have something to say
I shared memorable stories
Like, lightning striking my golf group
My acing all par threes at Tierra Santa
And being the fiddler on the roof
I was just warming up and wanted to say more
But the evil eye in my wife's eyes
They said otherwise, so I closed by saying
Mr. Reyna, I am seventy-nine and feeling fine
It's been a long but enjoyable ride
Made possible having my wife and son by my side
We've come a long way
After 25 years I guess you can shout
Hooray! They are here to stay!

Jose E. Hernandez
Donna, TX

This poem is dedicated to Maria Elena Reyna, my boss's sister who recently left to her heavenly home. Fifty years ago, my boss worked for me, today I work for him and celebrated my twenty-fifth employment anniversary. Double entry bookkeeping is of the past and so is manual calculators but playing pool and ping pong will never get old. Instead of memories written on a penca, they are etched forever in our hearts. Do you remember the secret of unlocking a file cabinet?

Untitled

My eyes and ears are open to God
What beauty in the world He created!
It is everything for mankind to enjoy,
My lips in thanksgiving bring Him praise.

To believe in God is to truly love Him.
For so much He has done for us.
Yet fools might be full of words
But lying lips are rejected of the Lord.

God loves those who deal in truth
His delight favors the righteous one;
Those who wait patiently for God
He never disaffirm in waiting like Job.

God is truth: He never lies
Lying lips are abomination to the Lord
Deceitful lips shall not dwell with Him
But He welcomes His children to His Home.

Rosa H. Collier
Clarkston, MI

[Hometown] *Clarkston, MI* [Ed] *teacher* [Occ] *retired* [Hobbies] *writing* [GA] *traveling to many European countries*
I was born in the island of Puerto Rico. Since very small, I wanted to learn to write and read. I developed a liking for poetry. There was a radio program coming from Cuba before it was changed to communism. I sent a poem there, which it was read on the air. I was encouraged to continue writing poems. I have continued to do so. Most of my poems express my love for God. I am a born-again Christian, and my poems show that sentiment.

The End

Bend, fend, lend, mend
 Pend, Send, Tend, Wend
Why not dend, gend, or hend?
Why don't these last make sense?

Bird, curds, girds, herds
 Nerds and Kurds
Why not ferds, tirds, lirds?
Why don't these last make sense?

Small words they are
Small thoughts, they do jar
Some make one's brain go far
As thoughts veer high and low.

These thoughts could go on and on
Until words appear thereon
Unknowingly a sense does become
Until, finally there becomes
 "The End"

Helen-Anne Keith
Chelsea, MA

Wow! I'll be 102 years old on August 25, 2022. Still walking (with a cane). I am blessed and still have something to do or I wouldn't still be here.

His Horizon

He sees the near horizon
Broad with promise, bright with hope,
All fresh with what can be.
It's all so reachable and good,
And all within the open world
That can be understood.
So simple! So dear!
So full of all that's pure!
He's sure it will endure.
He's just a child. But he will grow.
And, taller, he will see beyond
The day, the way, the new he now can know.
Then what of promise, brightness, hope?
Will broader scope of view then dim
The light, the future's glow?
Will cynicism darken all?
Will doubt and fear pervade
And stain his way?
Or will he find among his peers
Some truth that lets him see
That love and joy can be?

Charles David Poole
Prescott, AZ

[Hometown] *Prescott, AZ* [Occ] *retired* [Hobbies] *writing stories, painting pictures, writing songs and music*

Eyeglasses

She asked me
to help her find her favorite glasses—
you know, the green ones
with the round lens.
Of course I know, I say,
I've found them a number of times before.

On the second time through I used a flashlight
to better see under things,
but still no luck.
On my way out of the bedroom
I spotted her morning's empty coffee mug
on the edge of the dresser.

When I went to retrieve it, guess what I found?
Right next to her coffee mug
were her green eyeglasses
folded as if ready to be discovered!
How is it we can look and look
and never see what's right under our noses?

If it wasn't for the empty coffee mug,
I might still be looking.
All I can say is "thank goodness" for the empty coffee mugs
of the world or any others who, stained with use,
lead us, once again, to see.

Robert Skeele
Anacortes, WA

[Hometown] *Columbus, OH* [Ed] *BA (philosophy) BD (rel. ed)* [Occ] *college administrator (retired)* [Hobbies] *reading, writing, walking* [GA] *with wife, raised 4 wonderful children*
"Eyeglasses" is a good example of how I often proceed in writing a poem. I start with a common thought or action—searching for my wife's eyeglasses—and in the last line or two, apply that common experience to a more universal principal—learning to see, and understand, better from others who have been around the block a couple of times—that is, the "stained" coffee mugs of the world.

Don't Die, America

Remember when America was full of hope, love, and bright sunny days?
when the world would smile, wishing each other well—
good stories to each, we would tell.
Now America full of unemployed, the hungry, crime widespread,
seems no pride to be one's best; everyone looking for handouts,
a free ride.
We all have our ways to achieve in one's self, just need to believe.
Be your very best; help a friend to a happy end.
In one year, five years, in ten, will America be no more?
Will we fight for her? Will we have learned?
Hope, love and happiness for all, will we forget?
I hope not, I pray not, my friend.
I do pray for America, the country I love,
I think about those who have passed, those yet to come;
that leaves the present to get the job done.
A reach, a stretch, a prayer or two, then saving America will come true.
Stand up and fight for the red, white, and blue; Lady Liberty
is depending on you and me, too!

Thomas Dutcher
Myrtle Beach, SC

[Ed] *SUNY Degree Bus. Mg.* [Occ] *Retired* [Hobbies] *Golf* [GA] *Climbed the Great Wall, Hole in One in Golf Tourn.*
I write for different reasons depending upon the emotion I am feeling. "My Furry Friend" a poem in Collected Whispers, page 1, was written because a dear friend had lost her one year old dog. "Words for You (U Know)" my book, was dedicated to my wife, my love, who showed me the way back from depression and loneliness. "The Road Called Sadness" a poem written with heartache and pain after losing my son Shawn to drugs, depression and loss of self-worth. My hope is to reach others in time. This poem "Don't Die America" was written because I love America and worry about her soul. In the end, I write in hope that my words heal and guide those in need.

A True Love Story for All

A long time ago the world didn't exist but we
have a mighty God who spoke it in existence
and it came to be, but God wasn't finished
yet He took His time to make us all unique
in His own image and breathed into us a living
soul that is true love.
God came down from Heaven and robed Himself
in flesh and walk upon this earth, like us
He went through same things we went
through in our lives. He was a child just
like us and grew like us too, and went through
trials as well but Jesus never sinned once
that is true love as well.
As He became a grown up Jesus began
to teach and heal people, raise them from the
dead. There were miracles and wonders
Jesus did when He walked on this earth
because He was our Messiah who loves
us more than we know. That is also true
love for us all.
Jesus and His friends went to the garden to pray
for us all before we were ever born and
Jesus taught in the synagogues in front
of everyone. Some believed in Him and some
didn't; they wanted to kill Him instead.
"Jesus told them that I love you all"
That is true love.

Ruby Rollins
Ville Platte, LA

[Hometown] *Ville Platte, LA* [Ed] *high school* [Hobbies] *writing poems*
I am a person who loves animals and children and loves her job and going to church when I get a chance. I am also a Sunday school teacher and I love to write poems. One of my wishes is that they get publish and make money for my poems because the words I write are the words of Jesus Christ who gives me the words. It's a kind of way to praise and worship my Jesus Christ who is everything to me.

The Circle

Beginning at the end
Ending at the beginning
Unchanging in a changing world
Cyclical, circular, cycles
Rotating time into space
Reinventing, recycling, rearranging
Revolutionizing evolution
Infinite possibilities
Within finite space
Elective, electric
Keeping things in
While pushing them out
The eye of a storm
The nucleus whose radius can't be discerned
Self-sufficient
Creating creation
Focusing all energy
Into its vortex
Making a place for its inner space
In its outer core
All worlds within one world
    The circle

Paula Compo-Pratt
Westville, NJ

[Hometown] *Westville, NJ* [Ed] *BA, honorary MA, HDL* [Occ] *educator* [Hobbies] *oil painter who is a realist impressionist, author/illustrator of 5 children's books, and a certified floral designer* [GA] *becoming an ambassador general, 4 lifetime achievement awards, and 38 awards as an educator both national and international*

Love Conquers All

Why do I see so much trouble and violence?
It is because I live among rebellious people.
Destruction, injustice, and corruption abound.
The entire country is full of lawbreakers.
Fighting in the streets—cities full of violence.
Murders throughout the land.
Everything is confusion.
Evil people make evil plans...they commit terrible sins.
They do disgusting things, in private and publicly.
They don't care for the poor and underprivileged.
People with eyes, but they can't see what is evil.
People with ears that can't hear the cries of the poor.
I ask, "Lord, how can you stand for such evil?
How long must I wait for you to act?"
Almighty God replies, "People do what's evil.
Evil-doers will suffer for disgusting things done.
Woe to evil-doers...they are doomed."
The Almighty says, "I do not want anyone to die."
Thus, God says, I will honor My covenant of love.
Because of My constant love, I will be merciful.
In mercy I will seek those who seek me.
If the evil person turns and does what is good,
In mercy I will forgive all wrongs," says the Lord.
The Lord God says, "My covenant of love lasts forever."
Love conquers all.

Bill M. Watt
Junction City, KS

[Hometown] *Abilene, KS* [Ed] *doctorate Kansas State University* [Occ] *college professor (retired)* [Hobbies] *racquetball, chess, go* [GA] *smart enough to marry Katherine Ann (Young) Watt*

Petite Etoile

Tiny ebony paws reach out,
Then she jumps up on her toes
And hops around all about;
Threatening all is what she does.
She is black as the night
With one tiny star under her chin.
She thinks she will give a fright
As she dances around the bin.
A tiny menace to the mice
Both real and fake are filled with fear.
Catching flies is very nice;
These funny antics make her dear.
She is a tiny obsidian terror
Until her energy is spent.
Then she purrs with fervor
Of a feline sleep—she is the recipient.
She is like a little witch
With boundless energy and curiosity.
Her world is very rich
Spinning with great velocity.
She lights up the world with fun
As she spins like a little star.
She comes to love when she is done
My little feline friend, Merida Mim.

Judith Parrish Broadbent
Chapel Hill, TN

[Hometown] *Chapel Hill, TN* [Ed] *Master of Art plus 50* [Occ] *writer, adjunct professor, teacher* [Hobbies] *writing, gardening, sewing* [GA] *humanities teacher of the year TN and my children and grandchildren*
I am an old teacher and writer and draw inspiration from my children (grown now) and animal and human friends. Merida Mim is our new little cat and her antics are wonderful. She makes me smile. We need more smiles today!

Although the Mountains Wear Away

Although the mountains wear away by day,
Though limbs from trees do break and fall away,
And fruit does age and wither on the vine,
And life so strong does weaken and decline;

Though rocks do melt and much like water flow,
Though forests burn and put to flight the doe,
And lakes turn shallow, slow, as centuries grow,
And care does waver and in time let go;

As snows do melt and channel rivers wide,
As rain does fall and moves rocks down mountain side,
As streams do run to lakes and oceans fill,
And love does pleasure give and life fulfill;

My heart for you forever stays so strong;
We keep and hold, eternally belong.

To: Sarah,
In remembrance of our time together
on our Western Amtrak trip.

Kenneth Swan
Marion, IN

[Hometown] *Vincennes, IN* [Ed] *graduate school* [Occ] *teacher* [Hobbies] *bird watching, fishing, hunting, enjoying nature, and books* [GA] *traveling the world*
I have always had a love of books. Since my father was a minister, I read the Bible from Genesis to Revelation several times as a boy. This experience developed into a love of history and the classics of western literature. As a result, I became fascinated with a love of nature and traveling the world.

Make It Joyful—Make It Fun

Come and see, come and see,
take a fun-filled spree with me
Lush soft blanket beneath your feet
cool as a gentle springtime breeze.

Frogs and birds and dogs in a park
hummers, too, but they don't bark.
Bunnies with floppy ears quite long
even mice have joined the throng.

Snakes will sometimes slither by
paying no heed or wonder of why.
Wheels spin as breezes blow
adding to the magnificent show.

Beauty and grace is everywhere;
along fence rows, all give their share.
Golden, crimson, lavender, white
even more—they are so bright.

Angels and cherubs don't mind the showers
in their places for countless hours.
Tree and bush make complete
all the visions—each unique.

Anna M. Barnes
Sioux City, IA

[Hometown] *Sioux City, Iowa* [Ed] *high school* [Occ] *retired* [Hobbies] *writing poetry, flower gardening* *I am eighty-two years old. Love writing poetry! Also love flower gardening and my yards tell that! I have six great-grandchildren. Twin boys came first then two girls (cousins) born one day apart. Next, two more boys—one six years old and the last one five years old. I love writing and gardening BUT I love my "kids" more! They are my pride and joy!*

Your Homeplace

In memory of my friend Bill Lee, 4/25/1942 – 9/2/2021

As I sit here this cold January day
 and think how much I miss you since you went away.
Before when I felt lonely I could come by and visit with you
 but that I can no longer do.
The friendship that belonged to just us has been taken away
 if only you could have stayed.
Sometimes I am so lonesome I ride by your home
 and remember how it was when you were not gone.
Seeing your home from the road, it seems almost the same,
 but my heart knows it is different, your mailbox has a new name,
but in my mind it will always be yours. A place that I used to go.
 A place that I loved so.

Bonnie Watson Jolly
Cedartown, GA

[Hometown] *Cedartown, GA* [Ed] *high school* [Occ] *sewed in sewing factories, retired from Kellogg's bakery* [Hobbies] *writing poetry, reading, friends on Facebook* [GA] *being invited to poetry conventions—went to Washington, DC twice and Orlando, FL twice*
I mostly write about family and friends, my church, things that inspire me. My children are my daughter Richelle and my son Richard Jr. My son died in 1999. My husband Richard was killed in a traffic accident in 2015. The first poem I ever heard, my mom read to me when I was a child. I loved it. I love to read and keep up with my friends on Facebook. I have had around sixty of my poems published in different poetry books.

Did the Poets Lie?

I'm standing some place in the sands of time
between Heaven and Hell searching to find.

Searching to find what poets speak of,
that gift of the gods, that illusion called love.

I've searched so long to no avail;
weary of my journey, I feel I have failed.

I've failed to find the love that I seek.
Is there more to life or will this be my peak?

If this is my peak then I've not far to fall;
my heart cries out, this can't be all!

For where is the love poets said was real,
that makes strong men weak, makes honest men steal?

Did it ever exist, did it pass me by?
Is there such a thing, or did the poets just lie?

Daryl D. Brown
Burlington, IA

[Hometown] *Burlington, IA* [Ed] *Master of Science degree* [Occ] *retired teacher* [Hobbies] *poetry, Dodge Viper, Harley motorcycles, visiting casinos* [GA] *placing 1st in Iowa state track meets four times*
Before I met my wife I searched the bars and dance halls for something that didn't live there. Like a lot of destinations they were nice places to visit, but I didn't want to make them my home. During that time period, I realized I was able to find drinking buddies, but nothing meaningful. Disappointed, I wrote this poem, "Did the Poets Lie?" I have since met a young lady that has become my wife and the love of my life. The bars and dance halls have faded into a distant memory.

Life

A smile, a tear
A hope, a fear
A laugh, a frown
Some ups and some downs.

Good times, bad times
Happy times, sad times
Skies of blue, skies of gray
Time to leave, times to stay.

Going fast, going slow
What we learn, what we know
Guides our path to the end
Don't forget to be a friend.

Being brave, being shy
Say hello, say goodbye
Being grateful, being thankful
Asking who, asking why.

Showing kindness and forgiveness
Finding peace, peace of mind
Being open and accepting
What a blessing, what a find
Feeling love all the time!

Donna M. Mitchell
Kingston, PA

[Hometown] *Kingston, PA* [Ed] *BS early childhood and elementary education* [Occ] *retired businesswoman* [Hobbies] *writing, music, gardening, swimming* [GA] *being the proud mother and grandmother to four amazing humans!*

I have been married to a wonderful man for forty-nine years and have two daughters, Melissa and Laura, and two granddaughters, Alison and Emily. Writing poetry and lyrics has always been therapy for me since I was a teenager and continues to this day. Life has many challenges and wonderful experiences. How we handle or react to the ups and downs only comes from love, forgiveness, perseverance, and believing in yourself and God.

No Light!

No light!
There cannot be!
There would be no truth to humanity!
There would be no moon!
There would be no sun!
The light on the seashore
Would be done!
And there would be no music
To dance us to the light!
There would be only darkness!
There would be no stars at night!
Why do all the people
With wisdom in their brain,
Bring me so much sorrow
And show me so much pain?
Why do I have to see the truth
Every single day?
I am dancing on my rainbow
But the truth won't go away!
Indeed, I am so sorry
If I have brought you ruin on the way.
I would rather be an old man
And my hair was turning gray!
No light!
There cannot be!
There would be no truth to humanity!

Gilbert Reynosa
La Verne, CA

[Hometown] *La Verne, CA*
When I was a younger man, I had to spend several months in the hospital. I prevailed and emerged with a new sensitivity that embraced the very fabric of my soul. I developed into a singer/songwriter and taught myself how to play the acoustic guitar. I am a lover of life and remain humble in the face of God. I enjoy the sun, the stars, the wind. I am a poet with a truth, with my heart up in the sky...I dedicate this poem to my beautiful Lidia.

Earth Day, May It Be Every Day

Earth Day, let us view it as every day.
Let it be the new way.
Turn it over, un-fence it, un-dam it.
Let our mother's water flow.
Play in the dirt, wash your fingers, it won't hurt.
Maybe Earth Day can take on its own glow,
A human sunset reflected back at her.
Maybe nature can proceed on its own,
Slow, slow, repair now.
Let the consciousness grow.
Let it grow, let it grow.
Within the heart's mind, let it spring forward.
If we should return to this planet
A generation or two after we have left it.
Would we see it as with in our old imagery?
Comfort, fertility, generosity,
A sense of heritage defines we leave it as first seen.
Go ahead, pay your own postage,
Let your mind wander.
I'm betting you have already pondered.
Why does it rain so much?
Mother's letting go,
Her tears though granite and sand
Filling an ocean of need, purity, let it be.
Let it be what all of us need.
Earth Day now.

Gregory C. Sheppard
Issaquah, WA

I had a forty-five year career as a architectural woodworker. Building custom doors, windows, and staircases. My wife Bonny and I live on a pesticide free acre. It is our pleasure to care for God's creatures.

Solitude

I have a place I go to, whenever I want to think.
I walk up to the seawall, and watch the blue waves rise and sink.
Carved into the wall is a staircase that leads down to the rocks and the sand.
The vast sea is spread out before me.
The most beautiful sight in the land.

I slowly sit down on the stone stairs, as the sound of the waves fills my space.
I sit there until I am grounded, and savor the wind in my face.
Soon, my problems all fade on the sea breeze, and vanish without a trace.

Janet Sue Deckard
League City, TX

Island life has always been my inspiration. I was born, raised, educated, employed, and married on Galveston Island off the Texas coast. Besides the beach and Gulf of Mexico, the island has a very rich history. It has a history of pirates, ghosts, Mardi Gras, civil war adventures, and recovering from the 1900 storm, which destroyed the island. I love anything nature related and my beautiful family who is also a major inspiration!

A Time to Reflect

Independence Day is a time to reflect.
Will our freedom prevail or perish due to neglect?
Do we embrace freedom or try to escape from it?
Freedom comes to those who bear the cost to create it.
Do we choose security and safety at any cost?
Do we ignore the fact that our freedom will be lost?
Is freedom real or a grand delusion born of fear?
As evidence accumulates this will become clear.
We claim to be free even as our chains grow tighter.
The weight of oppression grows heavier, not lighter.
Are we free when government can choose to lock down life?
How free are we when hate and intolerance are rife?
We have a strong inclination to control others.
The cost of that power is the freedom we smother.
Are we too trusting of people with extreme power?
They dismantle our constitution, while we cower.
Will the right to defend our liberty be denied?
Is it the Second Amendment on which we relied?
Is safety our ultimate goal regardless of cost?
To forfeit liberty would be a catastrophic loss.
Are we too eager to give up our freedom to choose?
Allow government to dictate and we all will lose.
The fact we undermined our freedom is disdainful.
Learning we fueled our own enslavement is too painful.
Will acclimating to subservience serve us well?
Or are we willingly creating a living hell?

LeRoy F. Thielman
Oshkosh, WI

[Hometown] *Oshkosh, WI* [Ed] *master's degree in economics* [Occ] *retired* [Hobbies] *reading, writing, landscaping, traveling*
Freedom is under attack by people we depend upon to defend it. Government, our educational system and religious organizations are engaged in dismantling our constitution and the freedoms it was designed to protect. We claim to be free, but recognize that much of our freedom has already been lost. We know that our demands for safety and security have led to the undermining of our liberty. We fail to appreciate that we can never achieve total safety and security. Yet, attempting to do so could totally exterminate our freedom. Those thoughts inspired me to write the poem, "A Time to Reflect."

The Bombing

On Christmas day
Our state was woke up
By a bomb
No one saw it coming this way.

A man
Loaded up a
Van
And went to the city.

Right
In the middle of town
He exploded a bomb
That sent the town into fright.

He blew himself up
In the van.
It left people without jobs or homes.
What a crazy man.

A time of peace
Turned into war
By the devil unleashed.
No lives were lost but his and property cost.

Margaret Worley
Watertown, TN

[Hometown] *Watertown, TN* [Ed] *college* [Occ] *sales person* [Hobbies] *hiking, fishing, bird watching* [GA] *published poet and writer*
This will be the eleventh time I've been in a book by Eber & Wein Publishing. I love the outdoors and nature. I have also done hand crafts. I love poetry and writing most of all. I have done some paintings of birds, barns, and others that have been in Pancakes-In-Heaven. Have had articles in Farm and Ranch and Reminisce Magazines. Have written songs and now sing with a group.

The Farmer

He walked into the barn
And looked around.
Is this all there is
As he kicked the ground.
Forty years of working this earth,
As he thought of his worth.
The bank was after him again
To pay up on this piece of dirt.
He only had enough to pay
Half, and that hurt.
He reached down and picked
Up an old feed sack.
He turned it over to the clean
Side on the back.
Then he laid it on a hay bale.
And reached in his shirt pocket
For the pencil stub he always
Carried without fail.
The numbers raced through his brain.
No matter how he figured,
They came out the same.
Tears ran down his cheeks
As he thought about his family.
The insurance would pay off the debt,
And they'd be home free.
He reached down and patted his
Faithful old dog Blue.
With determination, he knew what he had to do.
The chill of the cold steel
Gripped his heart.
As he pulled the trigger, he thought,
"Forgive me, Lord," but I did my part.

Patricia Nienke
Ellsworth, KS

Miss Ruth's Battle

Miss Ruth, do you recall, at all
My bushy, matted hair,
On which was placed a scarf
Encasing tangles everywhere?
I'll bet you guessed my mom did best,
For you, not her, instead,
Were left to disentangle me,
You knew, and weren't misled!

I ducked; you pulled! I winced; you prayed,
A sad forsaken pair!
No comb was ever buff enough,
and ruled to our despair!
Each time you'd win that little war from underneath the grease
With one more week left to endure,
That first left us some peace.

Penelope H. White
New Kensington, PA

[Hometown] *New Kensington* [Occ] *retired* [Hobbies] *communicating with people from all walks of life, learning by reading, listening to good music, concerts, plays*
I used to visit her every two weeks when I was between nine and thirteen or fourteen years old. My hair, an African-American, was thick and hard to comb! It hurt each time!

A House—A Home

At first light, freshly hewned timbers, tall and erect,
Catch rays of sunlight that brightly reflect
Newly formed corners and shapes,
Once only visions, but now soon
to become double-glazed windows and spacious rooms.

Anxious anticipation for all that lies ahead,
each stage brings new concepts and ideas.
Never knowing what to expect or maybe dread,
forging forward with no time to face our fears.

Rolled papers reveal sketches and plans
more reality now than dreams.
Our future closer now, it seems,
Soon only contentment and satisfaction we'll demand.

Too much isolation and uncertainty fill these days,
Family, friends, love and laughter
We hope we'll exchange,
Today, tomorrow and forever after...

Here in this house,
Now our Home.

Renette JoAn Colwell
Prescott, AZ

[Hometown] *Carrington, ND* [Ed] *business/legal admin.* [Occ] *retired paralegal* [Hobbies] *writing poetry, short stories* [GA] *my son Eric Stangeland and publishing my poetry*

We Need Prayer for a Dying World

We look at the world today, praying for a brighter day.
We often forget
I see the crying and hunger in the streets.
When will we come together and become one.
The earth is groaning and people's souls are burning.
The world is full of disbelief and full of greed.
We see the signs of the Lord's return. Will you be ready?

Sonya G. Gafford
Oakland, CA

[Hometown] *Oakland* [Ed] *high school* [Occ] *caregiver* [Hobbies] *writer, cooking, reader* [GA] *learning to appreciate what God has given regardless how people talk against it*
God has given me a gift for writing; I choose to share it with the world. I praise God for His power and love and what He has gifted me with to touch heal and encourage his people. This is dedicated to the memory of the late and great Bishop Iona Locke. May you rest in peace 12/18/2020.

Falling Stars from Beneath

Close your eyes and wish
Will it come true?
Hopes and dreams
Will they disappoint you?
Did you wish hard enough?
Keep your wish secret?
Did you wish it out loud?
Shooting stars
Close your eyes and wish...

I feel like I'm breathing beneath the flowing water
Looking up through the waves and the weeds
Trying to speak, choking on the sea
Can you hear me?
Look down, reach below
Save me from myself, set me free
As I close my eyes and wish…

Stephanie Day
Long Beach, WA

[Hometown] *Long Beach, WA* [Ed] *AAS medical billing and coding* [Occ] *sales* [Hobbies] *photography, poetry, art making* [GA] *my boys and myself, work in progress*
I am a single mom of two adult sons. I live walking distance from the ocean. I am going back to college for the third time. Hoping to work from home and buy an RV to travel.

Shared Love

I see so much beauty in the love we share;
You have given me so much awesome care.
You have said all the things that say "I love you!"
I was that smart I heard them all, it's true.
When you showed me that beautiful diamond ring,
You gave my heart an awesome fling.
Now I wait for that wondrous day,
That day when we both say I do.
When we become one, as we will, too.
To stay close forever in every way.
You have made me smile,
Ever so much, for a long, long while.
With this wondrous love we share,
I surely will light up with that loving care.
Being together is so awesome on this day,
To hold each other's hand come what may
And stand by each other's side.
By one another in life we will not hide.
So in love still as our days fly,
Seeing all that joy and beauty up in the sky.
God gave me you. God gave you me.
Together we shall always be.
"Shared love are we."
The strongest force on the planet in love.
'Cause God shares it from above.

Deanna Maria Bacon
Colona, IL

[Hometown] *Davenport* [Ed] *college* [Occ] *retired after 20 years working at co* [Hobbies] *poetry* [GA] *first female unit supervisor with Alcoa Aluminum Co. of America*

The End

The End.
This, my last breath, I will breathe.
I am here without worry or fear.
When I die there will be one last sigh.
I will not cry or say goodbye.
I will see if an angel waits for me.
What lies ahead, I do not dread,
as I enter the world of the dead.
I do not know where I will go.
My words and deeds like planted seeds.
The things I did grow, I shall see as one last show.
Time stands still and nothing seems real,
no day or night, no reason for sight.
I shall die, please don't cry!
Will I go back because my soul did lack?
Is this the end or where it will begin?

Debra Jean Knapp
Ocala, FL

[Hometown] *Ocala, FL* [Ed] *critical care nurse* [Occ] *retired* [Hobbies] *taekwondo, kayaking, swimming, hiking, gardening, cooking, music, and poetry* [GA] *Marrying a wonderful man who has supported me in everything I do and shares hobbies and life with me!*
I grew up in a small town surrounded by nature. I married and had four children. Then I became a critical care nurse. Once retired, I began volunteer work. I drive a police car from two sub-stations and a river patrol boat. I take taekwondo two times a week with hapkido too. I am working on my second degree black belt. I enjoy hiking, kayaking, swimming, cooking, gardening, music, and sports cars! Writing poetry is a way to express my feelings and thoughts. A way to cope with life and touch lives.

The Beautiful Sea

I must go visit the sea someday
And watch the beautiful seagulls come into the bay

As I walk barefoot in the warm sand
I will try to find as many seashells as I can

To watch the tide come into the bay
And watch the beautiful sunset at the end of the day

Yes, I must go visit the sea someday
And watch the beautiful seagulls come into the bay

Bobbi Jo Hager
Ozark, AL

[Hometown] *Clarksburg, WV* [Ed] *14 years* [Occ] *retired US Army (SFCRCT)* [Hobbies] *paint by number, writing short stories, poems, writing songs* [GA] *hall of fame award in poetry 2017*

December 14

I do not need long gentle days to love you in:
Not a divan to rest on—
Not peace, solitude, a moon, fair weather's flowers—
No sweet spring breeze to carry you to me.
Dodging traffic on Fifth Avenue I saw a man
And called your name.
All through a raw, gray afternoon of rude legalities,
Crowds, haste, rain, alarms
You were upon me like a shot,
Bright madness.
Or I can be worrying a dollar,
Chore unhappy plan,
And feel your arms press me to shameless greed
In a cold street,
Buses, on a subway train—
I breathe away the seconds into hours
Till I can have your mouth and live
Reality again.

Olivia Ferrarini
New York, NY

[Hometown] *New York* [Ed] *life* [Occ] *living* [Hobbies] *growing things* [GA] *made it this far*

The Governess

The so-called lady dresses
like a Victorian in 2022
in the heat and humid Caribbean.
She acts like she comes from money,
a country girl who pretends
to be a sophisticated
city woman.
Plays the role of a
goody-two shoes, but
has the malice of a snake.
She hides under
a skirt that reaches her
ankles and wears a power coat
so no one can see her wrists.
What is she hiding?
The virginity of a 54-year-old woman.
At work pretends to be working
sitting with a straight back
making believe to be working.
She makes everyone's life miserable.
In the office she's always
counting pencils, controlling them.
She looks down at others, under her shoulder,
observing like a sentinel and imitating
the people she envies.
Ms. Perfect the poser wants to be like
her boss.

Daphne Martinez
San Juan, PR

[Hometown] *San Juan, Puerto Rico* [Ed] *PhD* [Occ] *professor* [Hobbies] *reading, dancing, shopping, exercising* [GA] *trying to be a good person*
Daphne has been working as a teacher for thirty-five years. She loves to travel, read, and meditate. She works at the University of Puerto Rico and at the moment she works in a TRIO Program that caters to students who are low-income, first-generation university students, and disabled.

Uncle Steve

Uncle Steve made everyone laugh
and spread happiness.
If you were crying he would
spread happiness.
He was liked and down to earth.
A joy since birth.
Laughing so hard you would cry.
My best friend, my uncle I
can't seem to say goodbye.
Tears roll down my face.
But a smile on my face when
I remember your jokes.
On some you would play a funny
hoax.
It was all in good fun.
Recognizing the pun.
You'll be forever in my heart.
Like you were from the start.

Kimberly Listro
Middletown, CT

[Hometown] *Meriden*
Hello, my name is Kim. I've been published for thirty-one years. I also love to sing, write lyrics (I started doing all of this before poetry at the age of twelve). Sometimes I write fiction stories. I love the beach, the movies, live music, etc. Most of my relatives are in Heaven now shining down on me. My grandparents really loved and believed in me. My best friend, my Uncle Steve, passed away recently and this poem is about him.

Our Silly Little Bug

Come quickly and see what the kitten has discovered!
You sigh and say girls and their silly little bugs.
Surprise—it is green, huge, and strange looking.
We have NEVER seen its kind before.
Our tortie would save us if she could but reach it.
It hovers in the uppermost corner of the doorway.
Wisely, it remains out of reach of all.
Free my home of this monster the kitten pleads.
Half a can of insect repellent stuns the fiend.
As it drops to the floor, its wings yet stir.
Actual stomping on it is required to subdue it.
Finally, it may be dropped outside the door.
The kitten now feels safe.
Off to bed with her humans.

Joelle Margarete
Fairfield, CA

[Hometown] *Northern California* [Ed] *high school* [Occ] *cat mom, poet* [Hobbies] *reading, crafting, and word/brain game puzzles* [GA] *Cold War naval service to bring down the Berlin Wall*
This is a true story about our first cat. Every one of my furballs has had a fascination with bugs. Atila-the-Hun was a beautiful tortoiseshell cat. We love her now and forever. She is the reason another eight cats have come into our lives. A beloved animal can never be replaced in your heart. You add a new friend to your life each time that you adopt. I hope that every pet parent is fortunate enough to love their charges as much as we do, past and present. All of my furballs were rescue animals that rescued me.

Still Grieving

It is hard for me to be believing
That after thirteen years I am still grieving
I have a montage of your pictures in plain sight
That I look at every day and night
I talk to you every day
It's mostly the same things that I say
Sometimes I tell you about family happenings
And a little bit of other things
I am still being true
I do not want to be with anyone but you
You gave me such a happy life
I am so glad that I took you for my wife

Chester Williams
Jewett City, CT

[Hometown] *Jewett City, CT* [Ed] *10th grade* [Occ] *retired trailer driver* [Hobbies] *sports and gambling* [GA] *marrying my wife*

Bliss

Blue skies
seagulls in flight
sand between my toes

  The taste of sea salt upon my lips
sweet scent of coconut oil

  Warm rays of the sun on my
golden bronze skin
  The rumbling of waves as
they make their way to shore

This is the place to which
I go to find peace within myself
  Yes, this is my bliss

Julie A. Gravel
San Diego, CA

[Hometown] *San Diego, CA* [Ed]. *dental tech* [Occ] *retired* [Hobbies] *writing poetry, bike-riding, rollerskating, zumba, fishing* [GA] *my love and following of God; winning the war in my battle with cancer*

Life

My life it seems was built on hopes and built on dreams, built on
promises of things still unseen.
But as the years so swiftly pass, I came to realize at last, life
is what you make it.
Dreams that fade, promises made that somehow you just couldn't keep
now at times still haunt you in your sleep.
Life is a game of give and take; at times you win when the stakes are
high but end up losing when the end is nigh.
Yet somehow I'm happy when all is said and done; through the years with
all its fears I've had my share of fun and with God's good graces
there will be a lot more still to come.
Epilogue
I wonder in my heart just what life is all about; I think I know as the
years may go, it's all in God's plan for woman or man, and only He knows
what the outcome will be.

James Harwood
Spencer, WI

[Hometown] *Spencer, WI* [Ed] *high school—military electronics* [Occ] *carpentry—retired* [Hobbies] *poetry, vintage electronics, old radios, juke boxes, etc.* [GA] *wonderful family, 6 children, many grandchildren*
I was born a year after the end of WWII, a baby boomer I became. After my dad was badly injured in a farm accident I was sent to a foster family on a farm near Loyal, WI at the age of twelve years old. I went to a one-room country school for two years then on to high school in the little town of Loyal, WI where I was fortunate enough to have an English teacher we affectionately called Mrs. B. She taught us to love prose and poetry which has stayed with me to this day. After high school I served in the US Army during the Vietnam conflict. Returning home I got married and raised a wonderful family of six children.

Ukraine Is in Flames!

Ukraine is in flames,
and Putin is to blame!
He thinks he's so darn smart,
but he was wrong from the start!

Meanwhile, Ukraine's economy is in the tank,
plus its grain crop is totally lost and we have Putin to thank!
Truly, Ukraine will suffer greatly due to this Russian invasion,
but make no mistake, this disaster will affect every nation!

Furthermore, as this war drags on, its costs will grow,
well beyond where Russia would be willing to go!
Where is the world court?
Is it only to be called upon as an absolute last resort?

Hopefully, it will all be over very soon,
and we'll be able to tend to our own various wounds!
If not, things are going to get much worse,
and Putin will surely have to pay from his shrinking purse!

Meanwhile, the Ukranians have been left out in the cold,
with very few resources, and even less dough!
My prayer is that nations all over the world
will help every Ukranian man, woman, boy, and girl!

Thomas S. Parish
Topeka, KS

[Hometown] *Topeka, KS* [Ed] *PhD in human development from the University of Illinois at Champaign-Urbana (1972)* [Occ] *emeritus professor of developmental psychology at Kansas State University (1976-2005). Currently the editor of the International Journal of Choice Theory and Reality Therapy (2010-present)* [Hobbies] *writing poetry, creating psychological inventories, and doing research* [GA] *selected as "One of the Top 100 Educators in the World" by the International Biographical Centre in Cambridge, England, in 2005.*
The times we live in are difficult, indeed, and few would argue with this point. In my poetry, then, I seek to confront some of these problems that we face, not by just a few but by the entire human race! In so doing, I hope to draw more attention to these problems and encourage others to work with me and other concerned scholars to develop solutions for these problems that we face today, and to those problems yet to come.

Thy Greatest Depths of Thy Most Blissful Oceans

Thy endlessness of his desires for thee
left me weak in thy knees... Singing
thy songs of thy serenading love birds.
Ironically beneath thy grains of rose
colored sandy shores and above thy
ocean tops of half hearted serene
secretly kept wishes...
Awaiting thee with thy most unforgettable
look in his eyes was he. As thy gaze
of his settled upon me a silent wish
of love and forever I make of he.
To thy greatest depths of thy deepest
oceans he shall swim just to fulfill
thy hearts desires of thee... For his dreams
of thee shield me from thy most fearful
frights hidden deep within thy darkest
coral lairs of thy oceanic bliss.

Gohar Minassian
Los Angeles, CA

[Hometown] *Los Angeles* [Ed] *The Art Institute of Santa Monica, animation* [Occ] *visual development artist specializing in rococo* [Hobbies] *yoga, aerobics, and singing* [GA] *2008 congressional award gold medalist*
My poem is inspired by a beautiful boy who fell in love with the ocean so early on in his life. He holds a place in my heart so grand, never have words been created with meanings powerful enough to be able to describe what I feel for he. I am a 2008 congressional award gold medalist and a first degree black belt in Tae Kwon Do.

As the Sun Sets

As the sun sets one more time I
think sadly how many young people
will not be here to see it come up
again. Our young children are dying
constantly by their own hands and
we are lost! Are they trying to be
like everyone else to fit in, or is
it they are trying to be true to
themselves and are different?
What could cause these beautiful
children to do such an unthinkable
thing as to take their own lives?
Whether it is done accidentally
or purposely it is heart breaking.
We as parents, brothers, sisters
grandparents, close family and
friends cannot see what might
be hurting these children enough to cause such pain
and desperation. If only they could see into their
futures to see what they might become or what their
life might be like once this troublesome time passes.
How do we help them if we
don't know. We need to learn
to recognize the warning signs
before it gets to this point;
before it's too late!

Margaret Beach
Mechanicsville, MD

[Hometown] *Mechanicsville, MD* [Ed] *high school* [Occ] *business owner* [Hobbies] *poetry, photography, crafts, jewelry making* [GA] *becoming a mother*
I am a wife of fifty-two years. A mother of four and a grandmother of nine and great-grandmother of two. I started my own business and writing poems in memory of my son Sean whom I lost twenty-seven years ago. He had a large heart and a sweet soul, so I try to put beauty back into the world in his memory. I wrote this poem because so many young people are lost and overdosing. I just had to hope that maybe the right person would read it and a life would be saved.

What Is Perfection?

What we had was far from perfect
But it's as close to perfect as I have ever had

When I look back on my life
I only see you
The fun we had and the love we made

We had both good and bad times
But I would not trade any of our times

My life here on Earth
Would be so much better with you in it

You were a perfect friend to me
Nothing and no one has been able to replace you

You are all that is missing in my life
I can only pray that God has a beautiful plan for me
so I am able to move on without you.

Elinore J. Krause
Renton, WA

[Hometown] *McKees Rocks* [Ed] *high school, some college courses and training* [Occ] *loan review, now retired* [Hobbies] *art and poetry* [GA] *my two sons*
I enjoy art and writing poems. Sometimes the words flow easily and I'll wake up from a dream and try to hurry and write them down before I forget them. My poems are very therapeutic to me and I hope they touch a memory for you, too.

Goodbye Shandong

You vibrant province of princely pagodas and aged sages.
Where cotton, corn, peanuts, fruit, feathers abound.
Carved mountains and grinning lions,
Rain falling at night, in just the right measures.

How I miss the sandy shores of Rizhao;
Vibrant bathers and beached ships;
Peddlers and fishermen's inns/houses/hotel.

Qufu schools and Qufu town,
Confucious, Mount Tai, and the Juxian church;
Myriad temples and princely pagodas;
Waning springs, rock gardens, layered fields.

Missed most of all are the people,
Ever-present smiles and friendly facades,
Whose kindness continues with curious abandon.

Where else can one buy a pen and gather a crowd?
With help just a vocal stumble away?
Appreciation paramount here; well-done work rewarded
With free-flowing fountains of gracious gratitude.

Goodbye, Shandong, from the physical,
But the spirit ever remains.

Douglas Allen Noel
Aiken, SC

[Hometown] *Aiken, SC* [Ed] *BA: CTCRF; MA: Southern Wesleyan University (also UNL); EDS Liberty University* [Occ] *retired teacher, minister, pastor, writer, singer* [Hobbies] *gardening, writing, traveling, singing* [GA] *the Lord has blessed me abundantly but I haven't achieved my greatest achievement yet.*

The Last Ditch

In my wildest dreams, this should not happen to me.
Now, I regret that I've been pretending that it happens only to others,
for I have been living in a false measure of illogical denial.
The very reason why I have been brought to this atoll labeled JRHCC*,
which separates me from the real world, is that they all said that I
would receive an enormous benefit from this isle.
They also incited me to stay here to expand my existence before
encountering dwellers in a point of no return, which can be reified
right here.
How dare they attempt to seduce me into becoming an actor to be on
the next stage?
Caught between this planet and the next, hoping to get a glimpse of
the great beyond, I've been eating out of their hands when I am told
what to do in the isolated arena in which I am expected to learn how
to get back to where I came from.
Would I be convicted of the reality that I would one day face
something which I could not avoid, would really, truly, inevitably
happen to me as I depart from this part of the macrocosm?
Fearing what would happen to me, I cannot but wish that someone
out there can teach me how to deal with fears of what will come to me
as a matter of course! In the end, I'll be coerced into searching for the
next stage!

*JRHCC = Jefferson Rehabilitation Health Care Center in New Jersey

Andrew K. Ha
Gibbstown, NJ

[Hometown] *Gibbstown, NJ* [Ed] *doctorate holder* [Occ] *retired professor* [Hobbies] *reading and writing* [GA] *one of TOP hundred educators throughout the world*
Several years ago, I had a chance to stay at the Jefferson Health Center, New Jersey to receive physical therapy, which lasted about a month. During my stay there, I felt as if I were dwelling in a foreign land, where I had a totally different time and space that cut me off from my own planet. This unique experience made me envisage what might happen to me someday outside this planet and this inspired me to produce this particular poem.

Your Eyes Are Red...

You scared me today, staring the way you did,
From horizon's ceiling, far out West, yonder.
Sporting your angry eyes; oh, were they beef red?!
Your silence too made me worry, and to wonder.

You couldn't be blushing, as strangers we're not,
Such good friends we were from my young years.
You used to walk with only me, and too, to hang out;
And you always flashed a smile from ear to ear.

The tricks you used to play, I remember well;
How you'd leave me each month, and vanish,
Deftly, later you'd peek, wearing a new veil,
Sickle, other masks you wore with relish.

Today's veil, never before seen, left me floored.
Numbing my mind, many questions flashed.
Had we let you down, your warnings ignored?
Your hopes for the heaven we inhabit quashed?

Answer came soon, as a news item scene;
"Wildfires ravaging West Coast prime land."
Billowing smoke filled the television screen,
Obscuring the setting sun's dwindling brand.

This is the reason why in anguish you cautioned?
Would we humans, the trustees of our earth,
Heed your dire warnings, match our actions,
To save our planet, with resolve, oft dearth?

Puthalath Koroth Raghuprasad
Odessa, TX

[Hometown] *Odessa, TX* [Ed] *MD,MRCP, ABIM, ABAI (London)* [Occ] *physician* [Hobbies] *painting, writing, inventing, poetry, astronomy/astrophysics* [GA] *21 US patents*

What Was I Saw

I was freely.
Looking of memory.
I saw free.
I was finally.
Finally, I saw free.
I saw freely.
Looking on memory.
I was free.
I saw finally.
Finally,
 I was free.

Derek F. Walsh
Millis, MA

[Hometown] *Millis, MA* [Ed] *writing* [Occ] *writer/poet* [Hobbies] *riddles, 3D puzzles* [GA] *building a dollhouse for my niece*
I grew up with a loving and supportive family. The memories of the times I have spent with them is what helped to inspire this poem. I am submitting this poem because of those memories and to take part in the world around me.

Magic

To be born
during the witching hour,
on the Ides of March.
To live in-between
the living and the spirits.
To know something
before it happens.
To sense and
communicate with
the beyond.
To have visions
while sleeping.
To feeling
other's feelings.
To using
herbal remedies
for healing.
To be someone
to have these
special abilities
is a gift.

Jessica Vollaro
Barrington, RI

[Hometown] *Barrington, RI* [Ed] *high school* [Hobbies] *reading, writing* [GA] *having my cats*
My great-great Grand'Mere was a high priestess for the Iroquois tribe. I inherited her talents and I'm slowly learning on my own. I'm learning how my abilities work and this was something I wish to share.

Grateful for My Life

Think about how you could run when you were young
All the energy that you used to have all day long
Then you got a job or had kids and things were wild
The older you got the more things started to slow down
You started losing family and friends who were way too young
Health issues started happening to you, your family and friends
Some people improved and others got worse
As time went on you lost more family and friends
Losing loved ones is so very hard to bear
Thankfully I still have my health and can still help others
Grateful for the Lord keeping me useful and still on my feet

Sharron G. Dorst
New Glarus, WI

[Hometown] *New Glarus, WI* [Ed] *high school graduate* [Occ] *retired* [GA] *having helped people all my life and so grateful I still can*

Gift from Heaven

Our sweet little precious baby child, into our lives you bring such smiles!
Ever since that awesome day, when you came down from Heaven to stay!
We marvel daily as you grow, teaching you what you should know.
Laughing at each face you make, until our funny-bones all but ache!
Adoring your eyes so vibrant and new, as they dance around to absorb the view.
With every stage of life you climb, we wonder what dreams are on your mind?
You love this time of day the best, when you lose your clothes and get undressed!
For the time has come for a bubble bath, where you wiggle and giggle and love to splash!
Then all the excitement tucker's you out, not before laughter brings hiccups about!
This "night-night" ritual is a blessing to go through, it's a precious tradition we're honored to do.
The ambiance is set with soft music and lights, with all of your "binkies" and friends for the night.
After rocking you gently and kissing your cheek, you drift off to NahNah Land as you sleep.
So many expressions cross over your face, as angels carry you to a secret place.
You laugh and play and have so much fun, then you're back at home before the rising sun!
When it's time for you to finally arise, you stretch and yawn, then open your eyes.
Eager to eat and eager to play, eager to start a brand new day!
New adventures are around the bend, just waiting for you to begin!
New challenges for you to master, another day, another chapter!
Peace and contentment blesses our lives, as we walk together in the footsteps of Christ.
So grateful to God for blessing us so, with our gift from Heaven that He's bestowed!

Darlene Ware Horzepa
Ormond Beach, FL

[Hometown] *Ormond Beach, FL* [Ed] *high school/administrative* [Occ] *retired/disabled* [Hobbies] *poetry, decorative artist, calligraphy, photography, murals, baby albums, graphic design, yearbook* [GA] *son (34)*

Love Is . . .

Love is...

Infinite...
All encompassing...
Hidden...
Messy...
Perspective...
Weak...
Hurtful...
Forgiving...
Helpful...
Strong...

Me.

Shay Maria Houlton
Manhattan, KS

[Hometown] *Manhattan, KS* [Ed] *military life for 30 years* [Occ] *administration* [Hobbies] *all types of crafts and my puppies* [GA] *my beautiful, wonderful daughters*
I'm learning to love myself unconditionally and to accept the love of others. I think when someone was shown situation love growing up, it takes a long time to accept unconditional love. Always choose love.

Hazel

I'm so glad you were my sister.
It was such a short time ago
A young lady set my heart aglow.
Your smile was so appealing—
How could anyone tell you no?
Even though you may not know it
Your smile just set my heart aglow.
You were sweet and you were gentle;
Your kindness just overflowed.
I'm so glad you were my sister;
I hope I let you know.
Now that you are gone
I will miss you so.
How much you do not know
I have always loved you.
During these last years together
I hope I told you so.

Vera M. Meney
Rochester, NY

[Hometown] *Ingersoll, Ontario* [Ed] *high school* [Occ] *retired* [Hobbies] *music—piano* [GA] *raising happy family*

From the First Moment

From the moment I first saw you
I have loved you...
God led me to you
God won't let me forget you
In my heart you truly are
My one and only soulmate
From the first moment I saw you
You have never left my mind
My heart is yours through eternity
Even when we are not together
You are always with me
My constant love without a pause
You are my strength and my belief
You flow through my every vein
You know my heart
As well as you know my mind
Please hold on tight hon'
To our love so very dear
For I truly believe in you and I
Knowing our love shall never die.

Debra Stuart James
Lexington, KY

[Hometown] *Glasgow, KY* [Ed] *Bachelor of Art, art studio, University of Kentucky and post-graduate certificate, human resources, Capella University* [Occ] *retired from healthcare* [Hobbies] *painting, poetry, love of nature and animals, and travel* [GA] *writing poetry for over fifty years*
I have been blessed with a passion for the arts from childhood. From the age of three I drew pictures in an art book that my mom gave me. In high school, I developed a love for poetry and that is when I started writing and never stopped. Painting and poetry are my life's passions fulfilled.

Uvalde, Texas

Robb Elementary School class gathers.
In walks the devil's servant with a gun.
Tragedy strikes. The innocent are killed.
The media reports this as they do.
A shocked, bewildered nation looks in tears.
The government comes to investigate.
Is God's hand of judgment on us all?
Have we committed great national sin?
If so, let us repent and be blessed.
As we were long ago and far away.

Lewis Walling Findley
Port Wentworth, GA

[Hometown] *Port Wentworth, GA* [Ed] *high school* [Occ] *janitor, retired* [Hobbies] *net surfing* [GA] *Hello, readers, I'm trying this one in blank verse instead of the usual attempts at Shakespearean sonnets I usually do. It's about the school shootings in Uvalde, TX.*

The Raven Cries

A raven cries amidst darkening night.
A bewildered lioness on a far plain
Sadly hugs close her remaining cub.
Earth's sorry plight is a loathsome sight.
Where is paradise?
Has a cruel artist, intent on destroying beauty
Taken the lives of imperiled species with stroke of plastic brush?
How may one explain this man-created charade of death?
The call of the wild is defiled.
Desire for wealth and expansion into
Nature's remote, vast waters and encampments is devastating.
Lives of elephants, bears, rhinos, reptiles, bees,
Ocean inhabitants, whales, and seals are imperiled.
Earth's species are poisoned, polluted,
Or become cheap trophies, food, or a rug.
Men gaze longingly at planets and stars yet often ignore Earth.
Is humankind ready to explore untouched distant places?
Until men find peace with each other and love the environment,
Perhaps intrusion into alien worlds should
Remain beyond human acquirement.

Gail Logan
Macon, GA

[Hometown] *Wellfleet, MA* [Occ] *taught English, worked for a few newspapers, and wrote book reviews for nine years* [Hobbies] *most outdoor activities, animals and nature are God's love* [GA] *I have two degrees from the University of Rhode Island (URI) BA, MA, wrote MA thesis on "Classical influence in Spenser's Poetry" (Edmund Spenser) and wrote 5 books, worked for satellite dish company, and traveled world. I've always been fascinated by ancient poetry. It is a link to understanding the past or what came before us. The Greeks, Romans, and ancient Hebrews left historic legacies found in writing. The ancient poetic texts are history. Mythology is sometimes telling us something other than myth. It tells us where we came from and where we are going.*

Sacrifice

My dad sacrificed his life
    for people's freedom of this world.
My dad put his life on hold
    when the government was concerned.
My dad made sacrifices daily
    and still has sacrifices to pay.
By the pain in his legs and his back he's suffering
    plus from agent orange in so many ways.
He sacrificed for our freedom,
    for yours and my freedom, too.
He fought for our flag to fly high,
    yes he fought for our red, white, and blue.
I take pride in my dad, in what he did
    and still does to this day.
For my dad is my hero
    in every way.
He has made sacrifices
    beyond what we know.
For this is a discussion
    that he does not disclose.
A sacrifice is a selfless thing to do.
When you sacrifice you are thinking
    of others and not thinking of you.

Marsha DeVoe Melton
Monroe, NC

[Hometown] *Monroe, NC* [Ed] *Parkwood High School graduate* [Occ] *disabled poet* [Hobbies] *writing poetry, going to nursing homes and singing to the elders* [GA] *having poetry published in newspapers and books*

God has blessed me with a talent to write poetry about anything and everything. But today, I used my talent to write about my dad's sacrifice and how he sacrifices everything for everyone else. I am so thankful and blessed to have a dad like him.

To Emilia

The little hands seem to know
When to hold on and
When to let go,
And there is no sleep
Without a story
Or two.

Her own stories
Starting always with
"Did you know..."
Being more interesting
And more complex than the printed one,
I fathom how could I ever
Match such fantasy and details.

A breath of fresh air,
Her curly hair tightened in tresses
And the ever-present smile in her eyes,
She hugs me
And the world is mine once more.

Tiziano Thomas Dossena
Yonkers, NY

[Hometown] *Yonkers, NY* [Ed] *BA in Italian, BS in liberal studies, BA in environmental studies* [Occ] *editorial director* [GA] *2019 Sons of Italy literary award*
I write to release internal energy that otherwise would be trapped inside me and cause imbalance and stress. Love and family are my topics and only rarely do I touch on other subjects. I edited many books but I found editing poetry the most challenging task. This poem was inspired by my granddaughter, who brought so much joy into my life.

Reflection

A picture I see through a thin glass
The reflection I see your true color.
It's a human being without any class,
I can see her soul without valor.

Can one truly see another's soul?
Through this reflection I see it clear.
It's another being I see not whole,
She's not as pure as the love I hold dear.

I can see a heart with a scar fresh.
Yet my love must remain strong.
A bleeding heart running down my flesh,
I can't help but take the pain as long.

A reflection within this mirror deep,
It shall show the truth within my eyes.
It shall test my strength at its peak,
In this reflection of melancholy cries!

What reflection are you that I see afar?
But I know you are within my reach.
I see those flowing tears in your heart,
I'd like to say it yet I cannot speak.

Carolyn Hines
Rosemead, CA

[Hometown] *Los Angeles, CA* [Ed] *legal secretarial Beverly Hills Bar of California* [Occ] *admin. asst.* [Hobbies] *writing, cooking, and spending time with loved ones* [GA] *being a published poet*
My experiences in life are what inspire me in writing poetry, and to add to this inspiration is the reality of evolvement surrounding worldwide events. I'm sincerely grateful to have acquired this gift of writing. I look forward to writing many more inspirational poems.

My Untamed Heart

My untamed heart is
like the ocean in rough seas
It feels like I cannot breathe
I have good days and bad
Wish I had someone to take
the pain away
A kind man with a great smile
Hopefully he would stay a long
While
A touch of his hands and
love from his heart would
tame
My untamed heart

Rebecca Bowman
Green Bay, WI

[Hometown] *Sheboygan, WI* [Ed] *high school* [Occ] *server* [Hobbies] *writing and training my pet birds, traveling* [GA] *raising my son and saving up money to travel*

A Letter to Myself

I am not worthless;
I am worthy.

I am not undeserving;
I am deserving.

I will not be a second choice;
I will be the first prize.

I will not be walked on;
I will stand up and fight.

I will not be unloved;
I will be loved.

I don't have to be liked by anyone,
Nor even liked by everyone else.

I have broken free of the norms,
I have healed all broken wounds.

I may have darkness in me.
I may have madness in me.

Now I am free to be me.
And me is who I am going to be.

John E. Weaver
Erie, PA

[Hometown] *Cambridge Springs, PA* [Ed] *Butler Community College, emergency medical services* [Occ] *emergency medical technician* [Hobbies] *writing, photography, traveling, cooking, spending time with loved ones and my cats* [GA] *receiving American Heart Association's HERO's award*
Helping others is my passion. Be it in their time of need or not, there is no greater thing that I love doing. Writing has been my escape from stress and the world. It has helped me stay in touch with reality and with myself for many years.

Layers

Fear in its many forms
Gallivants to derail my life's pleasures
And poisons the serenity of things we do for love.
I am the bearer of the web of pain that hangs around my neck.
Nobody but me makes sense of it all
And amidst the tumbling thunder that brings the utmost suspense
Presents an awful beat at the center of my very fainting heart.
Tell me "I am sorry" but take me off not from your prayers
With focus, guide me from the wrong to the right, you all-knowing!
As my imaginations creak in to sweep the balance off my thoughts
I yawn as I peep through my window of hope for grace
To get used to the dynamics of my nightmares for an escape
And thwart the desires of my future's monsters.
Deciding to be an artist of my dreamland
I say "NO" to being an everlasting victim of my life's vicissitudes
And as my hallucinations evaporate day-by-day
Behold, I see my haunting self-blame expire
As I ask for the resurrection power that wows my innermost being
To peel off the layers that torture my very self
And that tears down the strongholds of my fall-apart.

Raymond Obeng
Maynard, MA

[Hometown] *Nkawkaw, Ghana* [Ed] *Doctor of Education, organizational leadership concentration* [Occ] *compliance officer III* [Hobbies] *watching UFC Fight Night, movies, soccer, and international news* [GA] *an opportunity to teach at Harvard University part-time*
On January 29, 2022, we had a powerful nor'easter kick up blinding blizzard conditions with high winds that caused widespread power outages, giving me an opportunity to spend the time to watch Netflix's (2022) series 1 of The Woman in the House across the Street from the Girl in the Window, *that inspired me to write this poem. It was, indeed, a moment in my life to learn to seek for answers during the pandemic and make sense of the good and the bad as coronavirus variants creep into our overall lives and try to rip our very sanity.*

Abundance

Limbs of the tree
Bowed down to the ground,
Heavy with golden apples.

Neighbors came and friends came
To harvest the abundance.
Slowly the boughs rose
And took their rightful places.

In the top branches apples lingered.
Who would be able to pick these apples?
I wondered and worried.

Still, they clung to their high places
Until one morning they were on the ground,
Waiting for me to pick them up.

Jean Elizabeth Easterly
Hayward, CA

[Hometown] *Hayward, CA* [Ed] *EdD (education)* [Occ] *professor emerita* [Hobbies] *gardening, hiking, traveling, Bible study* [GA] *I have prepared elementary and high school teachers to make a positive difference in the world.*
We live in a home that overlooks San Francisco Bay. Our backyard faces a forested area where deer abound. Inside our fenced backyard we have a magnificent apple tree that faithfully produces apples every fall. We are blessed with great neighbors and friends who share in the abundance of the apples. We use a fruit picker that reaches up high but there are always some apples out of reach. Eventually, the out of reach apples fall to the ground and are quickly gathered up.

Push Pull

I push, pull, massage and manipulate
Words until they achieve symmetry
And my thoughts correlate and coordinate,
Arranged into rhyming poetry.
I push, pull, massage and manipulate
Emotions to feel the way they used to.
"Things'll get better." The situation'll ameliorate.
"I put cancer behind me. This'll pass, too."
But manipulation isn't good enough.
This new tragedy's making me a victim.
Things are starting to get tough.
I'm still suffering with the same symptom.
Will life be a downhill slide from now on?
Is this the beginning of the end?
How much more will I be able to carry on?
How far does "quality of life" extend?
The doom and gloom has its moments.
I'm starting to feel passed by.
At what point do panic attacks commence?
How do I tell the world "Goodbye"?
Tho I walk thru the valley
Of the shadow of death,
I have stubborn tenacity,
Living breath to breath.

Al Smith
San Diego, CA

[Hometown] *San Diego, CA* [Ed] *two associate degrees—computers, electronics* [Occ] *retired* [Hobbies] *poetry, dancing, playing cards* [GA] *blue ribbon at the county fair for crochet*
This poet publishes under the name of Al Smith. That way he can say he's doing his part for the environment. His name's been recycled. He was named after his grandfather. When he was born, his family was so poor that even his name's a hand-me-down. Al graduated from high school in Monticello, UT. Monticello's elevation's 7,000 feet. Since he now lives in San Diego, you could say that his life's gone downhill.

In Our World of Faces

Beaming, illustrious, vibrant are the faces,
Adorned in our churches; lofty ancient places.

Viewing...yet not so close, He watches and sees all
Seen soulmates so holy, wherein we are enthralled!

Museums show them; we are stunned as we gaze!
Labels, stamps and posters; paintings we often praise.

Colorful circus clowns, enchanting movie stars...
Before us, on large screens, those Disney avatars.

Surrounding all through life; bloom, parade, then mature
Organ rattled kisses; puckered cheeks swipe demure.

Great millions, none alike, taught how to stay freshed
Remembered just a few; eyes, skin, freckles; impressed!

Outliving many loved, among the world's given
Endlessly, moods expressed; fearless, happy livin.'

Watched young looks change so fast, Lo! Age brings grimaces,
Amazing countenance... in our world of faces!

Glenn Howard Voirol
Fort Wayne, IN

[Hometown] *Fort Wayne, IN* [Ed] *Central Catholic High School, Purdue UN* [Occ] *automotive design engineer, air force mechanic* [Hobbies] *building, crafts, travelling, hiking, camping, fishing, gambling, dancing bbshop, antique cars, writing, figure skating, and playing string instruments* [GA] *performing at an open skating competition at age 65, won ten gold metals*
The inspiration I had to compose poetry all began at age seventy, when my wife became a cancer patient. I started to use the time during her treatments to comfort her, and while contemplating, started writing. I began to set myself in a place where I describe, see, or feel what I think others have; also to show appreciation of the manifold blessings many take for granted every day. My school teachers told me to consider the journalist profession as they enjoyed my compositions. As for me, all forms of writing are a most fulfilling, enlightening, and rewarding endeavor.

Journal: Lavender Sails

I love the word lavender
I love the color lavender
I wish it were my name!

Lavender is soft,
Fragrant and romantic.
Lavender is gentle and
Easily assimilated
Into a pallette.

Have you ever seen
A rare lavender moon!
Does the touch of lavender
In the Almighty's rainbow
Excite you, too?

Sigh...
My all-time favorites
Are the lavender clouds
In the sunset that eventually
Separate to look like
Lavender sails!

O' lavender, take me away!

Rhonda S. Galizia
Zelienople, PA

[Hometown] *Kittanning, PA* [Ed] *TECU associate of Christian counseling/pastoral counseling & psychology* [Occ] *biblical wisdom & counseling/fully ordained minister* [Hobbies] *poetry, photography, art, singing/songwriting, piano/guitar, birds, plants & flowers, sunflowers & pumpkins* [GA] *graduating TECU with a 3.86 GPA, despite a massive stroke*

There's so much war and strife, division and downright wickedness in the world now, that I gratefully relish the special moments the Lord provides me! Remember being a child and lying on the ground with your siblings or friends, discerning God's sky art? What a wonderful time that was! Sometimes it evoked gasps, sometimes applause, and others times, even laughter. Praise the Lord there is no law against a senior citizen reliving those memories and enjoying what He has given to everyone so freely! How true His word, the heavens declare the glory of the Lord!

Hello, Mama

It's too long since I last wrote
You've been gone since forever
Oh how I miss you
So much has happened
You lost a daughter
I just lost a son
My husband died the year after you
I don't miss him, I miss you
You have six great-grandkids
I live in Missouri
It is so beautiful here
The silence is so peaceful
We can forget the trauma
Of Arizona and Michigan
We could walk by the Missouri River
Never to look back or remember
My youngest girl is a pearl of great price
She cares for me before herself
Even with a cancer scare
She and her mate came to Arizona for me
Now I am safe I love you Mama

Sharon Elaine Eoff
Moscow Mills, MO

[Hometown] *Moscow Mills* [Ed] *two years of college* [Occ] *retired* [Hobbies] *reading, writing, hiking, geology, astronomy, cooking*
I lost my oldest son eight months before I wrote this and I was feeling lost and missing him so much when a little voice in my head said write to your mama. So I did and this poem was what I wrote.

Prevention Any Way You Can

When you take it
One day at a time
Anything is possible
Write a poem, make it rhyme

Day or night
Put the poem down
Even if you must
Put on the light

Exercise whenever you can
Reduce the heart attack risk
Maybe the PTSD risk too
Dance, sing to your favorite disk

Morning, afternoon or night
Anytime of the day is just right
To take care of yourself
Your beauty will be out of sight!

Saundra Theresa Russell
Tucson, AZ

[Hometown] *Tucson* [Ed] *master's from NYU* [Occ] *retired* [Hobbies] *writing poetry, publishing poetry books* [GA] *Poetry Fest Hall of Fame*
Living with diagnoses of fibromyalgia, MS, and chronic sciatica, I write poetry to help calm some of the pain. I am a registered nurse with a master's degree from NYU in nutrition. I am a fifty-plus year registered nurse, (former thirty-five year registered dietitian and member of the Academy of Nutrition and Dietetics) and Food Service Director at Harlem Hospital in NYC. I am also certified image consultant and I am a multi-award-winning, independent published poet. I have published five books. I am in the PoetryFest Hall of Fame despite having lifelong dyslexia.

Beyond Broken

Storm around the horizon
Creepin' like a soldier
Turbulence has my scent
I tried so hard to lose her
This is me broken

Savage beasts let wild
Beneath rolling thunder
Misery has my scent
Refusing my surrender
This is me broken

The storm is "she"
She wields all power
She has my scent
She reminds me every hour
This is me beyond broken

Jeff Culling
Hollywood, FL

Rain

rain, rain
drops into tears
for the next day
for the next wrinkle crying
among trees
and disappeared somewhere
in the sky
where my birds
still flying high
singing about free
way of life
I heard you now.

Elizabeth Plater-Zyberk
South Miami, FL

[Hometown] *Miami, FL* [Ed] *philosophy* [Occ] *singer*
[Hobbies] *gypsy singer* [GA] *every moment of life*
I am still alive with my poetry.

Wish You Were Here

Wish you were here
Years go by
Wish you were here
But I still cry
Wish you were here
Pain still fresh
In my mind
These are my sorrows
For better tomorrows
Still feel
Empty and hollow
As dark clouds follow me around
Like a shadow
They're a part of me now
Happiness turned sadness
Love turned anger
Barely recognize myself
I've become a stranger
I wish you were here
Right here next to me
But I got memories.

A. E. Charles
Stone Mountain, GA

Life's Value

You don't know the true value of something until you don't have it anymore
What will you do then? When your heart's been ripped out from its core
When the sun no longer shines
And everything you once knew about a person is left behind
How do you move on?
When all essence of your loved one is gone
How do you just be
The person you were before this scene
One step forward and two back
It's impossible to move on without you, Pap
Nobody can prepare you for this life
Nothing will ever be alright
Now I'm left to pray
To see him again someday!

Tracey Zimmerman
Ashland, PA

[Hometown] *Ashland, PA* [Ed] *high school* [Hobbies] *writing poems, meditating, collecting pins and earrings* [GA] *having my poems published*
I live in a small town in Pennsylvania. This poem is about losing my grandfather in 2016. His death hit me very hard. And I expressed a lot of my emotions through my poems. I'll always miss him. But, I hold him close in my heart.

Unlawfully Awful

Can't walk around without being thrown to the ground.
Can't ride in my whip without being hit my lip.
PoPo still gets great joy out of calling me boy.
Used to happen only in the southern states,
Now it happens, you pick it, in any state.
What are you being taught in the academy or whatever school?
I know what it is called, don't trust black people rule.
Kick him, beat him, he ain't s—-,
He is always a target you can hit.
What happened to your cultural awareness skills?
You don't have any because you think you have a license to kill
Any black person and that's a fact.
Protect and serve that's a damn lie,
It must mean you and yours because it definitely doesn't
Mean my family and I.
You sat back and watched us kill each other and then you began to grin.
When you thought we were not doing it fast enough, you began to join in.
When is it going to stop—when, when, when?
The good ole' boys, yeah they're still prevalent,
Thought they were supposed to be irrelevant.
The good ole' boys are still up to no good.
They now wear uniforms and badges instead of a hood…

Raymond A. Thomas
Henrico, VA

I'm Proud to Be an American

I'm proud to be an American
To live in the land of the free
To know I will always honor
The flag of liberty

I know that I can live
I can work and laugh and play
And kneel before my bed
As to my God I pray

The men and women of this country
Who for us went to war
They shed their blood for all
As many had before

I want everyone to know
That justice will prevail
If we stand and salute the flag
Our country will not fail

One nation under God
Forever we will be
Let us stand together
America is free

Kayla Kimball
Blue Earth, MN

[Hometown] *Waupaca, WI* [Ed] *high school* [Hobbies] *writing poetry, being a Minnesota sports fan* [GA] *still being able to write poetry after being diagnosed with MS in 1967*
I worked outside my home for thirty-two years. I now live in St. Luke's Care Facility in Blue Earth, MN. I spend my days writing poetry.

Bright Rainbow Rising

I see a bright rainbow rising
I see hope on the way
I see healing and renewal
I see good times today
Good vibes tonight
Cause it's bound to enhance your life
There's a bright rebirth on the rise

Dorothy Ann Harris Moy
Southfield, MI

[Hometown] *Southfield, MI* [Hobbies] *writing poetry and doing artwork*
The inspiration for this poem was the Kadima/DSO music group and the Credence Clearwater revival song "Bad Moon Rising." My "Bright Rainbow Rising" helped me during my cancer fight in 2021, had chemo and surgery—a success, in remission since September 2021. My "Bright Rainbow Rising" is dedicated to cancer warriors and survivors.

Built with Faith

We have built our home upon rock and not upon sand alone. Our youth might be slipping away but the best is yet to be for you and me. With our trust becomes one love for we have built our home upon the rock and not upon sand alone. There will be times of sorrow and pain. There will be times of sunshine and rain. But for you and me will come the gain for we have built our home upon rock and not upon sand alone. For as we stand alone our strengths came together for we have built our home upon rock and not upon sand alone. When fears come knocking at our door with our faith fear can be no more for we have built our home upon rock and not upon sand alone.

Romona Newell
Peru, IL

We married in 1956; we had very different backgrounds. Donald went through the depression and I was in a orphanage from three till I was fifteen. In 1980 they found I had breast cancer; the prognosis was not good. Implant was put in it was a licker, had it removed. It left a lot of complications. We both knew we were strong together and needed to be for our family. I wrote this poem knowing this. I can't write the hardships we went through only how strong together. Donald passed away in 1997 grateful for almost forty-two years.

An Alternate Reality

We spend our time on Earth to play
and that's what they say—
but is there another day?

Where do we go when we leave—
leaving others to cheer or grieve.

Will they join us in another world soon enough
which can make departing for the living tough.
But is God more generous than we think
by giving us another chance to blink.

The producer of the play can only get actors from Himself
which is why the actors can never see the producer
who is disguised as the actors
and that is the strange and simultaneous factor.

Get that understanding clearer
and be to thine own nature—the seer.

Henry F. Mende
New City, NY

[Hometown] *Manhattan, NYC* [Ed] *high school, art school* [Occ] *artist, baker, retired* [Hobbies] *space art paintings, jazz keyboard improv, essays, poetry* [GA] *dealing in the moment and being myself*
This poem, "An Alternate Reality," was written in the passion of a truth that we are in reality multi-dimensional beings and exist simultaneously in a matrix of different dimensions. Aside from this I'm a normal person married with our two cats and retired from two careers in commercial art and baking. My main hobbies are producing space art illustrations and jazz keyboard improvisation. Poetry on the other hand has only dawned later within periods of writing essays on esoteric subjects. As an aging trekker I find myself spiraling down to Earth. Live long and prosper!

A Great Moment in Time

Kayla Kayla & Levi too we took the ride to Maryland to visit our jewels. It was a bright Saturday in March the sun was glowing in the sky the picture of an arc. It brought my heart joy to see Kayla the little girl grow into a young woman shaping her world. Little Levi, the little man he is reminds me of the King of Siam These are times when we must connect strong to our family and our people in spite of all that's going on! Kayla and Levi are our offspring to prepare. We must pour into them all that we have! They are our present and our future, too! They must represent truth and values in all that they do! They are an extension of us; they represent me and you. So please my dear Kayla, know that you are loved. Like a budding flower, you are coming into your own. Thank you for the opportunity to share your love. Let's make it the K&M connection, that'll be our way to hit a home run!

Marlene Theressa Lewis
Brooklyn, NY

[Hometown] *Brooklyn* [Ed] *educator* [Occ] *trained classroom teacher* [Hobbies] *listening to and attending musical concerts and other art aesthetics* [GA] *accepting the Lord into my life*
A meaningful relationship with Kayla, my granddaughter, began when she was five years old. As family members we believed we would have Kayla permanently. Being that the realization of that dream didn't occur, I wouldn't reconnect with her until she was twenty-one with a child of her own (a son whose name is Levi). This poem is the embodiment of the special moment when I saw Kayla, whom I was able to see during four stages in her life: when she was born, school aged, sweet sixteen, and more recently, a young adult. Consequently I have entitled my poem as an experience, "A Great Moment In Time."

luxury ride

empty promises
appearing all too real
dispense with thieves
and everything it is they
        luv to steal…

u've got nerves of steel;
u're banking the corner and braking hard
but, there, inside the turn—
who is that 1 driving u
from behind the wheel?

James W. Stonehouse
Delray Beach, FL

…perhaps, sum of us r better off flying planes or attempting to ride horses!

You Will Be There

Isabell all your beautiful
Thoughts and sensitive
Feelings seem lost.
This cruel disease is exacting
Such a tremendous, senseless cost.
I know they still exist
In the depths of your soul -
And someday will surface
Again whole.
You no longer remember
The words of life's song.
It's okay, Isabell, I will strive
To make right of this wrong.
When I listen to the beautiful music
We often shared—
When I smell the sweet aroma
Of a delicate rose—
And when the brackish smell of Barnegat Bay
Waifs through my nostrils,
You will be there.
And when your beloved daughters
and grandchildren fade into
The shadows of your mind
I will bring them forward
Hug and kiss them.
You will be there.

Stan A. Mendrick
Branchburg, NJ

[Hometown] *Branchburg, New Jersey* [Ed] *BA history, MA psychology* [Occ] *educator/counselor* [Hobbies] *playing harmonica, hiking, sailing, writing poetry, painting* [GA] *educating my three daughters* *My wife Isabell was diagnosed with Alzheimer's in 2010. She died five years later in 2015. I was, with help, able to keep her home to the end. Caring for a loved one with Alzheimer's changes who you are. Only if you had made the journey can you understand this. I am eighty-seven years old, blessed with three wonderful daughters and eight spectacular grandchildren who help make each day very special.*

If Only You Have Heard Me

I am the voice from the depths of the sea.
I would not be here, if only you had heard me.
But my echoes are so faint, my limbs so weak,
If you can hear me, I have a soul that breathe.

I have many questions from this deep abyss.
Wasn't I supposed to bring you joy and bliss?
Our eternal Father has created me with love;
The Lord has given you a free will from above.

If only you have heard me from your womb,
I will not be here and be home so soon.
I could have grown and been a world leader,
Or a devoted and loving mother or father.

But I no longer have a chance to have a life;
You have not heard me and had chosen the rife.
Then you told yourself, you are far away from me,
But from the depths, you are really not that free.

Even if I am gone, I still have a soul and a heart
Full of love for you, though we are now apart.
So, please hear our pleas, listen to our cries,
Don't let another unborn child join us, and die.

Virgilia Aberilla Smith
Marshall, MI

[Hometown] *Marshall, MI* [Ed] *Bachelor of Science in elementary education and registered nurse* [Occ] *retired registered nurse* [Hobbies] *traveling, writing, acrylic painting, gardening, reading, and playing the piano* [GA] *mother of two, retired nurse after 44 years, acrylic painter, lyricist of 12 songs in a CD, traveled to 19 countries and writing a memoir*

I wrote this poem on Mother's Day, May 8, 2022. It was written in honor of the many unborn children lost to elective abortion through the years. There is an on-going debate, increasing further division of our already divided country. Although some claim they have a right to have an abortion, they have forgotten that an unborn child has a right to exist, too. Life begins at conception. That is constantly questioned and debated. We are not here to judge anyone. Only our awesome God has the final say on judgment day. May the Lord forgive all of us.

Poetry over Breakfast

In my thoughts of you today
My heart is open to what you say!
The day is dawning into a beautiful day
Help me Lord show me Your way.
Give me strength
Give me hope
Shine Your light on me
So I can cope!
I see you in the sunlight
I see you in everything that is right
I will keep my eyes open all the day
I know you are near
So I have no fear!

Evie Hopkins
Kirkland, WA

[Hometown] *Kirkland, WA* [Ed] *Registered Nurse Degree* [Occ] *RN, Staff nurse for twenty-two years* [Hobbies] *Golf, sewing, writing poems and playing with grandchildren* [GA] *Becoming a nurse working with patients*
Evie Hopkins is a retired Registered Nurse: she worked as Staff Nurse for Dr. Kauth for 22 years also worked at Evergreen Medical Redmond WA for 3 years. She lives with her husband of 56 years Jim in Kirkland, Washington. They have three grown children Jim Jr., Steven and Tanya who all live in the area. They have 6 grandchildren; Cooper, Kesten (parents Tanya and John Delia,) a dog Patches. Samuel, Abigail & Hannah Hope Hopkins (she is called triple H), Caleb (parents Steven & Sarah Hopkins). Evie has written poems for pleasure since college. This poem was inspired by setting quietly after prayer before dawn in her favorite chair in the living room looking out the bay window sun coming up a beautiful sight to behold, "God is good His love endures forever".

Lost in the Dust of Time

Dead are conversations with a friend
Goals with others do not well blend
Separate ways seem to be the trend
Loneliness from distressing loss does not mend
  Lost in the dust of time

Remembered not where something was laid
Memories of yesterdays seem to fade
Overwhelming activities through which to wade
No longer is the mind sharp as a blade
  Lost in the dust of time

Tired of infuriating tweets and hostile roar
Good advice others seem to ignore
Each day, eyesight seems increasingly poor
Others seem to think you're a bore
  Lost in the dust of time

When moving about you're racked with pain
Caused by a problem no one can explain
Ointments, meds and herbs cannot tame
Be faithful, trust God through the hurtful stain
  God helps the faithful lost in the dust of time

Rom 8:26, I Cor 5:17, Psa 103:3

B. J. Boal
Des Moines, IA

Unfortunately, situations change. Nothing remains the same which can be disturbing. For some, things can be a challenge, overwhelming, worrisome, stressful, causing disturbing health issues. It seems helpful if there is close connection and relationship with God, our Creator, resulting in trust and faith, allowing strength and healing dissolving the crisis.

I Will Walk

I will walk with you up a mountain.
I will walk with you along the river by the fountain.
I will walk with you along the trail.
I will walk with you in rain, snow, and hail.
I will walk with you until day turns to night.
I will walk with you to the left and then to the right.
I will walk with you under a star.
I will walk with you near and far.
I will walk with you arm in arm.
I will walk with you because you have charm.
I will walk with you a golden mile.
I will walk with you down the aisle.
I will walk with you the rest of my life.
I will walk with you as husband and wife.
I will walk with you toward the light.
I will walk with you to Heaven because it's so bright.
I will walk with you because you're the best.
I will walk with you to our eternal rest.

Skip Clayton
Coraopolis, PA

[Hometown] *Beaver, PA* [Ed] *Beaver High School 1973* [Occ] *operations associate, Zamboni driver* [Hobbies] *writing poetry, reading, joke writing, walking, biking* [GA] *outstanding young man of America 1987,* Survivor *tryout (twice)*

I started writing poetry back in 2019 around the time covid started. I was always good with words and decided to challenge myself. When people told me my poems were good I wrote more. I started writing about any subject for variety—current events, news stories, history, or life in general. As of right now I have sixty-five poems that have inspired me. It gives me a sense of meaning and accomplishment. My wife's name is Lisa and we have one son, Daniel.

Hello Spring!

March, April, and May is supposed to be spring
So, Mr. Snow go away to do your thing.
Melt away and let the sun shine through,
So we seniors can do what we like to do.
Come to the center and see our friends and walk,
Drink a cup of coffee and have a little talk.
At the center, haven't fed the birds in days;
They probably think we have gone away.
But don't worry, we'll be back for bingo games,
And resume our walking and things will be the same.
So, hello spring and goodbye winter snow;
Can't say I'm sorry to see you go.

Barbara King
Clarksburg, MA

[Hometown] *Clarksburg, MA* [Ed] *high school* [Occ] *secretary to counsel on aging* [Hobbies] *writing poems and singing in choirs* [GA] *getting my poems published*
Since high school I have been writing poems. I have been married and had three children. I live alone now.

A Farmer's Thoughts

He heads down the orchard path
Having such the stress-filled mind
Carrying such a load
Staying ever so kind

Coming to a fork in the road
Wanting to be one that brings joy and light
Wondering if there is a secret code
That can be found in the dark of night

He learned just to go with the flow
To be in this act of the show
To be faithfully strong
To admit when he is wrong

Andrea Soller
Zanesville, OH

Daydreams

Dreams are made of wisp and whim,
of fluff and bits of nonsense.
They pay no heed to modes of prim
and proper stabs of conscience.

They plague us, young and old, by day
and by night—no less deceiving.
Our wandering thoughts their mischief play
and tangled webs go weaving.

A wistful look or passing smile
may give it vim and vigor,
and knowing we be fools the while—
we dream on...only bigger!

Our flights of fancy take us back
to when...and if only...
they never bother us with fact,
just soothe us when we're lonely.

But, lest we ever should forget
that brain—not brawn
has given us impetus,
however far we may have gone,
'tis dreaming that has led us!

Betty Paschall Grantham
Grantham, NC

[Hometown] *Grantham, NC* [Ed] *financial, investment, and insurance* [Occ] *retired* [Hobbies] *reading, writing, singing music, playing Scrabble with my husband Jerry, politics, Bible study and praying*
Dreaming inspired this poem! One of my favorite things is to take a few moments to sit on the front porch swing with the soft summer breeze blowing through my hair and just look out over the pasture with the horses frolicking with each other or quietly grazing and let my mind wander into day dreaming. It is so relaxing! Our great country of America is the envy of the world because we can dream and many of us fulfill those dreams! May God help us to retain that privilege!

Spiritual Me

In my shell, I rest calmly,
while the sound and fury plays outside.
As madness erupts and does its toll,
I sit back and try to make sense of it all.

On the outside, I look hurt;
My eyes make rain as I weather
the horrors that enter the ears and live in the heart,
but inside, the heart of a bull beats on.

Every day I awake with confidence;
the day's news unfurls from the steam of my coffee
and threatens to dim the sun like overcast,
broadcasting Ukraine, the ozone, and a school in Texas.

I stare adversity straight in the eye
like the way a dog eyes something he doesn't favor,
holding a needle and thread
to the face of a torn world.

Giulio Americo Bianchi
Middletown, NJ

[Hometown] *Middletown, NJ* [Ed] *Rutgers—currently finishing bachelor's degree in liberal studies* [Occ] *college student* [Hobbies] *writing, drawing, reading, bike riding, screenwriting, movie critique* [GA] *getting my associate's degree in liberal studies*

Every day when I turn on the news, I see a new terrible thing happening in the world. It hurts my heart to see people doing bad things to each other. Nevertheless, I stay strong and keep clinging to the hope that this world will change. I wrote this poem to inspire others to have faith and carry on, even in the darkest of times no matter how bad things may seem, to remind them that we are in this together and all we can do is love one another.

Up to Your Home

Oh, Great I Am, You had a plan,
Your children come up to Your home.

Each one You call, since Adam's fall
Can choose for You, the Savior true.

In life's hard walk and in our talk
The Spirit is here; we will not fear.

Oh, Great I Am, You had a plan,
Your children come up to Your home.

As life goes on, believe the Son,
Walk in His love, come from above.

This path leads home, the time shall come,
Eternal life will end all strife.

Oh, Great I Am, You had a plan,
Your children come up to Your home.

Darlene Wicksey
Independence, MO

[Hometown] *Independence, MO* [Ed] *college graduate* [Occ] *retired* [Hobbies] *writing, music* [GA] *writing several songs*
As a Christian I long to come "up to your home" O God. This is the heart cry for me to write this poem. All my poetry is from my walk with God. I am not always as close as I want to be but I know Him. He hears me and knows me. Jesus (Yeshua His Hebrew name), is God and I know loves me. He saved me from my sin, so I give Him glory when I write.

Star Dreaming

In the evening of summer solstice
the darkness slowly descends
upon the mountain's ridge as the
faint sigh of a cool breeze whispers
up and peace dissolves the heat
from the day's longest hours.
In stillness I wonder as I gaze
upon the serene stars dancing
for me in the night's cover of a silken sky.
The galaxy of stars sparkling
beautiful placing joy in my soul
as my imaginary footprints leap
upon the path of glittering constellations.
In my dream of timeless space
my steps are feather lite and
I start to feel as if I were a child.
I'll skip to play and hum a tune
then soon I'll rest upon sand's
sleep of a bright silver moon.

Debra Hollar
Lenoir, NC

[Hometown] *Lenoir, NC* [Ed] *East Wilkes High School* [Occ] *homemaker and poet* [Hobbies] *cooking, writing, home décor, reading* [GA] *editor's choice award—2004*
I am a senior citizen and poet living in the western mountains of North Carolina. I have written poetry for twenty years and I enjoy writing many styles and topics of poetry but I think the beauty of nature and my faith is what has inspired me the most in my writing. I have artistry published in several magazines and poetry books. I am always grateful for the blessing of having my work published by Eber & Wein.

Ocean Serenade

10,000 Leagues under the sea,
there's a black pearl for you
and a gold harp for me.
Neptune's treasures can be
found by the brave, but beware
thee abyss, be very afraid.
Strange creatures live there
sailors know well, or are these
silly stories from some fairy tale.
Where mysteries, seamonsters,
and mermaids have played.
The cries of misfortune weep
an ocean serenade.

Greg Werkmeister
Williston, ND

[Hometown] *Williston, ND* [Hobbies] *hunting, fishing, spending time with family* [GA] *wife, kids, grandkids, family*

The Mountain and the Lake

When we woke up this glorious sunny morning
Together we hiked these winding mountain roads
We wondered what it looked like a long time ago

Many streams must have been flowing
With mountain water so pure and clear
And all over the forest there were roaming
Lots of bears, mountain lions, and deer

Bluejays, hawks, ravens, and eagles
Soaring above the pine trees looking so regal
Squirrels and chipmunks searching for nuts
Their furry little tails swaying in a wind gust

Oh, these summer days when the rains came
With thunder and lightning we couldn't go out and play
How we anxiously waited for some glorious sun rays
For our plans have been delayed for too many days

But today we set sail on a grand pirate ship
So glad to see a blue sky it will be a fun trip
Many wonderful sites to see and pictures to take
As we sail across the beautiful Big Bear mountain lake.

Judy Russell
Big Bear City, CA

[Hometown] *Big Bear City, CA* [Occ] *retired* [Hobbies] *hiking, playing guitar, cooking vegan food, photography* [GA] *recording a Christmas CD at JEL Recording Studio, with Mom playing piano and family members singing and 7 poems published by Eber & Wein!*
This poem was inspired by my granddaughter Marlene, fourteen years old. She came up to our mountain cabin and we had rain and thunderstorms for three days, canceling our many plans. On the fourth day it cleared up and we were able to set sail around Big Bear Lake on The Pirate Ship! We all had a wonderful time and made many memories that will last a lifetime.

God's Saving Grace

God is love;
His love is true.
He loved you first
Even before you were you.

He came here
So long ago
Bearing a message,
That we should know.

He loved His Father,
and this was His will.
To take sin to the cross,
this He would fulfill.

While even as a child He preached of Heaven.
Sermons to all
that their sins could be forgiven.

He preached of grace to all
Who repented of their sin.
With mercy and gladness,
A new life is to be born again.

For you death will soon come,
But let it not be in vain.
But plant your eyes in God's word,
Repent, and be saved by His grace. Amen.

Lawrence Melvin
Greenup, KY

I am seventy-three years young, country-born and raised in Greenup County, KY. I have a GED education. I served in Vietnam. I've been happily married to my wonderful wife Ruth for fifty-three years. We have four children, eight grandchildren, one great-grand and another any day. I write poetry about my Lord and Savior. I try to witness to those lost of His love and mercy and to better help educate them of His coming again. May God bless us every one. Thank you and pray continually. Godspeed.

My Other Mother

Sally heard her stepdaughter talking
Two girls sharing the talk
The remarriage of her parents
into this new world Sally walked
Other friends did tell the tales
making new families after divorce
Some were easily adjusted to
Some were nightmares of worse force
Sally didn't mean to be eavesdropping
Curiosity made her silently stand
She treated this stepdaughter like the others
Being stepmother had never been her plan
Sally wasn't prepared for the secret
her stepdaughter told her friend
She choked up as she listened
She would soon be given a special pin
Mother's Day would be the occasion
Sally's heart felt all aglow
The pin would inscribe *my other mother*
Simple words to her heart she would hold.

Loraine Faschingbauer
Bloomer, WI

[Hometown] *Bloomer, WI* [Ed] *1 1/2 years college* [Occ] *activity director/assistant* [Hobbies] *writing, biking, hiking, sewing, traveling* [GA] *assistant pastor to folks inside and outside of church*

The Sea

I gaze across the vastness that is the sea
It touches something deep within me
I feel the wind across my weary face
Nothing compares to this place
I feel the ships pitch and roll beneath me
I am awed by the power of the sea
Of all the things I have seen
Of all the places I have been
The ocean touches me most deep within
I feel so small and insignificant
I am amazed by its wonderment
The ocean seems so vacant and lonely
It touches me inside my soul as it can only
I ponder all the wonders of the world around me
This is the one that holds and talks to me
This is where I belong upon the sea
She caresses me and blesses my soul
Wherever I go I am alive within her hold
As I stand here alone gazing across the sea
I feel most in touch with God as he is beside me

Morris S. Adams
Jacksonville, AR

[Hometown] *Sherwood, AR* [Occ] *retired* [Hobbies] *fishing, auto mechanics* [GA] *twenty-four years in the United States Navy*
US Navy retired, auto mechanic, truck driver, father to three, grandfather to eight, great-grandfather to five.

Words of Sand

Words of sand written on a deserted beach
Scattered as if swept by the savage wind
As tempestuous as sheer hopeless ambitions
Unforgettable words, chiseled in the marble
Just like bitter tears extracted from a tormented soul
These became ageless pearls at the bottom of the seas.
One day, when the storm will have subsided
And the old tears once shed on the deserted beach
Have become pure crystals along the years
I would come to think why had I cried?
Then time would have told me to forever abandon
This already calcified heart reduced to sandy dust
Prone to be blown and gone with the wind!

Quoc Sung Truong Ducam MBA
Santa Clara, CA

[Occ] *retired* [Hobbies] *photography, writing poetry, reading* [GA] *former technical advisor to the United Nations Development Program*
Born in Vietnam in 1934, I was educated within the French system through high school, then earned my Bachelor of Technical Science and Technology (United Kingdom) in 1962. In 1975, I emigrated from France where I had been living and working since 1962, to the United States as a refugee. The theme that inspired me to write the poem "Words of Sand" came from reminiscences of promises not kept and betrayed in my earlier youth. Now at eighty-seven years old, I enjoy creating music for piano black keys, writing poems, and learning foreign languages.

Follow Your Dreams

Your dreams are the
beginning of your success,
no matter what your
journey may be.
If you cannot see the end,
there is no beginning.
The mountains you come
across will be broken by
your determination to reach
your destination.
Don't give up; winners
never do!
If you have a dream, it could
be the start of greatness.

Ernest Asselin
Richland, WA

[Hometown] *Richland, WA* [Ed] *barber school and high school* [GA] *book self-publisher and writing poetry*
I'm sitting here—my cousins keep me thinking and going. Millie Ann, Linda, Tim, Greg—owner of the Shaw Cattle Co.—Mary my sister who I love so much, TG and Skeeter are great cousins. My kids say my work is great. I have written a book of short stories and won a lot of poetry contests. If it was not for God I would not have been able to do all this. I cannot forget my beautiful wife. Thanks to everyone who reads my work. Linda and her husband are retired. Tim is retired. More cousins I love.

Calling Mother Mary

Hail Mother Mary, blessed among women for your divinity,
and Blessed Virgin Mother of our Lord Jesus, His God-identity.
Pray for us who are mislead outside the Garden of Eden
to know we all are God's blessed children,
born to glorify Life's innate gift of divine grace to be certain
identities we personify on Earth merit eternal life in Heaven.

Thank you God almighty, our Supernal Father and Creator,
for Your sacred breath of transmutable life that sustains us.
And thank you Blessed Virgin Mother Mary for guiding us
to our Father's kingdom. Let it be...

Carol A. Sustarsic
Willowick, OH

The truth of Life's spiritual nature and the function of divine grace occurred to me after I read the Gospel of Saint Luke from a decoded version on its presentation in the Bible. Since the birth of Jesus was a momentous spiritual event in the life of the Virgin Mary who, along with her cousin Elizabeth, conceived inexplicably, resulting in the births of John the Baptist, and Jesus the Christ Child, I thought of "Calling Mother Mary" while praying for healing and world peace on a small rosary for praying to Bonne Saint Anne; not knowing at the time she was Mother of the Blessed Virgin Mary and grandmother of Jesus her Divine Grandson.

The New Normal

At evening sitting on my terrace
When the sun from the west beyond the mountains depart
I look up and I see swallows
I see swallows flying so low
Suddenly I see a cacophony of events
Office closures
Business closures
Movie theater closures
People sick with a virus
People unable to breathe
People angry
People in physical, emotional, and psychological trauma
People in isolation
People quarantined
Feelings of emptiness
Feelings of numbness
People wearing masks everywhere
Faces hidden behind a mask
People succumbing and dying from the COVID-19 virus
I sit, stare, and ponder about what has come upon humanity
A pandemic of unimaginable proportion has befallen mankind
People are scared, weary, and filled with questions and a great feeling of nostalgia
People are longing for life to be normal again
All we hear about is "the new normal"
Oh how humanity longs for a pre COVID-19 normalcy

Anne Uzoigwe
S. Salt Lake City, UT

I was inspired to write the poem "The New Normal" to depict what humanity has had to deal with during the COVID-19 pandemic. Millions of people died as a result of the afflictions of COVID-19. That indeed was a turning point. I consider myself to be an advocate, a humanitarian, a philanthropist, a floriculturists who fees a deep connection to living things.

We Are...

Framers of a new constitution,
Race and gender,
Ethnicity, lifestyle, and religion without discrimination,
Equality without an arbitrary measuring stick,
Determination, courage, and sweat built a community,
Overcoming the daily distress of oppression,
Maintaining a quiet resilience...

...Freedom.

Lynette Bajsarowycz
Philadelphia, PA

[Hometown] *Philadelphia, PA* [Ed] *AAS in accounting* [Occ] *retired (municipal government)* [Hobbies] *collecting 1960s memorabilia, vacations by the shore, attending cat shows, and 1960s memorabilia exhibitions, reading* [GA] *This is a tie—being invited to read at a poetry event for the first time and winning a poetry prize for the first time last year.*
I was active in the "poetry/spoken word scene" since the summer of 1985. I enjoyed reading poetry as a child. I wrote my first poem at age fourteen, an assignment for English class. And I didn't stop writing. I contributed poems to the high school literary magazine, and had a poem published in the College Poetry Review *in spring 1982. My work has appeared in* Poetry Forum Anthology, *several Eber & Wein anthologies,* PoetryInk Anthology, *and the* Free Venice Beachhead *newspaper. And I continue writing about "this thing called life!"*

Sophie's Poem

I forget you're dead.
Still leave the
Toilet seat down for you.
The Tuesday of your funeral
A yellow sun glowed at the graveside,
But a cold January wind
Still blew in from the north.
You had drifted off to sleep at 8:00
And never woke up again.
I didn't have the chance
To say goodnight or I love you.
Now you sleep eternally,
And all I can do
Is scribble this poem
To say goodnight and
I love you still.

Richard Stepsay
Aurora, CO

[Hometown] *Denver* [Ed] *BS creative writing* [Occ] *retired peer specialist* [Hobbies] *writing, coin collecting* [GA] *upcoming book of poetry titled* Sophie's Poem

Two-Minute Warning

We too together:
Fish, mums, and perspiration
Permeate the air.

Glynn Holmberg
New York, NY

I grew up in an age when sex was considered a basic need. Love was considered a growth need. We ended up having sex with people we did not love simply to satisfy a basic physical need. Love is an emotion we need and the heart is the seat of human emotion. Hence, we ended up loving those we never had sex with simply to satisfy a growing emotional need. Having sex without love is like writing a poem without rhythm or rhyme. It might be pleasing for the moment. It might even be noteworthy. Nevertheless, it will never be momentous.

Unseen Pain

Can you hear the beating of the drums so loud?
It is the same as the beating of my heart against my chest.
You may hear the sounds of the drums, but
you will never hear nor ever feel the pain within my chest.
The silence of this pain can't be heard or felt for it is within me.
Sometimes people look into my eyes and some of the pain is revealed with the tears forming
but tears shall never flow.
The more one denies it the worse it gets every day.
How much pain can one take until they begin to unravel?
Losing and caring about the events and people around them.
This pain of silence will never be heard nor seen, for the tears shall never fall.

Consuelo Giron
Denver, CO

Life's Expectations

I realize life expectations
My life like a book turning pages
One by one
Do this do that
An unending twist of events
From being a small child
To a teen
To an adult
Where has the time gone
So fast
I don't where the time went
Then suddenly I am older
With family around still
I love them so dearly
From afar as I miss my relatives from afar

Marielou P. Pascua
San Francisco, CA

[Hometown] *San Francisco, CA* [Ed] *associate's degree, various trainings* [Occ] *poet/artist* [Hobbies] *Zentangle art or other forms of arts, poetry writing, listening to music, writing* [GA] *getting my poetry published*
Some say I'm quiet and reserved. But through poetry and through art I am fierce and outspoken and strong. My poem is about growth and maturity.

Country Folk

I was raised out in the country,
on a dirt road, full of pot holes.
Some as big as gallon bowls.
Open fields with many farm gates
To keep the animals in with their mates.
A big pond for animals to get water, the right spot.
They gather around as the day is hot.
Plenty of kittens love milk, this makes
their fur feel like silk from the cows' milk.
Children are playing in the yard
Watching people go by in their car.
Many on their way to church.
A sermon given by Uncle Bruch.
At noon lunch is on the table.
Everyone eats, all that is able.
Country folk like to help each other;
People treat each other like a brother.
Gardens full of vegetables,
laundry blowing on the line;
They work hard every day, but that's fine.
That's what country folk do,
Country poor, country proud.
With a howy-u-do? Real loud.

Wilma Lee Shifflett
Mount Crawford, VA

[Hometown] *Mt. Crawford, VA* [Ed] *high school* [Occ] *cashier/retired* [Hobbies] *gardening, writing, cooking, crocheting* [GA] *having my poems published; my children*
This poem of country folk is the way I've always known. Grew up in a small place, or town, where we worked real hard. Everyone knew each other. A lot of kin folks all around. We grew our own food, raised our animals, didn't have much money. Wore a lot of hand-me-downs. But we were happy. Families were close. Mom and Dad, Dad worked, Mom stayed at home with her children. We did the chores at home, worked hard.

Mothers and Dads

God bless all mothers, faithful as the oceans tide.
Their kindness, love, and care last forever as a guide.
We would love to give you treasures, our means you're surely aware.
So please accept gifts more precious, our devotion, love, and care.
And God bless dads who helped pave the way
for all of us to be here today.
When a boy is just a little tyke
it's his dad he wants to be like.
Dad is also his daughter's source of pride.
She always counts on him to take her side.
And dads are versatile in so many ways.
They know when to holler and when to praise.
Because you're a dad, you need to know,
you're very important "so way to go."

John E. Luckovich
Edmonds, WA

[Hometown] *Edmund, WA* [Ed] *college grad* [Occ] *retired credit manager* [Hobbies] *exercise and yard work* [GA] *community recognition award through education*

Born Again

I have the word
of the Lord
Living in my heart
Jesus saved my soul
and He set me apart
His love is so real
It gives me a "Thrill"
Praise the Lord
I've been born again

I've been born again
by the blood of the Lamb
Jesus Christ
gave His life
on the cross
for my sin

I am living for Him
His love will never end
Praise the Lord
I've been born again

Doris Cox
Tunnel Hill, GA

[Hometown] *Dalton, GA.* [Ed] *High School Graduate* [Occ] *Textile Shaw Plant 81* [Hobbies] *Riding my bike* [GA] *Having my poems published*
Inspired by my brother Charles Pilcher who is about to enter Heaven's gate to be with the Lord.

The Poem

I try to write a poem or two
To wile away the time.
It stimulates the mind, you know,
And doesn't cost a dime.

I'll not compete with Robert Frost,
And a Shakespeare, I'll never be.
The lines are crude and simply put, but
I'm just trying to be me.

I manage to have an idea or two
As I type along the line.
It sure is fun to vent my thoughts
As I wile away this time.

Some day my kids will find
This book of little rhymes.
"Now look at that" they all will say,
"He had a real good time!"

Arthur C. Elvin
Greeneville, TN

[Ed] *some college* [Occ] *accountant* [Hobbies] *poetry, all kinds of music* [GA] *I have met and become friends with hundreds of wonderful people from all over the country and several foreign countries. I am a US Navy veteran.*
As I near my "90th" I revel in memories of my wonderful life. I would not change a thing.

Let There Be Life #3

June ninth, two thousand twenty-two
Our luminous moon was an alluring view
Aloha! LoveLeiella Dey Jones
The heavens blessed you with beautiful skin and strong bones
This world has given me a gorgeous pearl
So grateful that God has blessed me with a little girl
You're our number three, even though you're the first
I promise to always be here for you, for better never worst
Mommy was determined and truly invested in your home birth
Daddy is thankful and now knows the true meaning of "a woman's worth"
Today is the third day that our family lives on forever
Artist II, Aquarian, and Daddy will protect you, through any weather
Here on O'ahu, Hawaii, "you" made this tropical island paradise
Our Gemini with two sides, Daddy's fire and Mommy's ice
Innocence and purity
Your brothers and I are your security
"Parental anxiety of having a girl"
Your brothers and I will crush any nut from a squirrel
Celebrating seven joyous years together created you
The night you were conceived, Daddy told Mommy "I do!"
God said once more, "Let there be life"
Thanking your mom every day for becoming my best friend and wife!
I wished upon a star and my dreams came true
Proud to be a girl dad, thanking God for you!

Artist Clay Jones
Wahiawa, HI

[Hometown] *Tampa, FL* [Ed] *MS logistics management* [Occ] *government* [Hobbies] *writing, running, traveling* [GA] *father of three beautiful children*
Hello again Poetry Nation! This is my tenth published poem! This poem was inspired by the birth of my third child, who happens to be my first and only precious little girl, LoveLeiella Dey Jones! Having LoveLeiella here at home was an amazing and incredible experience! Her mother, LoveLeigh, two brothers, Artist II, Aquarian and I, are so excited to finally have her here! My wife, LoveLeigh delivered all three of our kids natural without any pain medication. She is a true champion and "I love her more than most!" God continues to bless our family and I'm truly thankful!

Pop's Prayer

Dear heavenly Father almighty God
Forgive us of our sins, of which there are many
Regardless of our status in life
We all have many blessing to be thankful for
Be with those who are less fortunate than us
Guide and direct us through the coming days
Send an army of angels
And put one on everybody's shoulder
To help us make wise decisions
In Jesus' name we pray
Amen

W. V. Sadler
Powhatan, VA

The Headache

Could everyone stop talking now, please?
Put that noisy trumpet down.
Please leave the room if you must sneeze.
I'm sorry my headache is causing your frown.

My head is pounding a monster drumbeat.
I can't balance loud noise with peace.
Impossible to be comforted sitting in my seat.
Even as I imagine tranquility under the trees.

Thank God I'm tired and I'll be asleep soon.
Worn out and burnt out, after letting off steam.
The goal is set and that is tomorrow at noon.
Hopefully when I wake, it will all have been a dream.

Darryl Monteiro
Fall River, MA

Progress for Man and God

World is divine! The heavenly twinkle of the stars is painted magic. The wonderful people of all trades gives us prayers. Our movie stars, our inspiring nurses, and scientist gives us health. The church! The state! Who cares about animals and charities who feed the poor. Word shineth! With gold, hope, and harmony and our red, white, and blue stripes flowing in the silvery wind. Music of love spreads; bells ring for our forefathers teachings.
The song of progress is set in brilliance of diamond stones.

Catherine C. Inserra
Clifton, NJ

[Hometown] *Clifton, NJ* [Ed] *high school/writing school* [Occ] *retired; nurse aid at home caring for the sick* [Hobbies] *poetry, music*
I love to write about God. Wrote a book of poems titled Vigil of Religious Poems.

The King's Highway

Today I started walking up the King's highway
It's the dawning of another new day
Not a cloud in the sky
Just a private moment between my Lord and I
The sun was shining oh so bright
Brighter than all the stars in the night
Sin had once covered my life
But now I am trying to be a good Christian wife
I now shine in God's love
Enjoy His blessing from up above
I will forever walk with Him on the King's highway
And make the most of every new day

Diane Updegrove Delcamp
Milton, PA

[Hometown] *Milton, PA* [Ed] *associate degree* [Occ] *domestic engineer* [Hobbies] *writing poetry, latch hook, reading*
I am a born-again Christian, like to attend church and church functions. My husband and I enjoy gospel concerts.

The Dream Team

We, who are trekkers on Tennessee trails,
Meet the able-bodied, strong, and fit at the trailhead.
Through winding wooded paths, we share our tales
Of woodland flora, fauna, birds, and bluffs.

But today, we meet a hiking team extraordinaire.
Melanie, born with spina bifida, sits in a wheelchair;
Trevor, her faithful partner, is blind from glaucoma.
He—the strong burly one—lifts her onto his back.

She grasps his shoulders as he belts her onto his hips.
Melanie emerges as the wide-eyed, vocal avant-courier,
Leading Trevor down the winding wooded trail.
She shares the vision and gives the commands.

They are a "Dream Team," modeling a lesson for life—
When we lay bare our strengths and weaknesses,
We can plug into a partnership niche to serve another,
As we trek through the twists and turns on life's journey.

A life of purpose and mutual merit may be found
In discovering a niche in someone else's "hitch."
Our temporal trails may be uphill and rocky,
But a dream team partner is a priceless treasure!

Rachel V. McKeel-Abrahamsen
Crossville, TN

[Hometown] *Crossville, TN* [Ed] *BS degree: German/English, plus advanced degrees in marketing, business management* [Occ] *retired HS German and English teacher* [Hobbies] *golf, hiking, writing and reading good poetry (classic and contemporary); writing letters to, and keeping tabs on, my 3 children and 10 grandchildren* [GA] *encouraging and ministering to drug-addicted women in jail*

During my community's annual hiking marathon, I met handicapped hikers, as well as people with limitations, who have found ways to cope with their limitations by engaging mindfully with people who are great partners. As we recognize the limitations we all have at various stages of our life, we may be fortunate enough to find a partner who is a "Dream Partner." Thankfully, I have found a dream partner in my second husband whom I married after losing my first husband in 2019. Hence, the hyphenated name change above.

The Shadow in the Night

I was walking through the dark one night
When I saw this shadow on the ground.
Then I heard a voice with a weeping sound.
I stood there startled as I knew,
This was the voice of my little boy who had died so young.
I started to cry knowing it was just in my mind.
Then I saw the figure in the dark, the figure of my son.
He said, "Don't leave me as I will always be with you in your heart."
Then the shadow faded, leaving me in the dark.

Darlene K. Lannholm
Galesburg, IL

[Hometown] *Galesburg, IL* [Ed] *high school graduate* [Occ] *retired from Wal-Mart* [Hobbies] *working with different organizations in the past* [GA] *raising a family of 4 children and have a stepdaughter*
I'm a mom and grandmother of many grandchildren. My loving husband and I are both retired. The inspiration for this poem is for two of our children, who each lost a son at a young age, one in his thirties, the other at seventeen. The oldest died in a tragic motorcycle accident, the younger just died an unexplainable death one night while watching the stars. They were both good, loving young men.

Today's Tophet

The fireplace
It's sooty black bricks
Are my dark future

It's fitful fire
Is my life being spent
In hopeless striving
The fire is increasing
My thirst for you

The log burning is my mind
It is the last log
Heart and soul are the ashes
Along with my past

Stanley A. Walls
Savannah, GA

[Hometown] *Savannah, GA* [Ed] *substitute teacher* [Occ] *musician/teacher* [Hobbies] *swimming, fishing, golfing* [GA] *opening a show for Chubby Checker*
I have enjoyed my life as a musician and substitute teacher. Both of these careers have been a joy and now I am retired and have more time for fishing and have learned the art of "couch potato." I enjoy watching The History Channel *and game shows. I picked up writing poetry as a hobby.*

Working Retail

Too many questions
with obvious answers.
Too many arguments
to our team leaders
and who's right and
why policy is wrong.
Too much laziness
to look for what is
wanted, but not required,
thereby ensuring more
insults not needed.
Too much larceny and
false sloppiness accusations
with greedy lawsuits.
Too much name-calling
or too much apathy
for those working hard
from paycheck to paycheck.
Too many wanting what's
unavailable than what is
presently stocked.
Too much stress and
pressured weight
until the pot finally
explodes.

Krisann Johnson
Richmond, IN

[Hometown] *Richmond, IN* [Ed] *fine arts and creative writing* [Occ] *retail associate* [Hobbies] *crafting, painting, writing fiction novels* [GA] *being published as an independent fiction writer*
I am a retail associate, mainly in customer service, and though my poem describes a lot of negativity I deal with, sixty percent of the time I have the nicest customers from both Indiana and Ohio since our store is on the border. I feel that everyone in customer service goes though days like what I described and I hope this poem will move people to appreciate us a little more.

Little Lies

As I sit beside my mother and I stare into her eyes,
I wonder just how many times she told me little lies.
Like the times she told me someday everything would
be alright, then he would come home drunk again and
start another fight.
Or when she told the neighbor how she got that big
black eye; she tripped, she said, how clumsy
and I knew it was a lie!
A busted lip, a broken arm, the accidents kept
amounting, and with them all came little lies—
so many I stopped counting.
Many years have flown and he is gone;
the incidents are now in the past.
As I sit beside my mother and I stare into her eyes,
little lies are finally gone at last.

Brenda Sue Morajka
Crown Point, IN

[Hometown] *Crown Point* [Ed] *I did not finish high school but I have a world of knowledge.* [Occ] *retired childcare* [Hobbies] *gardening, crafting, singing, and sewing* [GA] *my two sons, Jacob and Mathew*
For my mom, she survived domestic abuse to enjoy sixteen grandchildren and thirteen great-grandchildren. At eighty-two I admire her for her courage and strength. I love her with all my heart! I wouldn't be who I am today if not for her. I am married to a wonderful man for forty-two years; Albert is the love of my life. We are both retired and enjoying our best life, along with my mother.

Notches

I'd like to know just how He felt When He added those notches on His belt There were three within a year All of whom I held so dear How could anyone be so mean To ruin the life of a naive teen How was I to deal with this reality check With enough strength to finish my life's trek? I tried not to live with constant fear As notches were added year after year Learning to deal with the emotions felt I won the game with the cards I was dealt All has led to where I want to be A notch on His belt - when it's time for me!

Richard Charles Fitzgerald
Hermon, NY

Just Thinking

As I sit and think of words to write
They come slowly one, by one
Some are wrong, some are right
Some are to finish, and some to be done
Some are cheerful, some are sad
Some are good, some are bad
But all are there to use
To sooth the loneliness and the blues

William N. Arnold
Fairborn, OH

[Hometown] *Fairborn, Ohio* [Occ] *Retired*

A Hug from the Sun

The sun is so kind,
she warms my face.
When I cry she wipes away my tears;
when she comes out she takes away my fears.
But I wish the sun would help humanity.
I wish the sun would hug those who
need it more than me.
She would wipe the tears of the ones who
have no sun to take away their fears.
You can take some of my sun;
I won't mind and neither will she,
because she, the sun, is kind.

Kaitlynn S. Anderson
Keizer, OR

When you read this poem, I want you to see that we all have a sun within us, and it doesn't take much to give a little to those in need.

His Blessings

He was taken from them so very long ago.
Such innocent of minds, however could they know.
Living in a land of plenty, with a destiny,
insidiously being robbed of their minds, money,
and their dignity.
Sent to another country across the Atlantic sea,
known as the land of plenty,
where the children could be free.
He was taken from us so very long ago.
Such innocent of minds, how could we have ever known.
Living in the land of plenty, with a destiny,
insidiously being robbed of our minds, money,
and our dignity.
There is no other country with such prosperity
and only with His Blessings will we remain free.

Cecilia Hattendorf
Apple Valley, CA

[Hometown] *Apple Valley, CA* [Occ] *retired* [Hobbies] *writing*
My poem is about children who were sent to another country to escape apostasy and the plight of the ancestors of those children.

Travel Musings

I've traveled the world and I've seen so much.
Each new place has its own unique touch.
I love the thrill of seeing new places, as well as
meeting new faces.

I've climbed to high places in order to view great sights
and have loved looking down at the twinkling lights.
Have sat on the beaches enjoying each view, each time
seeing something distinctly new.

I have traveled by plane as well as by ship. I have gone by
bus and sometimes by train, just to see and enjoy
the terrain. I've had good things happen as well as bad,
but I always think of what a great time I have had.

I have lots of pictures and souvenirs. Looking at them
really makes me feel glad. Being able to travel is such
a great treasure. I look forward to each trip with much
pleasure.

Marilyn S. Vatter
Oskaloosa, IA

[Hometown] *Oskaloosa, IA* [Ed] *BA degree/grad work* [Occ] *retired teacher* [Hobbies] *writing, traveling, and singing* [GA] *taking my advanced French students to France*
I taught French, German, and English for many years. I worked many tours to France and after retirement have been traveling by doing many small ship cruises. I have sung for a long time, both for church as well as doing old standards for a few shows on board ship. My travels inspired my poem.

Gethsemane's Hope

Blessed is your heart that you might see
the sacrifices that Jesus made at Gethsemane.

He prayed for you to the Father above
with a compassionate heart filled with love.

Take heed that you remember His sacrifice for you.
The foretold agony He already knew.

He prayed urgently there upon His knees
as the Father listened to His urgent pleas.

He prayed passionately there in that lonely garden
to take away your sin and give you His pardon.

He said, "Father if it be possible take this cup from me."
Please save your people and set them free.

He knew His future there that day
as the Roman soldiers led Him away.

Bonnie F. Tucker
Clarksburg, WV

[Hometown] *Clarksburg, WV* [Ed] *BS accounting* [Occ] *retired banker* [Hobbies] *gardening* [GA] *salvation*
Hoping to make a difference in someone's life. To God be all the glory.

In Search of Peace

I thought to go to a mountaintop
Or sit by a peaceful stream
But the mountain was on fire
Blocking the sun's brilliant beam

The stream was so polluted
The water resembling soup
I hung my head in sorrow
I felt I had been duped

I looked toward the sky
And what I saw was haze
My God, my God I cried
I was suddenly in a daze

I stumbled down into a valley
Seeking shelter under the trees
But they were all cut down
I sank slowly to my knees

What has happened to my world
Why is it falling all apart
What has happened to the beauty
That was—from the start

I made my way back home
There I crawled into my bed
The only peace I found
Was under the covers pulled over my head

Laura P. Smith
Pinebluff, NC

A Tale of Two Kitties

Black as coal, green eyes like the sea,
A little handsome fellow if you ask me.
Full of life, so warm to hold.
Who wouldn't be smitten with this kitten?
A ball of ebony, energy and love,
Just six weeks old, the size of a glove.
It was in August of eighteen,
The fluffy one met Bebe the queen,
A bit of a bully, huge and mean.
Bebe did not need a brother,
Since she already had another.
The mini kitty grew lean and bold,
An explorer like in days of old.
Marco Polo was his name.
His fluffy black tail brought him fame.
A mini panther you don't antagonize,
His whip-like tail cut all to size.
Larger and older Marco became.
Really he remained quite tame.
Marco rarely crossed Bebe's path,
Not wanting to incur her wrath.
Then one day they declared a truce;
Marco was too old for Bebe's abuse.

Illene Gerard Powell
Myrtle Beach, SC

[Hometown] *Oyster Bay, NY* [Ed] *BA in English St. John's University; MA in humanities Hofstra University* [Occ] *advertising, now retired* [Hobbies] *travel, swimming, fishing, hiking, riding my one speed bike* [GA] *keeping a sense of humor in the midst of this crazy world*
Living on Long Island my entire life, I jumped at the chance to move to South Carolina in 1995. It was the best move of my life. I was able to share the experience with my husband Dennis. We traveled to French Polynesia, Hawaii, Bermuda, Europe, the Caribbean. We enjoyed visiting historic sites, cruising and meeting people. In my next life, I want to be an investigative reporter.

Alzheimer's

Knowing I know you.
Seeing you coming and going
Talking at me and then blowing
out the what you call it,
Yes, the door,
Saying I can't stay home no more.
Even home seems so nice,
But I can't remember at any price
Where is home and what is it, anyway?
Yes, yes you cannot stay.
The grandchildren need you
So run along and have fun.

Nurse, who was that woman?

Jutta Janotha-Woitscheck
Vero Beach, FL

Salutations

Salutations
Aslan's greetings
Aslan the great is lion, lamb and man!
Aslan's readings
He who has an ear
Listen to the praise of Aslan!
He who has no fear
Hasten to the faith of Aslan!
Salutation is revelation's prophesy
Salutation is revelation's sanctity
Salutation is revelations mystery,
Clap and shout: Salvation is Aslan
Clap and shout: Revelation is Aslan
Clap and shout: Salutation is Aslan
Aslan the great is revelations's salutation
Aslan's greetings
Salultations

Timothy A. Wik
Elkins Park, PA

The Inner Crux

Not satisfied with the present,
We search out something new,
Only to find a future
Filled with unhappiness, too.

We think our search will end
With a happier tomorrow,
But even with the best of efforts,
We only find different pains and sorrow.

They say the 'grass is greener,'
But only when seen through unhappy eyes.
For once we cross over the fence,
Grass still lives and grows 'neath the same skies.

We think a change of surroundings
Will give us happier lives.
But only when change occurs within us
Will we find that happiness thrives.

Ken Frjelich
Deerfield, WI

What Will I Be?

I may just be a door knob
Or maybe just a stool.
What must I be
That God can take
And use me as His tool?
A mouth to speak,
An ear to hear,
An eye to see the good,
A nose to smell the flowers,
And always be kind and good,
A hand to help another,
A foot to walk beside,
What plan for me
While I am here?
His arms will open wide.
Maybe in a choir
Or a teacher I will be
It will be very joyous
To be what He makes of me!

Virginia J. Long
Grand Rapids, MN

[Hometown] *Grand Rapids, MN* [Ed] *college, driver* [Occ] *musician* [Hobbies] *sending out cards* [GA] *singing and playing music in 8 of our beautiful states*
Mother of six children, five girls, one boy.

My Sacred Space

In such days of tumult where nothing seems real,
watching war and greed take hold.
Where most do not care about future things.
One needs the solace of a place quiet
and soul satisfying to help get through it all.

I have such a place and it requires little effort
to arrive there.
It is a place where the occupants do not know
what a fragile and endangered world
they make their home in.
The go about their business as though
their business is all that matters.

Nancy S. Haydock
Turlock, CA

[Hometown] *Turlock, CA* [Occ] *retired teacher* [Hobbies] *watching all of nature* [GA] *teaching about nature*

I am just a nature nerd. I love walking in the forest and birding. I love watching metamorphosis in butterflies, especially monarch butterflies. I love trees and love to learn what they can do. All the books I read are science and nature information. The book, Finding the Mother Tree, *by Simard is a great example of what interests me. I also love helping injured wildlife at a wildlife center.*

Where Are You, Little Boy?

Where are you, little boy, head butting without warning
Where are you, little boy, wanting to play in the morning
Where are you, little boy, you did not sleep all night
Where are you, little boy, with hugs so tight
Where are you, little boy, asleep your ear to my heart
Where are you, little boy, time and distance keep us apart
Where are you, little boy, when I close my eyes, I see you
Where are you, little boy, in everything I see and do
Where are you, little boy, you always wanting to assist
Where are you, little boy, constantly questioning I miss
Where are you, little boy, you grew into a man
Where are you, little boy, brave enough alone to stand
Where are you, little boy, as your idol nimble and strong
Where are you, little boy, for you I could do no wrong
Where are you, little boy, no longer am I your hero
Where are you, little boy, on your own you must go
Where are you, little boy, your head on my chest
Where are you, little boy, praying you do what's best
Where are you, little boy, in each lonely tear
Where are you, little boy, son my heart says, right here

Bobby E. Hopper
Jemison, AL

[Hometown] *Jemison* [Ed] *doctor of ministry, Samford University* [Occ] *retired/bi-vocational pastor of Mt. Carmel Baptist Church #2* [Hobbies] *woodworking, restoration of old vehicles, horticulture* [GA] *three children*
Time, distance, and things separated my son Aaron and me. I wrote this poem as a reminder to us that some things will never change. The moments that he spent with me will always be etched in my heart and mind. I love my son and thank God for allowing me to be his dad. I prepared him for twenty-six years to leave home and teach the next generation of Hoppers. It is and will always be a blessing to me to have been part of Aaron's life.

My Child I Pray

I pray while you slumber
Your greatest dreams come true
That you always have a full belly
If you ever make a mistake
I hope you learn and rise from it
Oh my dearest child
I pray that you never know fearhorze

That your heart is never broken
May the only tears from your eyes
Be those of happiness and laughter
Oh my small child
I pray your strength never wavers
May your feet carry you
To the world's tallest peaks
And I hope your arms
Might reach for the farthest stars
But above all others
Oh child who saved me
I pray that you will always know
The deep love I have for you

Joseph Hawkins
Saint Joseph, MO

True Beauty Dwells Within

Beauty is only skin deep
so we have been told
unless it dwells in a heart
of gold and to be good as
gold in a heart that is
fine is a treasure to all
if it's gentle and kind
We all look for a pearl
among the jewels because
it stands out and is more
precious than corals
God knows true beauty
dwells in a good heart
along with love and wisdom
we impart. Let us be true
to ourselves and do what
our heart tells us to and
show others what true
beauty can do

Virginia Sanders
Chapmanville, WV

[Hometown] *Chapmanville, WV* [Ed] *farmer* [Occ] *farmer* [Hobbies] *gardening, writing poetry, Bible reading* [GA] *learning the truth in the Bible*
I was inspired to write this poem because the Bible shows true beauty dwells in a good heart and our Creator Jehovah God can read our heart and He can see true beauty when He observes a good heart. May we all try to have one. Thanks for reading my poem.

Matters of Fact

Something people truly believe
Something that is reality
Something that made history
Something from ancestry
Something that was in the news
Something written in reviews
Something that has not changed
Something that is ungrained
Something you can talk about
Something you cannot doubt
Something that has been proved
Something that remains unmoved
Something with a solid base
Something you can't erase
Something signed and sealed
Something you can't repeal
Something with ample accuracy
Something in a documentary
Something displayed in a museum
Something preserved for a reason
Something that is vastly known
Something that is set in stone
Something that maintains exact
All these 'somethings' track...
    Matters of fact

Judy Thornton
Leavenworth, KS

She Wrote This to Me

Sent last night.
With smiles and eyes that draw you towards
The memories of her.
Three are sleeping.
Nine are playing.
One is reading a message to you upon the skies.
My struggles are over if you believe in me.
The best way to show me is to pray for me.
No suffering, no tears, because I am near
Within the center of your chest where you feel me.
Upon the anger or hate that change into care and love
That save me with each beat that keeps me safe upon
The heart of the skies.

To my loving daughter Marylane Gonzalez
Pass 3-21-22 born 3-8-84.

Sendia Gomez Gonzalez
Far Rockaway, NY

[Hometown] *Far Rockaway, NY* [Hobbies] *painter and writer* [GA] *becoming a mother of four girls and seventeen grandchildren*
My name is Sendia Gonzalez. I am a poet and painter. I have three girls left: Jenny, Julie, and Olga. And bless upon the living.

My Favorite Club Is a Tree Iron

Before a long night of drinking,
often we don't do much thinking
when we plan a morning tee time.
Dehydration with a headache
does not make any golf game great;
the first nine holes might be a grind.
That day I felt like an old fart
softly asking for a golf cart,
I was sure feeling pretty poor.
At hole six later that morning
down the fairway we were cruising
on an average length par four.
Just left of the green in the rough
the shot should not have been that tough,
it was only stroke number three.
After my partner hit a dud
and up in the air went his club,
the wedge wound up stuck in the tree.
Please re-read the first fifteen lines
the same story ahead in time
a year to the day, there were we.
Left of the green it was gleaming
my partner's wedge lonely sitting,
'twas something we could not believe.

Ian M. W. Norman
Mobile, AL

I Owe

At seventeen I felt my country's call
voices whisper you owe. Time to pay.
Remember it's my turn I've got your six this day.

So, I went, took my oath the beginning
before I knew I was halfway through.
This decision to serve I'll never regret
for country, my parents—I'll always owe a debt.

All too short my career came and went
I miss my fellow airman the security we had.
Now retired missing the military scent
for each and every day away I'm a little sad.

It was my honor to have served
thank you all who served others who will go.
In serving my country much was learned and earned
after all these years—to vets my country. "I still owe."

James Edward Horton
Sutherlin, OR

[Hometown] *Sutherlin, OR* [Ed] *high school graduate and some college* [Occ] *retired* [Hobbies] *writing poetry, guns, sports, and mechanical work* [GA] *my children and being published*
I am a high school graduate with a little college. I enlisted in the US Air Force and retired with over twenty years service. I've worked many jobs—gas stations, retail, etc. I'm very active in the Veterans of Foreign Wars being a post commander as well as a district commander is what inspired me to write this poem. It's my way of telling others who have served, those who might, and to thank my country for what it has given me along with my parents.

Magic

Magic by air, magic by night, chills with fright.
What's said is said. What's done is done.
The evil that shuns, admiring the nuns.
Twist to the left, twist to the right,
Struggle for what's right.
Perspective, interpretation,
Misguided communication leads to faulty perfection.
Hearts are sinking into an empty sea.
One of a kind, that's scary enough.
Where there are two of a kind, they can never touch.
Where havens above with clouds of fluff.
Surreal dreams turn to mush as though times were tough.
There once was a shadow encased in lust, turned to dust.
Fiery spirits could not trust.
Believing in something beyond the brush.
Time fades away into a new day.
Sacrifice and settle for something, even just a little.
Tease the pain within a riddle as if to strike a chord on a fiddle.
Magic by air, magic by night,
Let the wings take flight.

Christy Schroeder
Canyon, TX

[Hometown] *Canyon, TX* [Ed] *social work* [Occ] *case manager* [Hobbies] *hiking, swimming, camping, jigsaw puzzles, and learning.* [GA] *surviving life and graduating higher education*
I look forward to these events each year. Being able to submit my poetry is fun and allows me to be creative. Each poem reveals a little bit of truth, fantasy, and emotion. Each poem reflects a different time in my life with various thoughts and events going on in the world. Each poem has a story to tell. Innuendos help encapsulate my poetry in a creative and fun story. Thank you for reading it!

Hold On

Hold on to your dear loved ones
as much as you can every day.
Show them how much you care
in all that you do and say.

Show your love and care to others, too
not only with money but also in word and deed,
bringing happiness to everyone you meet,
especially to those who are truly in need.

Try to live a Godly life as much as you can.
Shining Jesus light for all the world to see.
So that others will want to be Christians
and want to go to Heaven like you and me.

Live each day as if it is your last.
Hold on tightly to your heavenly Father's hand.
Keep strong in the faith always
until you reach the promised land.

Debora Ann Robbins
Temple, TX

[Hometown] *Temple, TX* [Ed] *BA in English* [Occ] *USDA clerk for Head Start* [Hobbies] *writing poetry, reading, sand art*

I am sixty-two years young. I was born and raised in Temple, TX. I have been writing poetry since I was in high school I have written many poems. I was inspired to write this poem when I think about how fast time flies. I praise and thank God for giving me the ability to write. I am currently working on a book of my poems and a devotional book.

Fourth of July Jubilee

Fireworks, parades, celebrations, ballgames,
ice cream, and cookouts—all to celebrate
the Fourth of July. It represents the
greatest nation on Earth—the USA!

Spark the chorus and join the fun to congratulate
the nation on its birthday. Time is not
wasted so partake and shout, hurrah!
and cheers! May God bless the USA!

Ralph Whitley
Concord, NC

[Hometown] *Concord, NC* [Ed] *retired educator* [Hobbies] *art, uni bowling, cornhole, traveling, walking, listening to music* [GA] *church life achievement award*
I am a retired educator who taught history for thirty-five years at Central Piedmont Community College in Charlotte, NC. I taught part-time at Rowan-Cabarrus Community College in Salisbury, NC. I have written a book of poems entitled Reflections Poems by Ralph Whitley. *This past July 4, 2022 I live in Morning Assisted Living of Concord, NC and several residents caught the covid virus. I was inspired to write a poem on the Fourth of July due to the greatness of our country. Enjoy!*

Walk a Sunbeam

Walk a sunbeam to the mountain
Feel the rivers, fields, and trees
Taste the freshness of the breezes
Smell the colors of the sunlight
Filtered through the forest leaves.
Walk a sunbeam to the mountain
Watch yourself among the trees.

Robert B. Aukerman
Centennial, CO

[Hometown] *Centennial, CO* [Ed] *social work* [Occ] *human services and health administration* [Hobbies] *reading, fishing, gardening* [GA] *maintaining my family*
Living at the foot of the Rocky Mountains for more than fifty years has given me the opportunity to occasionally attune all my senses to our world's natural wonders. The mountain moments, though not many, have been memorable. Like fishing at dusk on a mountain stream when I suddenly heard and felt the swoosh of a snowy owl above my head. As he flew on toward the meadow I knew he was letting me know I was encroaching on his hunting time and territory. I recovered from this close encounter and left the area. The communication was direct. I was attuned.

Anxious Pleads

Sad voice, let me smile
I grow tired of your tears.

Scared voice, let me breathe
I have no room for fears.

Angry voice, let me love
Not everything should be war.

Hurt voice, let me heal
And be happy like before.

Jacob Paul Shada
Linden, TX

[Hometown] *Atlanta, TX* [Ed] *Linden Kildare High School* [Occ] *writer* [Hobbies] *writing, martial arts, reading, photography* [GA] *being published in poetry anthologies*
I'm from East Texas and over the years I've learned that everyone and everything has a story, if only you care enough to turn the page.

Heaven

Jesus whispered to me in the night
You know your husband is dying, right
Don't hold on to him too tight
Because he will need to go to the light

Heaven is waiting his return
Of what he did right or wrong, he will learn
He will meet St. Peter and turn
At the gates of hell, he will not burn

For the Lord will give comfort and peace
And the rewards, He will release
Because my husband's faith will please
The Lord above who gives us mercy without cease

May God bless him as he goes
To the mansion the Lord shows
With the beauty, my husband's eye glows
As the love and peace flows

Peggy S. Collier
Canyon, TX

[Hometown] *Canyon* [Ed] *high school, secretarial degree, bachelor's degree in marketing, and broker's license* [Occ] *retired* [Hobbies] *enjoying my family, cross-stitch, reading, enjoying my dogs, writing* [GA] *having my two children and getting to see them grow into wonderful adults*
My husband has Alzheimer's and has had it for nine-plus years. He is in a memory facility at this time and I know his time will come. I wrote this poem knowing that and wanting to encourage myself in knowing that he will be in a better place when his time comes.

Love the Lord

Love the Lord with all your heart, with all your soul and mind.
Trust in Him for all your needs, those of every kind.
Our God created all the things that our eyes do see.
Come before Him now in reverent humility.
No longer mock the name that is above all names.
Lift your arms in praise. Let this be your favorite game.
Come into His house and worship there today.
Bend your knee in holy repentance; this I humbly pray.
Let go of all violence and hate for your brother.
Replace it with peace and love for each other.
This is commanded by God on high;
those who live and believe in Him will never die.
Christ has gone before to prepare us a place.
He will come again for those who accept His grace.
They will live forever in His heavenly home.
Never again will they thirst or cry or ever be alone.
He will be their light and life, fulfilling every need.
Sustaining them in all their joy, as through life they do proceed.
He is our resurrected Savior; He lives with God on high.
He's preparing a holy banquet for all who repent and draw nigh.
The only thing we need to do is to come and joyfully receive.
His crown will be placed on the heads of those who believe.
So won't you come to His house today?
Let His word penetrate your heart I pray.

Sonja Lee Goldsmith
Vero Beach, FL

[Hometown] *Mora, MN* [Ed] *high school/vocational* [Occ] *banking—teller* [Hobbies] *writing faith poems, photography of God's creation* [GA] *sharing my faith through my poems*
Graduated high school in 1957, married a sailor in 1958, and spent the next twenty years as a US Navy wife. Very adventurous but at times lonely. As a naval air controlman during the Vietnam War he did a two year tour aboard the USS Enterprise. I and our three-year-old son went back home to MN. It was a blessing our son got to really know grandmas, grandpa, and cousins. This is when I started my faith walk and the poems started to pour into my mind and onto paper.

A Glimpse of Nature

The sky is clear, no dark clouds there,
Where you can see rays of sun
White clouds in bubbles of laundry soap.
Rocky road is bumpy, no fun.
Tunnels of trees make shade to adore,
Green grass under foot,
Feel the soft soil under it all.
Long brown snake, no, just a root.
Off a way, but still close by
Fresh water stream, flowing clear,
Murmurs tiny words,
Makes a tinkle inside my ear.
The path to walk on, low rolling hill.
Scurrying little creatures under a log,
High in a tree limb
A squirrel all agog.
Now in the quiet a
Soothing sound is heard.
Another gift is given,
A melody, the comforting song of a bird.

Patty Montag
Colo, IA

[Hometown] *Whiting, IA* [Ed] *University of Northern Iowa*
Patty Montag, 93 years old. Born in Whiting, Iowa, and lifelong Iowa resident. A husband and six children, all graduates of Iowa State University. Avid gardener, bird watcher and reader. Inspired by words that rhyme. A liberal lady.

Molly's Imagism

Ellipical Oort cloud, onlooking word painter
Luminophore, Island Universe, lool's mock moon
Ambit, shoal actinism ray, picturesque aboon
Pangea, splate rammed Earth, whimsicality
Tachyletic fossils, Dragon Tree, factuality
Monssonean, ancestral red jungle fowl spoorer
Reginal reconnoisance, deterent datum doer
Cradle to grave priscan, brash odyssean legerity
Imperceptible oneiric peal, echapper rarity
Reasoned juriprudence, keyless heterbox
Esteemed, lidless inspiriter, pouncet box
Osiered foreshadowing, windage pasture rose
Primavernal crooning, nidificating otiose
Eclipsed plumage, jocundities, Annica netted
A haute voix sub-song, moxie au vol abetted
Idoneity melanges, graminae to juneberries
Midmorning jack-daw, owl butterfly memories
Aspian, adret cobble, logging stone meliot
Tactuality of mountain avens, touch-me-not
Unstinting lamprids egral, airglow royalism
Nyctitropic alpine gardens, peridot fairyism
Priggish rainbow cactus, labor of love punnet
Overtly! Quaggy, ubique teliosporic runnet
Mid Heaven, joie de vivre, intermingling
Ab in tra! Society verse ting-a-ling

Mary R. Martinez De Arellano
Chamisal, NM

[Hometown] *Chamisal, NM* [Ed] *associate of arts degree in fine arts* [Occ] *DI Turner's Syndrome* [Hobbies] *Keeping tradition alive "Quiltéra"; homemade soap, jams, foods; nature daily interaction* [GA] *In Mindfulness, my words are therapeutic seeds of kindness. "My gift to the world"*

Her Name Was Robin

I know not why, we had such little time together. Nor
why they had to take our sister away. They broke our
family apart, that left a hole in all our hearts.
Come and go she came and went.
Sometimes many years apart.
With each visit we always thought she was back to stay.
But it was not meant to be this way.
Then again she would appear, as if from thin air.
She never stayed for too long.
But she would dance and sing and make us laugh
and sometimes cry. We made the most of times together.
But off again she would go.
She was like a bird in a cage flapping her wings against the
bars. Now she is finally home with wings of her own—our angel up above
watching over us and sending us her love.
She is the big sister she always wanted to be.
So when you feel lost or feel alone just whistle and before you know, she will be by your side
giving you a hug.
Her name was Robin and was always meant to fly!

Cissy DeCroce
Toms River, NJ

[GA] *I am one of four sisters and a half-sister we found one year after our sister passed*
I am one of four sisters and a half-sister we found one year after our sister passed.

God Is Number One

We need to put God first,
Especially when we have hunger and thirst.

God shows us His love
In the path of a dove.

Even when we push or shove
Or even raise every glove.

God is the best!
He's well above the rest.

When we're with God,
We need to follow every trod.

If you want to stay in the game,
You must remember to praise His name!

It's a huge shame
If you share the devil's blame.

You must be willing
To get the holy filling.

Talk to God to have peace
And to get your soul rest and release.

David A. Ott
Wapakoneta, OH

[Hometown] *Wapakoneta* [Ed] *associate's degree* [Occ] *disabled—seizure disorder* [Hobbies] *poetry* [GA] *publication of my poetry*

In 1981, I was born C-section because my body was upside down in the womb. My life was somewhat normal until 1995. I suffered a grand malseizure. In 2001, to help me fight seizures, I received an implant called VNS. (Vages Nerve Stimulator) to help fight seizures and depression. I still had bad seizures. In 2008 they watched me have seizures at the Cleveland Clinic, then said they had to do brain surgery. They then gave me five to ten years to live. It's been fourteen years!

Little Boy Gone

When you were young, you were my pride;
My love for you I couldn't hide.
So many things we used to do
I now must face without you.
We went to the doctor's office for you to be checked;
Little did I know then that my life would be wrecked.
He said that you were very sick, and nothing more.
I could feel the tears welling up in my eyes as we walked out the door.
There were other doctors we went to see
But none of them would say, what was most important to me.
As time went on, you became very ill;
I felt your pain, as I always will.
I held your hand as the days passed away,
Praying to God for you, that was all I could say.
Near the end, when you looked up at me,
I almost wanted a merciful God to set you free.
You're gone now, as I watch the setting sun,
Part of my life will always be missing without my only son.

Louis M. Graziaplena
Orlando, FL

[Hometown] *Baltimore, MD* [Ed] *high school* [Occ] *retired state employee* [Hobbies] *reading, sports, writing poetry* [GA] *my poems have been published in 22 different books*
Lou was born on September 16, 1942, at University Hospital on Greene Street in Baltimore, MD. Both of Lou's parents were of Italian heritage. He attended the Catholic parochial schools, St. Brigid's and Our Lady of Pompei. He attended Patterson High School in Baltimore, graduating in February 1961. His first significant job was for the Motor Vehicle Administration in Maryland as a state employee for thirty years. Lou served four years and four months in the United States Navy. After the military, he went to work with the State of Florida, from which he retired after six years.

Wait a Minute

People are addicted to quarter hours
they use them all the time
They don't like those other minutes
and that, to me, is a crime

To say "half-past" when it's 8:26
or quarter-to-five when it's more
is a sloppy way of telling time
that you shouldn't be noted for

What's so weird about 12-after-12
or 13-minutes-to-3?
Why aren't the minutes on any clock
as equal as you are to me?

When you ask a man what time it is
his answer will be right on the nose
He'll say, "Let me see, I've got 8:43"
'cause that's what his wristwatch shows

No train stops around 3 o'clock
and no bus leaves at 4ish
so please start talking like schedules do
just be sure to be charming, not boorish

Jim Alfred Healey
Aptos, CA

[Hometown] *Aptos, CA* [Ed] *MBA* [Occ] *retired college marketing instructor* [Hobbies] *magic, baseball, tennis, cornhole, pickleball, Laurel & Hardy, Chrysler cars, Route 66, singing, road trips, writing poems, Robert Paige, shaggy dog stories* [GA] *pitching for our undefeated Giants Fantasy Camp team in 1989, winning the Willie McCovey Hall of Fame contest in 1986—an all expense paid trip for two to see him inducted into the Baseball Hall of Fame*
My brother Jack inspired this poem. He's not odd but he prefers odd times on the clock.

Is Today?

Every morning I awake fresh and rejuvenated;
I can't wait to see
What kind of day it'll be.
Will it begin with a slight and even
Sometimes fragrant breeze?
With a solid canopy of blue sky?
Maybe this day will have a blue sky; but in
The mass of blue, there might be
Dozens of gigantic clouds forming
An endless amount of fancy designs.
Will the sun be warm and strong?
And shine early in the morning? If it has
A gentle breeze, blue sky, huge white
Clouds, and warm penetrating sun;
Then to me it's a perfect day, and I must
Be out enjoying it. And you know what?
It is! Today is a perfect day!

Patricia Jo Long
Terra Bella, CA

[Hometown] *Terra Bella, CA* [Ed] *1 1/2 years of college* [Occ] *housewife* [Hobbies] *writing poetry and reading* [GA] *having my poems published in Eber & Wein's Who Who books*

Pause

She sits quiet as a breath
  deep in reverie, dreaming
dreams...

her eyes are dark,
  and full of stars...

hair pools in little myriad lights
  at her feet, and there is
a golden dusting a mist about her
  and a radiance too,
So much light -
  and a kind of waiting....

Joh Cambilargiu
Tooele, UT

[Hometown] *Tooele, UT* [Ed] *High School, College, Arts Studio* [Hobbies] *Piano teaching, playing music, reading, writing and drawing*

A Stinking Walk

I took an evening walk down the beautiful garden trail
Among the flowers so grand with colors bright and pale
Then down to the woods with trees majestic and tall
Leaves turning bright colors it was the beginning of fall
The trail came to a creek where the cool waters flow
With fish swimming lazily where the water lilies grow
I crawled through a fence into a pasture lush and green
Watching for that big bull he's mighty ornery and mean
The path went by the corn field with corn ready to pick
The soybeans were also ready the crop was ripe and thick
A field of alfalfa hay was cut and dry and ready to bale
We might have some left over that we can put up for sale
Walking past the big red barn coming home the back way
Past the cows and the horses who were eating their hay
Saw some deer in the pasture and stepped into their dung
Should watch where I walk because on my shoes it hung
The chickens were scratching they were out of the coop
Then I made a big mistake by stepping right into their poop
As a walked through the lot and please don't ask me why
My mind was on all that poop and stepped into a cow-pie
That flock of sheep down by the shed left a big pile, too
As I was walking past stepping into that with each shoe
As I was shaking my shoes trying to loosen all that goo
Walked my Rover's doghouse and stepped in his dog do-do
My walk started out so great the first part was a big hit
But the second part stank no more evening walks [I quit]

Marvin H. Hitzemann
Waterloo, IL

[Hometown] *Waterloo, IL* [Ed] *10th grade military high school GED* [Occ] *railroad carman inspector 43 years* [Hobbies] *collecting and repairing Lawn Boy lawn mowers approximately 300lb collected* [GA] *married to my wonderful wife (67 years), my children, and grandchildren*
I started working for the railroad on February 12, 1953 and worked for forty-three years. After serving in the army I took a repair small engine course, then started repairing and collecting Lawn Boy lawn mowers.

The Country Sparrow

Simple and plain her feathery garb of gray,
She sings and scratches in the scattered hay.

She nests high in the henhouse eaves,
A jumble of feathers, straw, and leaves.

She lives well with friends, the flock.
And drinks from their heated pot.

Happiness and joy resonate from this little bird.
She's accepted and mingles with every herd.

On frigid days when few birds venture,
The sparrow sings of the adventure.

She's up at dawn just before the rest.
Following the farmer, she eats the best.

Perhaps she's one of twelve made from clay
By the hands of the child master while at play.

Tess J. Wilke
Durand, IL

[Hometown] *Durand, IL* [Ed] *two years college* [Occ] *retired—quality control rep Aerospace-Honeywell* [Hobbies] *illustrating, painting, song writing, reading, quilting, horticulture* [GA] *raising a loving family* *My poem was inspired by my early years on a farm. I grew up in Northern Illinois and helped with farm chores. I loved to take care of all the animals, domesticated and wild. Up early before school I experienced peace and trust from them. Farm life taught me so much about the natural world and unconditional love.*

Melanie

Tenderly as the lovelight
In her gentle blue eyes,

Willingness to assist in
any way in need,

Filling the room
with joyous laughter,

Add the gentle kiss of
her patience,

Mothering in perfection
to three special children,

Too much Irishness
it would be hard to find,

Who else but my daughter
Her name is Melanie.

Margaret Coralie Pearce
Englewood, CO

The Dandelion's Magic

I saw dandelion seeds today,
flying through the air.
One little seed
flew 'round and 'round,
as if without a care.
When you pick a dandelion,
you make a wish
and blow.
You open your eyes
and watch the seeds
fly away into the unknown.
Dandelions are magical;
they hold so much mystery.
They take your wish
and carry it away
to a land
that knows no misery.

Jennifer Melissa Ragan
Boone, NC

[Hometown] *Boone, NC*

To My Daddy

Years have passed since you left this world
I hope you're proud of your baby girl
Junior in high school, published author and more
After I graduate, I'll travel like we planned
Sorry I'm not going to college
But some days I still need you
What I do know is if you were here my snake
Would never leave your arms
It's funny how the years have passed
But my memories will always last
I miss your voice, I miss your smile
Overall I miss my time with you
I'll finally admit you were right
When we would laugh and fight
About who was who, Norbert or Dagget
Spoot or not
I'm the spoot
And our favorite dog Lilly is the poot

I love you, Daddy
—Your Bird

Ayla Gilliam
Dickson, TN

[Hometown] *Dickson, TN* [Ed] *junior in high school* [Occ] *student* [Hobbies] *reading, writing, and music* [GA] *this book right here*
The end of the poem is what my daddy called me. Bird was my nickname when I was little. Our favorite show to watch when we were together was called Angry Beavers *and would constantly joke on who was the silly one. His death took a toll on me and I wrote letters to him. Poetry was another escape. In my freshman year of high school I participated in what my theatre teacher called "*Mental Health Monday.*" I shared a poem with the class and continued to write more poetry. I noticed they told a story, from weakness to strength.*

The Proposal

The toxin of humanity lingers within the air,
Safeguarding her heart,
She builds a wall around it
Becoming as tough as concrete.

His Majesty came along,
Dealt with all the darts she thrown at him,
Witnessed the beheading of the last Love Bird.
Still, he finds this woman attractive.
She makes it twice difficult,
Even more she is his perfect match—
Not too sweet and rough around the edges.

He types all day admiring her mastery of swords,
Thumping away his fingers glancing at her beauty.
She became his conquest, seducing her with red hearts.
Santorini voyage determined his gallantry,
Feasting lobsters, bubbly by the blue water

At the greeting room he descends to one knee.
Will you marry me?
Affixing a ring to her fingers
She responded "Yes."
A knight worthy of the honor
My Queen is who you are now and forevermore.

Monique Susan Murray
Weymouth, MA

[Hometown] *Weymouth, MA* [Occ] *artist and founder of Nokamo Apparel Llc* [Hobbies] *relaxing by the beach with the children.*
Every woman at a point in their life thinks about the moment when the guy they are madly in love with will request their hand in marriage. The poem was inspired by my husband Michael Moradian who proposed in the most romantic way, and I love him dearly.

Time Will Tell

If you think they'll always listen to you—
They don't!
Or think they'll do what you advise them to—
They won't!
The time will come when they say to you
"Don't advise me anymore, what I should or shouldn't do."
You'll stare and you'll wonder, how could this be.
How could they forget they belonged to me?
We clothed them and fed them and helped them in school.
Host friends for their parties and swimming
in the pool.
At holiday times, the house would be filled with family,
games and toys. We could hardly keep them quiet,
there was always so much noise.
But, although we had some bad times, mostly we had good.
They never got in trouble, always did as they should.
Now we must accept the fact, our children all have grown.
They'll live by their decisions when
they go out on their own.
So! When they say the time has come, you're
not needed anymore.
Still, always love them and help them,
venture out the front door.

Marie Klein
Staten Island, NY

[Hometown] *Bensonhurst, Brooklyn, NY* [Ed] *high school* [Occ] *ladies health club instructor* [Hobbies] *writing poems, stories, letters; drawing, painting, crafts, reading* [GA] *2 daughters, 2 sons, 12 grandkids, 1 great; survived car accident*

My family inspires me the most. With my kids and grandkids, there's a lot going on. My feelings about me with them, or them with each other. It's better to write, then express verbally. Writing can be erased. First, use a pencil and don't use anyone's name. I write about the world, special occasions, funny things and whatever comes to mind. Someday, I'd like to make a book of my poems to leave for my kids. Then, maybe, I'll write their names. Nah! I won't. Just kidding.

M.A.G.I.C. C.R.Y. C.L.E.A.N.S. S.K.Y.

Making a gem in Colorado
Colorful radio's youth
Can love erase a nasty smile?
Seek kind youngsters!

Cloud proud prince
Castle loud since
Car ride rinse
Keeps female fence independent intense!

Walker Hayes
Columbia, MO

[Hometown] *Columbia, MO* [Ed] *GED, vocational school* [Occ] *self-published writer* [Hobbies] *listening to music while reading my poems* [GA] *American Legion award at the end of sixth grade*
I was a phone interviewer for CASR on MU campus here in Columbia, MO from 2000 to near the end of 2003 where I received one raise in 2001. I've also held many telemarketing jobs and been an elections official on many occasions (1992 through 2004). I was hired as an election official when Wendy Noren was the Boone County clerk (Columbia).

Dance of the Spanish Moss

The lacy Spanish moss sways
With every gentle breeze
Whether sunny or stormy days
The lacy Spanish moss sways
Like the hula skirt it portrays
Flowing from tall oak trees
The lacy Spanish moss sways
With every gentle breeze

Joan Patterson Yeck
Moosic, PA

[Hometown] *Moosic, PA* [Ed] *Mercidian School of Nursing* [Occ] *homemaker/retired rehab nurse* [Hobbies] *reading and writing poetry, playing accordion, water aerobics and walking* [GA] *my children and grandchildren*
I love to write about the beautiful areas of our country that we visit. They all have something unique about them that makes them memorable. I especially like the warmer weather and tropical scenes of the southern states. The graceful Spanish moss of Hilton Head Island, SC and Savannah, GA inspired this poem.

Inevitable

A sentence of death—handed down
Adorning invisible cloak and crown
We are chosen
When it is our time
We choke on the knowing
And like a pill, bitter
It is hard to swallow down
Reality grips like a tight rope
As your last breath escapes
Leaving silence in your chest
Your light begins to fade
Like the flicker of a candle
Burning out
Death will be our final chapter
But also, our new beginning
And when it is that we finally take "the fall"
Our spirits will rise
It is our human nature
We are all prone
Where death one day abides
And still remains
Inevitable

Shelly Marie Gambino
North Liberty, IN

[Hometown] *Mequon, WI* [Ed] *college and self-taught, educationally read* [Occ] *administrative officer* [Hobbies] *playing my 12-string acoustic guitar, walking my dogs, lyrics and poetry, writing* [GA] *being self-published (but not marketing my poetry), touching people's lives through experiences*
Death is a subject that comes to my mind and heart. As I was a thirty-five year old widow of a Vietnam veteran of the United States Army. Now, my best friend, Marc suffers his same fate—that of lung cancer stage IV. I lost a four year old nephew to brain cancer and have learned that life hurts but also happens to us all, the inevitable. Live every day like it is your last. Dream big and never forget to dance!

Love Is the Greatest Gift

Are you just captivated by her beauty?
And will you stick with her through thick and thin?
With true love, there is no boundaries
For two hearts entwined together,
Shall always win!
We must truly understand each other
With communication at all times,
For when true love flows like a river
We know what is on each other's mind
True love brings trust, which keeps us together
Through all the ups and downs
And through stormy weather!
With true love we shall weather the storm.

Lois Ann Gassdorf
Rogers, AR

[Hometown] *Rogers, AR* [Ed] *high school* [Occ] *retired* [Hobbies] *arts & crafts, sewing, painting, and decorating* [GA] *my church, which supplies my spiritual needs and where I enjoy the fellowship*
I love painting, sewing, and decorating! I have been writing poetry over twenty years! I live on a beautiful golf course which offers me good country living. And it's beautiful here especially in springtime! This poem is inspired by someone I dated a long time. Seeing his love was weak and with him was no good standard, I knew marriage would never work for us, so we parted as friends. My special achievement is my church with faith-filled friends who are Christian believers. My Sunday is the highlight of my week! My veteran husband has been deceased twenty-two years. My life goes on with Jesus.

Looking on the Bright Side of Life

While looking on the bright side,
A snag comes now and then.
When all goes smooth and quiet,
The shadows will creep in.

When many lives are taken,
In a frightful, careless way,
We all feel hurt and laden,
Heavy-hearted with dismay.

We each must keep a happy heart,
And show it to all others.
'Cause all the people far and wide
Are our sisters and our brothers.

Make the world a better place
By our actions and our love
And keep in mind that God, our healer,
Is shining from above.

Keep looking on the bright side,
Heal hurts along the way,
So all can be a blessing
In our living of each day.

Gladys Thornton
San Diego, CA

I wrote this because of the latest shooting of Uvalde school. If only there was a way of stopping this kind of madness...

The Mind Feels

Here I am watching the birds soaring through the blue sky as they seem so free up there flying so high.

Knowing they have no worry of this cruel cruel world or being judged whether your a boy or a girl.

The feeling of the wind blowing against my skin somehow gives me a sense of peace, as I close my eyes I feel I have released.

Released my thoughts into the wonder of the clouds so they can take it all away, like an innocent lost pet what most call a stray.

The sound of rain gives me calmness from overthinking my past troubles, as I clear my mind to focus the thought of it all is as if I'm working a double.

My shadow follows me; I keep it near. It sees and hears what I sometimes don't and therefore it protects me so I have nothing to fear.

The world is at war with each other also with the demons you have inside. Breathing in and breathing out, a sigh of relief is a technique from panic that you try to abide.

I prefer to be like the birds, the ocean, the wind because they seem so free, instead of the fire, tornado, and demons that rage inside of me.

Terria Denise Williams Alexander
Dothan, AL

[Hometown] *Dothan, AL* [Ed] *high school diploma, associate's degree, Bachelor of Science in nursing, Christian, certified in medication administration, certificate of recognition for unity* [Occ] *former supervisor for persons with disabilities, former contracted with DCF, former hospice care provider, and former in-home support worker* [Hobbies] *reading, writing poetry, spending time with loved ones* [GA] *my daughter Kailani D. Alexander*

It's Been Awhile

It's been awhile.
Riding my bike down the gravelly road,
Baseball cards strategically placed;
Flapping wildly against the spokes,
My excitement as I caught sight
Of people marveling at my ingenuity
As I peddled by.

A twilight night, a mason jar,
Air holes skillfully pierced through the tin lid.
Filled with excitement as I capture
A lightning bug in full flight,
Then tenderly place it in my jar.
In stillness I watch the graceful movement
Of this tiny, fragile creature
As it casts darkened shadows
That dance in mystical rhythm.

The richness of these splendid moments
Of my youth come to life,
Beckoning me to call upon them again.

Mary Marlene Daley
Roseburg, OR

[Hometown] *Roseburg, OR*
I marvel at how far my journey of writing has come. I never truly felt that I could ever consider myself a writer until I stepped forward to write as often as I could and in doing so I was accepted by other writers. It has been the most inspiring experience of my life, always waiting for the next prompt to work its way into my thoughts.

Dangerous Passion

Walls built around her that no one could touch,
until, him.
She felt him looking at her; he reached for her,
holding his hand out to her. She smiled at him
as she placed her hand in his.
His flame drew her in; there would be no resisting him.
He was dark, wild, and dangerous; she would
surrender and drown in her desire for him.
His soul whispered her name as it branded her
his, calming her inner storm, bringing peace to
the dark corners of her mind.
She was his.

Margaret Rene Mendez
Decatur, IN

[Hometown] *Decatur* [Ed] *nursing school* [Occ] *retired* [Hobbies] *writing, painting* [GA] *my sons*

A Birthday Poem—70 Unleashed!

As I turn the age of 70
I look back at the life that was
My mind is filled with memories
Of my family and my love

Sunday church and family dinners
Table manners and good behavior
Catholic school and daily prayers
The holy nuns kept us in favor

Teenage years were a total blast
Beatles, Elvis, and Maryjane
Boys and love-in's that didn't last
Sitting at the park and feeling no pain

The love of my life, children and their children
Bonded in love, together we clung
Heartache came, and he was gone
But for a moment in time, we were young

After 70 trips around the sun
A simpler life I could never erase
With family and friends and lots of fun
My year of 70 I will embrace

Margi A. Spurgeon
Phoenix, AZ

This was the first birthday my husband missed in forty-eight years. Larry passed away on October 20, 2021 of cancer. I dedicate this poem to him.

Starting Over

I cannot believe you two are really still together. Why can't y'all just wave the white flag and surrender? You know that you deserve better. Hence, why are you deciding to just settle? There are plenty of fish in the sea. So, maybe it is about time to just run and be set free. Surprisingly, this poem has nothing to do with you and everything to do with me becoming the woman that I was always meant to be.

Chelsea A. Hoffner
Dover, DE

Temporary Sensation

Some people prefer coffee, others tea, but my preference was the TV show, *Glee*.
When I started watching this program, I became interested in the character, Kurt Hummel.
To me, he appeared to possess a heart of an upright gentleman. Kurt was also well known for not being straight. Out of his own free will, he decided to walk in this opposite direction.
Many times, he was mocked for living this way but instead he chose to be brave. While attending his senior prom, he wore a skirt that raised many eyebrows.
The TV show itself produced many CDs and DVDs. At one time, a full length 3D movie was made.
On the night of March 20, 2015, was D-Day for *Glee*. Gone now is Kurt Hummel.
To this very day, since this TV program was so popular, why didn't toy manufacture companies bother to produce either a Kurt Hummel doll or bobblehead for my collection?
As an old wise man Solomon once stated, "A time to be born and a time to die."

Hans Jurgen Hauser
Queen Creek, AZ

If Only

If only I had smiled more,
If only I had spoken,
If only I had told the truth,
My heart would not be broken.

If only I had watched my tongue,
I wish I hadn't said it.
If only I could take it back,
Why then I'd not regret it.

Next time, I'll have to smile more,
Next time I'll show more kindness.
Next time I'll simply tell the truth.
Next time I won't be mindless.

Next time, I'll keep my mouth shut,
And reach out to the lonely.
Next time, I'll use more common sense,
Then I won't have to say "if only!"

Marian Louise Malone
Lincoln, NE

[Hometown] *Eagle, NE* [Ed] *Volunteer* [Occ] *Retired* [Hobbies] *Freelance writing, genealogy, knitting, reading* [GA] *Getting poems published in Eber & Wein*
I am enjoying my retirement. It gives me a chance to volunteer, travel and spend time with my cats. I volunteer for charities, the public library and the local food bank. I have traveled to Europe, Canada and the USA. My cats are my babies and very important in my life.

Oh My God

How many times a day
Do we hear people say?

Oh, my God, in expressing
Their circumstances in many ways.
But using His name is breaking
One of the few commandments is
Thou shalt not use my name in vain.

When you really need to call on God,
You will find yourself in a different situation.

There is a difference
In expression or in need.
But think about how you use
His name, remember not to use
His name in vain.

Thou shalt not take the name
Of the Lord in vain, for the
Lord will not hold him guiltless
That taketh His name in vain.

Deuteronomy 5:11

Elizabeth Fredricks
Port Saint Lucie, FL

[Hometown] *Lico, WV* [Ed] *graduated 1952 Wheeling High School* [Occ] *retired - riviter* [Hobbies] *jigsaw puzzles, sewing, poetry, church* [GA] *I've been a Christian since Jan. 7, 1961*
I am sorry to say this will be my last entry. I have always enjoyed poetry but I have trouble writing and concentrating now. I was eighty-eight years old in May and I have arthritis in my hands. I really enjoyed seeing my poems in your book and all the other poems, too.

The Seagulls' Lament

They fly majestic
Over the land
Sounding their cry
To the group
Like a band of angels
Moving like an army troop
Ore boats come into the harbor
To go through the docks
To get another supply of ore
Mining is quite the chore
Then they leave for other ports of call
Beaver Bay to Thunder Bay
You can hear their cries
God's band of feathered angels
I see before my eyes

Barbara L. Page
Two Harbors, MN

[Hometown] *born and raised in Austin, MN* [Ed] *high school graduate 1965* [Occ] *retired since 2010—cleaning services* [Hobbies] *knitting prayer shawls and writing my poetry* [GA] *learning to drive at 30 (better late than never!); gave cleaning service to many*
I'm currently living in Two Harbors, MN just a block or so from Lake Superior. At times, I go to a sitting area and bring along some bread or popcorn, tossing it out to the seagulls. The make quite the racket! I only have to look out my windows to see them flying overhead. This inspired me to write "The Seagulls' Lament."

Good Ol' Boy Syndrome II: Code of Silence

From the very beginning
There's been a code
A conspiracy was growing
Their souls they sold

We are not always privy
To things behind the scenes
The unwritten oath of secrecy
Revealed when the task-force convenes

So to eliminate the undesirables
Has always been the plan
To take out the deplorable
And destroy your fellow man

The country is so divided
We can't make a stand
All our opinions have collided
God, please heal our land

Latitia Mariner
Happy, TX

[Hometown] *Happy, TX* [Ed] *high school* [Occ] *Happy's poet laureate* [Hobbies] *writing, reading, rock polishing* [GA] *realizing it's okay to be different and unique, it's okay to be yourself, being a loner has its advantages*
I see the world around me differently. I have always been a people-watcher, on the outside looking in, with the tendency of staying to myself. My poems are based on experiences and interaction I have had with people. Basically life in a small town.

Spirit of America

So long ago and far away; searching for a brand new day
Here to follow all our dreams—that's what America means.
Our "Lady" stands for freedom—to be just who we are;
One bright light in this great big world—free to touch the stars!
We all stand beside her—raise our flag up high
Cherish all this life she gives and honor those who died!
From one shore to the other—cross deserts and great plains,
Through valleys and the mountainsides—we fight to defend her name.
God placed His hand on this great land—we join together hand in hand;
Every heart now beats as one—proud to be an American!
The "Spirit of America"
Your light shines on and on;
Stars and stripes—forever
this country—brave and strong.
We're the "Spirit of America"
where truth rings loud and free;
Yes, the "Spirit of America"
Lives on in you and me.

Shines on—In you and me!

Arthur Maurice Zohn
Brownfield, TX

[Hometown] *Colorado Springs, CO* [Ed] *BA—education/1973* [Occ] *education, marketing, music* [Hobbies] *painting, camping, hot air ballooning, animals, the west, film* [GA] *writing poem/song "Spirit of America" all veterans/America*

My life has been an adventure of special moments and poetry has helped capture these windows. Reflections include—family, friends, pets, hopes and dreams, events in history, love, spirituality—and our world. A musician, singer/songwriter, many poems evolve into songs. Adopted at four in Germany, with great parents and childhood, I have lived the American dream. My father nurtured a hidden talent—and here I am today! A renaissance man of art, poetry, and music. "Spirit of America" is heartfelt and is also a song honoring our heroes and America!

Rockin' at 98

I can't rock and roll "no more"
At least the way I did before
So
Hand me down my "walkin'" stick
I'll show you a real neat trick
I rock and slide, rock and glide
To the kitchen—make some "brew"
And
Next to the powder room do my "updo"
Go to shop, do the same move, too
But rock and slide—rock and glide
Is not for me, you see
So
I'm getting physical ther-a-py
So I can rock and roll once more
The way I did before!

Jean Hickman
Auburn, CA

[Hometown] *Auburn, CA* [Ed] *high school* [Occ] *accountant* [Hobbies] *antiquing, sewing, writing, coloring*
I was born in 1924 in Spokane, WA. Later lived in Hawaii and California. Enjoy writing poetry, antiquing, sewing and coloring. High school grad and music studies. I'm proud to be a mother of a daughter and son—one a teacher, one an engineer. At ninety-eight I am happy to enjoy and partake in easy activities!

The Children of Uvalde

It was a very special day
For these young children
As they came up for their
Awards and trophies
As that stranger came in
And as we heard the sad news
Of so many children's voices
And of their young lives taken
Gone so very early in life
And nothing gets us prepared
For what happens as life goes on
But parents will remember how much
Their children loved them
For life will be better
In that heavenly place
For who can therefore grasp
And look into the life and faces
Of these amazing so loved children
Now they will never know pain
As they enter Heaven's gates
You see, all had amazing journeys
As they lived day by day
To tell of their journey with friends

Magdalena Charles
Cuero, TX

[Hometown] *Cuero, TX* [Occ] *retired senior with flower arranging experience* [Hobbies] *writing poems, short stories, painting with acrylics, sketching, reading devotionals* [GA] *writing my poems and having them published; having my paintings on display*

My poem was inspired by the tragedy of the life of the children of Uvalde, TX. When I heard of this story I was shocked. But in all I'm promised that we have hope. As God always opens the doors of my life. As I have always loved to read books of Christian faith. I have also loved music. As a little girl I used to sing with my brothers in church. When I grew up I grew up running track in school and in my thirties, forties, and fifties I started jogging. I love to also help others in need because all of us go through struggles. But there is nothing we cannot face without the love of Jesus. Now more than ever.

Rainbows

This beautiful arch of colors, I truly love to see
Pops in the sky to show us the promises for you and me
Way back in time when people...
Didn't listen to what our Lord has said...
He sent the rain to flood the earth...
To give it a new rebirth.

Now just like in those Bible times...
People won't listen to His Word...
He sends us storms into our lives...
Then gives us our rewards.
Storm clouds clap with thunder
Then lightning brightens the sky
And after the storm is over, He sends a rainbow to the sky.

Some think there is a treasure... maybe a pot of gold
But certainly if you believe, your treasure will unfold.
Cherish every rainbow you see up in the sky...
Because you see a treasure unfold right before your eyes
The sun brings out the rainbow...
The promise from above... with hope and peace
Our gifts from God... He sends us down His love.

Martha A. Breakwell
N. Belle Vernon, PA

[Hometown] *N. Belle Vernon, PA* [Ed] *associates in business* [Occ] *retired* [Hobbies] *baking, flower and vegetable gardening, walking, sewing, reading* [GA] *becoming a gramma*
Since I was a child I loved rainbows and the stories from Sunday School about its promise God gave us. Since we have been having some crazy storms which seem to end with rainbows, it inspired my thoughts.

He Knows

When the sun rises and when it sets
even when you were thought of and
the day you were born.
What you are thinking, every fret all
wants, needs and your inner thorns.
Each thunder roll, each lightning bolt,
all the earthquakes and floods.
When the wind blows, and the time
for each plant to bloom and grow.
Just for us, He was given, He gave his
blood, and was risen. He knows all
above and below, every bird chirping,
each seed that is sown.
Your happiness, sadness, your love or
anger full of questions. We are only
human, with innate abilities.
Our mistakes in life's bungling way, you
can just hear Him say. 'I am bringing unto
you a brighter day.' Upon each gifted
day, He knows our ups and downs every
twist and turn, still I say to you.
Trust in Him. I hear He is coming soon.
He listens, are you aware of the Son.
We His children, our father in us resides
The Father the word the truth are one.

Ethelyn Barnes
Kansas City, MO

[Hometown] *Kansas City, MO* [Ed] *business management* [Occ] *retired/data transcriber* [Hobbies] *writing, swimming, reading, TV, Internet* [GA] *grandmother/great-grandmother*

The Blink of an Eye

You sit and reminisce about climbing the ladder of life
You can't wait to reach twenty one years of age
You then blink your eyes and you are twenty five
You blink again and a family appears as kids and a wife

Another blink and you hit the age of forty fast years
These years reward you with experience and careers
You blink and the big number fifty shows in your face
So far the years in the ladder have flown as in a race

You blink again and the years of sixty-two are here
The memories of career, family, and Medicare appear
You blink and scratch your head and where did time go
Three score and ten is the blink of your life's flow

Blinking your eyes causes life's time ladder to speed by
Each rung in your ladder is here and gone as time flies
The time on a clock's face you see and its click you hear
Your blinking has caused life's passing like a running deer

You look at the reflection of your face in the mirror
You blink your eyes and time of passing age becomes clearer
When you reach the age of borrowed time, just give a sigh
Just remember the length of life is only the blink of your eye

Benny R. Peoples
Saraland, AL

[Hometown] *Fort Payne, AL* [Ed] *college grad - law enforcement* [Occ] *retired law enforcement* [Hobbies] *travel, hunting, grandchildren contact* [GA] *a life of accomplishment and adventure and great family*
I started writing poetry approximately forty years ago. I am pushing eighty years old and have had an adventurous and wonderful life. I had a great childhood and wonderful parents who taught me right from wrong. I hold three college degrees. I married the love of my life and lost her after fifty-three years. We raised three children who have become outstanding citizens. I am a United States Air Force and Army veteran. I am also a veteran of state law enforcement. I write poetry that relates to present and passing life that most people can relate to.

Is It Still Spring?

It is still spring, so I can still beat the clock, today the basement got a brand new look, cleaned so good, I could walk over the floor in a white sock. All the old unnecessary junk carried outside, sorted, burned, or cleaned to be put away with pride. I see the early flowers gone that showed their colors in April or May, replaced by late bloomers, tall orange giants, starting to show after a rainy day. So many young rabbits using the land as a conservation spot, feeling unafraid, safe and secure from any hunter's shot. Beautiful birds of all colors, size, and breed, daring to fly close to the house for daily feed. Stinging bees, wasp, and other flying insects, welcoming the beauty of nature, fulfilling the urges of the opposite of sex. Making a garden, tending to it with love, watching the young spouts being nourished by God's touch from above. Riding down the highway seeing all kinds of animals big or small, wanting to stop to save the ones that crawl. Waiting anxiously to pick the ripe berries, that earlier I did see, but fearing an unknown something might take a bite out of me. Pulling weeds to make the yard look neat. Making room for flowers to grow, tackling vines of poison ivy, thorns, and itching plants that can take over so. Being so hot, feeling the sun's rays and terrible humidity, wishing for a cool breeze and a tall glass of iced tea. Enjoying going on a picnic or just barbecuing with a few friends, splashing in a pool, river, or feeling a sudden rain, trying to forget what winter sends. These are just a few of my many memories in my mind, I know there are more in my brain's attic, to be written another time!

Julia B. Saunchegraw
Bonne Terre, MO

[Hometown] *Bonne Terre, MO* [Ed] *12th* [Occ] *retired from elderly care* [Hobbies] *writing, Cardinal games, going to church, being with family members, working outside in yard* [GA] *my salvation and being a poet*
I love to write on what I see, feel, whether the past or the present, future thoughts still evade my writings. I can be inspired during my loved Cardinals game, a movie, a TV news happening, nature, or even by the loss of a loved one. I write on whatever is handy, that's later rewritten in my big book for my family. I am grateful to my God that my RA hand and mind still function together. I am thankful for the PA publishers and my children liking my poetry.

Holy Poetry

I sit here and write, the time is 4:43,
Stuck in my head are the words "holy poetry.
Each poem I write is not very long,
I don't want to be late, that would be wrong.
Why should we worry and watch the time,
We're talking about Jesus, is that a crime?
No, it's not, it cannot be,
So I'll sit here and write my holy poetry.
Through Christ I'm free,
You could be too,
If you would open your heart to Him and see.

Shannon Louise Young
Jacksonville, AK

[Hometown] *Las Vegas, NV* [Ed] *bachelor's degree in communications* [Occ] *kitchen person at Little Caesar's* [Hobbies] *writing, singing* [GA] *being published by Eber & Wein*
This poem was written during a time when I had to leave and go somewhere, I forgot where, but I couldn't get the words "holy poetry" out of my head, so I was inspired by God to write this poem about the poetry theme I wanted to maintain, but later poems will reveal that I got off track from that for a while.

Daily Prayer

Dear Lord,
You've taught me that You love me,
A lesson so hard for me to see.
Your arms reach out like a mighty tree,
Why should You love a child like me?
When I awake and think I'm lost,
I pray my "daily prayer" at any cost.
I say, "Oh, Lord, please help me now.
I know You'll help me no matter how."
At times problems make my vision dim,
As I bow my head and call on Him.
Tears are running down my cheeks;
I'm feeling pain in my heart so deep.
Suddenly the answer is so plain,
I do not know why I complain.
I start to smile as the sun comes out;
I know what my day will be about.
Thank You, Lord, for helping me out;
Again You saved me, there is no doubt.
Thank You, thank You for all You do,
The times You've helped are many not few.
Now comes to mind the "The Perfect Prayer";
I never forget it—I would not dare.
"Our Father who art in Heaven,"
My day goes on without a care.
With this last line I say "Amen."
"Thank You, thank You once again."

Frances L. Kalapodis
New Franklin, OH

[Hometown] *New Franklin, OH* [Occ] *teacher (30), Elementary School Principal (16), retired* [Hobbies] *reading and writing poetry and shopping for fashionable clothes* [GA] *as an elected official, made Franklin township into the city of New Franklin, OH*

My favorite poet is Henry Wadsworth Longfellow because in the olden days reading and writing poetry was a cultural thing to do. One of his famous poems was "The Midnight Ride of Paul Revere." In the days of Longfellow, being religious and praying were expected. I am thankful for the legacy that Longfellow left our country. In 2022 reading and writing poetry is a blessing and my prayer for our country is that religion and praying remain a freedom.

Tic-toc

Tic-toc, tic-toc, time passing by
As my eyes watch the numbers
As sleep escapes me I sigh
And my mind wanders through things
Through things I should have done
And pushed aside for another tide
And I let them slide and slide and slide
Until it was too late
Too late, I ran out of time
Out of time, and the clock still runs
Tic-toc, tic-toc, it grows louder in my mind
No refrain
Never to regain
Simply gone.

Jill Taylor-Keck
San Rafael, CA

[Hometown] *San Rafael, CA* [Ed] *high school graduate, Royal Ballet School* [Occ] *former ballerina, ballet teacher, fitness trainer, teacher's aide, mom, and wife.* [Hobbies] *writing, music, movies* [GA] *my amazing children and the realization that no matter what life throws at you, it takes you through a new door into a new possibility and new growth*
As a ballerina, during my time touring around the country, I started writing poetry. It became my special place and time, just for me. This continued throughout my performing career, my teaching career, and my time raising three children, each with different levels of autism and health issues. Poetry and writing were my place of healing, joy, creativity, and escape.

The Weeping Willow

In its ancient grandeur, the weeping willow
With its thin silken lace of gold and green and
Burnished brown—
An attestation of its glory in other times,
Is still a splendid tree, a ginormous tree—
On this silent sunny day, standing in the shadows,
An innuendo of pride granted, long ago.

A story, perchance it means,
Waiting on the once loved grounds,
Trusting its splendor is evidently apparent,
For one to discover, to wonder,
To want, to imagine—
What does it eloquently, seemingly, implore?
To be essential, to be loved, once more.

Olivia Serena Snead
Harleysville, PA

[Hometown] *Harleysville, PA* [Ed] *high school, bachelor's degree in business administration, certificates in creative writing* [Hobbies] *exercise, writing letters, reading, walking*
I went on a walk one day, and I was astounded by the greatness and glory of a gigantic weeping willow that may have been dying. And yet the brownish gold, mingled with gold and green, gave the tree an almost aristocratic bearing. It was the most magnificent tree I'd ever seen. It was standing in the shadows of a neglected yard that still had evidence of a time when the owners had lovingly taken care of it. I stood there for several minutes in awe. I had to own it. And the only way I could own it was by writing a poem.

A Part of the Whole

Welcome, like our state name of South Carolina
Named for King Charles I of England
We treat you like kings and queens.
Welcome, like our South Carolina climate,
We are warm and friendly.
Welcome, like our largest South Carolina rivers—
The Pee Dee, Broad, Savannah, Saluda and Santee;
We are consistent and steady.
Welcome, like our South Carolina peaches;
We look good because we are good.
Welcome, like our South Carolina gardens—
Middleton Place, Brookgreen, Swan Lake
Iris, and Edisto; our buildings are beautiful
And colorful.
Welcome, like our beaches and islands—
Myrtle, Hilton Head, Daufuskie and Kiawah;
We are fun, entertaining and relaxing.
Welcome, like one of our South Carolina mottoes,
We are prepared in mind and resources.
Welcome—to a part of the whole.
Welcome—to our Nursing Home.

Jessie Epps
Whitmire, SC

Suddenly Is the Word

All of a sudden lessons are learned
Violence diminish, hate and arrogance
Going with the wind.

Bad attitude and racism
Selfishness and egoism are becoming null
A pacifist conversation clearly is on the way.

The devil is running away, giving back to us
What to us pertain
Our God is good, like He always being.

The KGB is defeated
Its agents are ruined
Their boss will pay
Just like he well deserves.

We were always confident
That lessons are learned
Taking the right steps
Loving and not hating
Bad attitude is hell.

Let us start all over
By becoming happy again
Good persons at Heaven
Bad people to hell.

Raimundo Matos
Spring Hill, FL

[Hometown] *Spring Hill, FL* [Ed] *business admin* [Occ] *US Army retired* [Hobbies] *writing songs and poems in Spanish and English* [GA] *wrote the story of my life in 5 volume binders*

Life

When I look at my life I feel happy and sad
All the things I have lost and that I have had
Some things were important and some were not
Some things really put me on the spot
Important hurdles that never got crossed
Important goals that have gotten lost
Most important of all, and all that matters
Love, health, and dreams that never shatters
To be loved by many and be in good health
This is more important than all of the wealth
Look around at the old, sick, and dying
To say you don't care, hopefully you would be lying
We none want to face it, although we must
Sooner or later we will all be dust

Maggie Flanigan
Sun City Center, FL

[Hometown] *Hermon, NY* [Ed] *high school and some college* [Occ] *retired* [Hobbies] *walking, singing, dancing, writing* [GA] *to live in a country with the freedom to be me*
Over seventy years a lot has occurred to write about. One's complete psyche is shown in lines written. Good, bad, or ugly, it has to come out. Any piece of poetry can touch someone. Let's hope we all can do some good.

My Star...Shine On

My star
 Will always
Shine on
For you... for me

I will lead you on
I will lead you far
Listen to what star
 I say
I will lead you on

I will tell you stories
I will tell you
Listen to what
 I say
I will tell you stories

I will tell you about life
I will tell you about love
Listen to what
 I say
I will lead you on

My star
 Will always
Shine on
For me... for you

James Fred Brinkman
Bismarck, ND

[Hometown] *Palmyra, NE* [Occ] *Welder* [Hobbies] *Playing guitar, Writing*

Living Life

Our lives are touched every day
By strangers stepping in our way
Most of them just come and go
But special people we try to get to know.

In a restaurant, over time,
I sat where the waitress would be mine.
We joked and laughed and became familiar,
She was delightful as I became sillier.

Life is drear when special moments are lost,
Lost moments come at a vital cost.
If I had not stepped from my "comfort zone,"
Our acquaintance would be lost and gone.

I thank you Mady for your style and grace,
Your comforting banter, the smile on your face,
Your stately presence, your regal aire,
Your personality has no compare!

Clay Thompson
Pocatello, ID

[Hometown] *Aberdeen, ID* [Ed] *12th grade/hardrock miner* [Occ] *underground miner* [Hobbies] *collecting comics, action figures* [GA] *7 children*
This poem is for essential workers all over. I appreciate them all. One, however, affected me with so much positivity I had to write a poem in her honor. She greets everyone with a smile, her service is professional, and she makes me (and everyone) feel so special and important. We don't always live life to the fullest, sometimes we step out of our comfort zone and meet magnificent people.

Life Matters

It was dark in the bedroom
light under our queen size bed
I saw a shadow of a male
under the bedside.
I was a female curious to touch
the male with my bare foot on the
small males back a stroke on his
back, straight down his black colored
hairy fun.
I was surprised I don't who it was
and we enjoyed the stroke down his back
and we enjoyed and liked each other.

Janie Jo Crowe
Silverdale, WA

[Hometown] *Forks, WA* [Ed] *writer, wife, mother* [Occ] *wife* [Hobbies] *friends* [GA] *my husband 33 years, kids raised, my books*
I'm married of thirty-three years to Ray Crowe. I'm a writer of Eber & Wein for fourteen years. I write poetry and I help others in writings. I have with my husband four children who are adults with their families. I'm proud to be a writer of Eber & Wein. Thank you.

Dying Vicariously

I wet my cracked lips against the sting
Of my last sip of whiskey
Living vicariously through these unknown
Souls that haunt this bar room,
Stumbling corpses of self-indulgence
Each drowning. Each alone.
My existence is not so different from theirs.
Evening approaches and the pulse of the city
Thunders in my aching head,
Breathing and drinking
All that I'm really good at anymore,
All that I have left.
Each drop a condolence.
A familiar kiss.
A love letter.
A promise to always be there.
My bloodshot eyes burn,
Tired of searching for the shore.
I'm drowning like the rest.
Dying vicariously.

Howard Boling
Senatobia, MS

[Hometown] *Senatobia, Mississippi*

Morning Ritual

Three little faces framed in wool caps
Eyes pretending to be intently closed
Flickering eyelids prying to see
The winter morn snow through a circle
Hole on the foot board rusted under rug
Mom in the front seat still trying
To shake off her sleepless late night

Both mittened hands held in prayer
Holding their breath in...in all earnest
The children murmur 'please, Jesus...
Please, let the car start, please!'
As dad keys in the ignition and turns
Apprehensively... with a jolt
The old Mercury Monarch roars

Clapping and cheering the children
Shout a prayer 'Thank YOU, Jesus'
With a sigh of relief, mom and dad
Both grad students, join in
The morning ritual
Of family tenacity and gratitude

Our early years...
Of migrant verve
Making home in Wisconsin!

Veeraramani S. Rajaratnam
Franklin, TN

[Hometown] *Franklin, TN* [Ed] *PhD in developmental molecular biology* [Occ] *scientist-turned-poet, artist and author* [Hobbies] *reading, writing poetry, painting, gardening, traveling, and being in awe of God!* [GA] *having and raising three young children while pursuing my doctorate degree*

I commend the strong Christian educational environment, rich culture, and joyous nature of the people I enjoyed growing up in Ceylon (Sri Lanka), and the luxuriant natural beauty of both Ceylon and my current home state Tennessee for stirring up my creative spirit. This poem depicts our early years in the US as a young immigrant couple still in graduate school, raising three young children, managing within our grad-student stipends. I am in awe of our tenacity as a family and feel very proud of our children for keeping our spirits up while enduring hardships.

Memories of You

I can hear sounds of you, memories in the air.
How you smelled so sweet after a shower.
The way you put your socks on you'd stretch them out of shape.
All the little things you and I would give and take.
Today's such a lonely day as I sit here all alone waiting for
a chance to hear you walking through our home.
Just now as the phone rang, I thought it might be you.
I looked at your picture, the smile on your face and I
realized all the phones in all the world could never
take your place.
I can hear sounds of you memories in the air.
The way you put the chair down when it was time to go to bed.
The warmth of your body, the way you lay your head.
The sound of your breathing that echoed in the night.
I'd give all I have to have you by my side.
I can hear sounds of you, memories in the air.
Tears that stain my eyes, the reason that I cry.
Memories in the air.
RIP my love.

Viola Bowden
Lancaster, CA

[Hometown] *Lancaster, CA* [Ed] *high school* [Occ] *retired* [Hobbies] *dancing, gardening* [GA] *family The loss of my husband, the love of my life. I love to dance, work in my yard, spend time with my children and their children. I travel as much as I can.*

Twosday's Memory

I thought that I would write a poem;
today's a special day.
It's 2/22/22 you see,
and I'd just like to say...
that doing something memorable
just seemed like it was right;
forever I will have the poem
I wrote on Twosday night!

Linda Mikula
Youngstown, OH

[Hometown] *Youngstown, OH* [Ed] *Chaney High School and Mahoning County JVS Adult Education (now known as MCCTC)* [Occ] *executive assistant/accountant* [Hobbies] *poetry, drawing, painting* [GA] *I've had poems published by Eber & Wein in* Across the Way, *the Best Poets books, in* Who's Who in American Poetry 2021 *and I'm happy to be in this 2022 edition as well. I've also participated in several invitational art shows at Pleiades Gallery in NYC.*

I was inspired to write this poem because of the unique date. I wanted to have completed some special little thing on 2/22/22 to make it memorable on a personal basis. I believe that it's good to celebrate even the small things in our lives. I enjoy creating poetry that's uplifting and/or simple. Poetry doesn't have to be complicated to have an impact on someone. It enables us to be able to articulate our emotions and ideas. If this poem can make even one person smile, I've accomplished my goal!

A Mouse Ran up the Clock

A mouse ran up the clock
And found a kitten on top.
Up on the edge, he stopped to stare,
Wondering why the cat was there.

Plucking up his courage, he politely asked,
"Why have you settled on this lofty mast?"
The kitten opened an eye and licked a paw.
"You know my kind," she said. "We like to be above all."

P. Clauss
Mesquite, TX

[Hometown] *Edinburg, TX* [Ed] *Doctor of Veterinary Medicine* [Occ] *veterinarian and novelist* [Hobbies] *reading, writing, arts and crafts, and watching streaming channels* [GA] *being married to a wonderful man and being a proud mother of two adult children*
We are a household of clocks and cats. More than once, we have found a cat curled up on top of one of the clocks, whether it be a grandfather clock, grandmother clock, or wall clock hung high up on the wall. Somehow, they find a way!

Small Daisy

A small daisy in a large flower bouquet
That is who I am.
Searching out through my white petals
And yellow face
I know COVID-19 virus across the planet Earth
Invading human cells of every race, gender, and age.
And looming are AR-15 bullet holes in flesh of school children.
Rage, depression, suicide, disease betrayal monster about.
A small daisy in a large bouquet
That is what I am.
Out beyond me
Are gushing galaxies of moons, suns and black holes,
And beneath me slither the fantasy creatures of earth oceans.
What is this universe to me?
A small daisy in a large bouquet.
I am awaiting what is unseen by the eye
But visible to all creatures' hearts.
It is a rebirth of compassion
Of kindness and of curiosity
Which mysteriously and gently must blanket all creation.
That's what I know
As a small, white, yellow daisy in a large bouquet.

Phyllis Jeanette Tyler
Camarillo, CA

[Hometown] *Sioux Falls, SD* [Ed] *Masters of Divinity Wesley Seminary 1971, Doctor of Divinity Claremont School of Theology 1990* [Occ] *retired United Methodist clergy* [Hobbies] *writing, gardening, bird watching* [GA] *surviving and dancing through 76 years*
Poem was inspired by a bouquet of flowers at hospital where I volunteer. Shaping my life was growing up in South Dakota and adopted at age six. Blessed with two remarkable husbands, four sons, and five grandchildren blanket retirement. Gratitude for tears and laughter flow through my moment. Forty years as a United Methodist clergy amazed my soul. Curiosity drives me in retirement in California. AMD and fading of vision is challenge. As I await eighty years old I sense death, life, life, death two sides of same coin.

Deers Kiss

I was sitting outside
Midnight hour was upon me
My head tilted back, looking up
The stars twinkling back at me

Out of the corner of my eye
A movement was seen
Five lonely dear, walking so near
Single file they moved, so silently

I was in awe as they move quietly by
Four of them passed, by without a sigh
The last one stopped and turned its head
And walked over to me with sad eyes

We stared at each other
Don't know for how long
When he bowed his head
And licked the back of my hand

He raised his head
And trotted back to his friends
A voice, I heard
Here's a kiss from your son, in Heaven.

Jerry Wayne Yates
Jacksonville, AL

[Hometown] *Jacksonville, AL* [Ed] *auto mechanic and food service* [Occ] *retired* [Hobbies] *coin collecting* [GA] *raising my only son to be polite and well-mannered until his passing at 20*
Navy vet with forty-six years in food service both military and commercial. My poetry or writings come from losing my son in 2011. My writings come from memories and emotions that run rapid.

Summertime Euphories...

"Objets inanimés, avez-vous donc une âme qui s'attache
à notre âme et la force d'aimer ?" (Alphonse De Lamartine}

"Lifeless objects, do you have a soul which
Attaches to ours with the strength to love?"
Wandering in my heart, yet dwelling in my mind,
Like reminiscing, remembering my youth.
Sitting on the beach, watching the wildlife,
Listening to my heart, reasoning in my memory,
While a cruiser on the horizon slicing through ice,
Leaving in its trail a plethora of tiny isles
And through the mist surfaced humpback whales.
A rumbling sound separating an iceberg from its base
Leading horned puffins-pelagic exotic swimmers
Padding back and forth scoop up fish in their beaks,
Fly back to their nest from the sea to the shore.
The clumsy marching of the female penguins
with inflated bellies glide away from the waves,
To feed their peeping chicks, gaping with greed.
A polar bear on ice approaching between floes
To stalk and hunt the leopard seal...
Bold testimony to territorial power.
These enormous feasts of natural grandeur,
These icy peaks formed through Divine origins,
The combination of Silence, Faith, Reflection and Love,
the deepest beatific agenda of our human life,
Inspire our souls to transcendence beauty and peace
In communion with beyond, the providential,
In amazement with the seraphic, in ETERNAL perception!!

Rose M. Akian
Belleville, NJ

Rosemarie Maljian-Akian (AMBEAR): A native of Aleppo, Syria and further educated in Beirut, Lebanon. She immigrated to the US during the 1960's, and her vocal talents took her to Carnegie Hall and NY World's Fair. In 1988, published

Satin Beauty

Explain to me the world in satin beauty
the breakers on distant shore
explain your greatest mind to me
explain the essence of your mysteries.

For I am a wanderer lost
adrift among the mighty seas
forever lost from mine to yours
not fearful but of greatest serendipity.

Myriah Barringer
Tumwater, WA

[Hometown] *Tumwater, WA* [Ed] *master's of multicultural English literature and languages* [Occ] *instructor at college level* [Hobbies] *creative writing, oil painting, and archaeology* [GA] *having been published nine times*

Myriah Barringer is a nine-time published poet and author. She has two undergraduate degrees and graduates with her master's this fall. She dabbles in archaeology on the side as a member of the Association of Ancient Historians. She writes short fiction, poetry, and novels.

Today and Every Day

Today is a bad day and I wanted you to know in hopes that
we could take things slow. Yes, of course we can take it
slow. Is there anything else you want me to know?
My brother and I were up all night listening to our parents
fight. My homework is not done, my hair is a mess, my
clothes I detest because I'm out of uniform making me
different from the others and I had no breakfast.
Okay, let's see what we can do. I can fix your hair, check
for any uniforms to spare, call home to check on your
brother and any others if you wish, as well as getting you
something to eat. Don't worry, it will be okay. You have me
the rest of the day.
Thank you so much for being you. I don't know what I would
do without you today and most other days. You are my
parent when mine are off task, my mentor without being
asked, my cheerleader moving me toward success, and a
teacher, one of the best.
Our needs create situations that require you to wear way
too many hats and I for one appreciate that. Thank you for
choosing the profession of teaching, reaching those of us
who really need you. My goal is to someday be like you,
a mentor, tutor, cheerleader, dreamer, and maybe just
maybe a teacher.

Cathy A. Clark
Chicago, IL

[Hometown] *Anna, IL* [Ed] *educational leadership* [Occ] *educator* [Hobbies] *hiking, biking, canoeing, puzzles, reading* [GA] *becoming a published poet*
Poetry can touch individuals in many different ways. When people read poetry they can relate to it and find meaning based on their own life experiences. This poem "Today and Every day" was written about a conversation between a student and a teacher. While writing this poem I remembered many of the conversations I had with my students and wondered if I had made a difference. I have accepted the fact that I have made a difference and will continue doing so.

The Encounter

Deep within the forest
Hidden by the trees, dense and dark,
There is a creature who lives there
In the caves of a molten park.
He's out there for I have heard him
Bugling like an elk,
Growling like a grizzly,
Yelling a scream within itself.
It roars just like a lion.
It barks just like a dog.
It laughs hideously, yet human
Then croaks just like a frog.
It makes the forest quiet;
Not a sound when it is near.
I'm sure within an instant
It can catch a leaping deer.
It came there to tell us
It was the owner of the woods,
To get out, stop our camping,
Pack up, stay out for good.
But we could not move
So frozen and with muddled minds
Standing there in terror
With a creature lost in time.
Breathless, we stand and wonder
Will it ever go away;
An hour and a half it bellows
And haunts us to this day.

Andrea G. Lafazio
Lyle, WA

The Puppeteer

Fragile marionette
Who pulls the strings?
Empty eyed, yet sorrowful
Dance for me.
Anguish, disdain
Push it all down.
Your perpetual smile
Meticulously applied
Smile for me.
Insignificant marionette
Forsaken, apathetic
Are you hollow inside?
Hush, I know what you'd say.
Stammering, stuttering
Lamentable words, such
Enfeeblement, dismay.
Little marionette
Ivory, pristine
Do you know your place?
Sit upon your shelf
Wait for me.

Gabrielle Leva Nichols
Saginaw, MI

[Ed] *cosmetology, social work, psychology* [Occ] *retired* [Hobbies] *reading, writing poems and children's books, comic book collecting, Pomeranians* [GA] *being a mother and wife*
Gabrielle Nichols was born in January of 1973 in Michigan. She is of Greek and Native American descent. In 1996 she gave birth to her son, Austin. In September of 2015 Gabrielle married the love of her life, Edward Economous, in a traditional Greek Orthodox wedding. Her poetry is inspired by personal experience and her observations of the human condition.

Outside My Mind

The land is flat, trees a pale line.
This place is slate; it's thin, withered, missing
The colors my mind's eyes provide.

In the distance—the only life seeming
To spark—dots of yellowish gold,
Which fleck thickets wreathing an old stump.

As I draw near, the golden flecks
Take flight, and rise in complex formations,
Lifting, confetti-like whirlwinds.

I watch in muted wonder when they sweep past.
The little things take to choosing
A cardinal point that suits them, then leave.

I consider my prior thoughts
On this place, as I stand upon the stump.
I must try to remember this:
The world outside my mind is still worthy.

Trevor Daniel Otis
Constable, NY

[Hometown] *Westville* [Ed] AAS: *computer graphics & design* [Occ] *associate at Walmart* [Hobbies] *videos games, listening to music, reading, walking* [GA] *publishing my book of poetry*
I grew up on my family's dairy farm near the Canadian border, and got serious about writing poetry in college, when I took a course in creative writing. Three of my poems were printed in the campus literature/ art magazine. Since then I have written a book of poems entitled Dream Deep: A Poetry Collection Based on Dreams. *This poem was written as a reminder to myself that things are okay.*

Tomato Juice

I witnessed once the result of the collision of owl vs
skunk in a raptor hospital full of birds who only hunt.
A great horned owl with fierce yellow eyes met her
match.
Though human beings had to take a putrid whiff of her
catch.
What to do with a two foot tall smelly bird
with talons like scimitars long and curved?
Why you buy out the store of tomato juice?
Get a big vat, drop in bird and begin to sluice.
As owl stares malevolently, turning bright yellow eyes
every which way.
Clacking her beak, hooting, hissing trying not to stay.
Immersed to her head in tomato juice soup.
Covered with mesh so she cannot fly and swoop.
If a bird that resembles a tabby cat with wings could
blush.
At her failure with the skunk she had made to flush.
She killed the skunk and injured herself in the wing.
Which caused her tomato juice wing to be in a sling.

Elana Elisabeth Renata
Brooklyn Park, MN

[Hometown] *Minneapolis* [Ed] *degree in psychology* [Occ] *retired* [Hobbies] *singing, writing poems, watching TV series* [GA] *junior recital with voice as my instrument*
Leanne, the great horned owl perched on my left hand. She pirouetted counterclockwise and hooted softly, hoo hoo hoo hoo hoo hoo hoo hoo. *She was my favorite raptor at the world renowned Raptor Center on the University of Minnesota, St. Paul campus. She stood two feet tall and was in perfect feather. Her coloring was mottled black, white, tan, and brown. Her eyes were round and bright yellow. She swiveled her neck around three quarter of the way to watch the crowd.* Hoo hoo hoo hoo hoo hoo hoo

Enlightenment

The cloak of nobility is not seen,
It does not shine nor does it gleam,
Unannounced among the masses,
Working silently,
Persevering,
A grain of sand,
Drifting in a universal desert,
Finite yet infinite,
Integral to the grand design,
On a journey of self=discovery,
Visible in eternity.

Richard A. Sano
Sammamish, WA

[Hometown] *Albany, NY* [Ed] *BS State University of NY Oneonta, Master of Arts liberal Studies Wesleyan University* [Occ] *retired federal government/science teacher* [Hobbies] *playing jazz piano, reading non-fiction, cooking Italian, hiking/walking, attending concerts and theatre* [GA] *Improvising on the piano, college education*
I enjoy science and the arts and believe each enhances the other. Being creative is both objective and subjective. Having a philosophical approach to life enables self-development and inspires aspiration to strive toward individual potential.

Pets

Pets are a gift from God
They are cared for and loved
Familiar pets and odd
Touched petted softly rubbed

Pets give companionship
Follow where owners go
Near them on every trip
To soothe when they feel low

Care for pets is not free
It may come at great cost
Pet love turns the cost key
Such money is not lost

Pets give glimpse of Heaven
Where the Lord will bless us
With goodness times seven
With love that is generous

Carl Arthur Schomberg
La Crosse, WI

[Hometown] *La Crosse, WI* [Ed] *Northwestern College and Wisconsin Lutheran Seminary* [Occ] *retired minister* [Hobbies] *writing poetry* [GA] *reading my poems to Pastor Dayton Fritz who was blind.*
Carl Arthur Schomberg graduated from Wisconsin Lutheran Seminary in 1976. During his 35 years of pastoral ministry he served congregations in Washington and California. He enjoys writing poetry and finds it to be a good way to say a lot with just a few words. His goal is to help people know Jesus Christ and see the many wonderful blessings Jesus gives us as our Lord and Savior. This poem was inspired by our family cat Pieces.

The Cutting Tree

It all started at the tender age of eight,
an overwhelming urge to self-mutilate.
The tree itself was shady and pine,
perfect place to think, even hide.
Often I climbed under its sappy branches
just to get away from the world and its mid-evil dances.
Suddenly, as quick as a flash
my whole life changed, as my mind and my hands soon began to lash.
For I was drawn into the temptation
that many refer to as self-mutilation.
First it was simple, actually quite small
but before I could grasp upon it, it began to spiral out of control.
Under the tree I climbed time after time,
always ignoring the fact, I just might die.
Family and others say, "It's just a phase."
I myself knew only I can make it change.
Years flew by with no closure in sight
but therapy helped me put up a fight.
I have a road map of scars, miles of shame;
people now ridicule me, my life isn't the same.
But the cutting tree is now gone
so is my desire to self-harm.

Angela Sills
Cambridge, OH

[Hometown] *Cambridge, OH* [Ed] *high school graduate* [Occ] *disabled* [Hobbies] *writing, reading, drawing, crocheting* [GA] *overcoming my battle with self-harm*
I am fifty-two years old. I got the inspiration to write this poem after overcoming my battle with a really severe self-harm addiction. Writing poetry and journaling has really helped me through the rough patches of dealing with my self-harm addiction, depression, and anxiety. I have been free from my never-ending battle with self-harm for almost twenty years now, after battling with it for twenty-five years. Hopefully my poem will help inspire others like myself.

Little Did I Know

It was just another day;
Ready to give up, to surrender.
Another bad date, another bad guy;
The solace rolled in like early morning fog.

As if I hadn't been through enough;
What's one more chance, what the hell.
I sent my message, quietly hoping,
Longing for something greater than myself.

Little did I know, you were longing too.

The first message took my breath away;
Trying not to panic, Lord, what do I say.
Keep it cool, breathe, patience;
Screaming deep inside, hope ignited.

The first night, all my fears flooded my heart;
We walked, we talked and it felt right.
In the end, we hugged, and I fell
Like I had never fallen before, fearless.

Little did I know, you were falling, too.

Then it happened, standing in the kitchen.
You offered me a rose; of course, I cried.
You asked me to be yours.

Deanna Willenbring
Kimball, MN

[Hometown] *Arlington, MN* [Occ] *quality assurance* [Hobbies] *photography* [GA] *being published*
I write what I call poetry; it's always open to interpretation. Some are made of the darkness inside me, some are glimpses of my past, some are the happiest moments in my life. Writing saved my life, and being able to share it with others has been a life long dream. Enjoy!

A Maritime Mare in Morning Tide

Amidst the sea and a pristine pink, streaked sky
A maritime mare enjoys the morning tide
Frolicking in funneling foam with splashing stride
She releases glee's energy bubbling up inside

The ocean curls and caves with its wanderlust waves
As if it understands the crazy way she behaves
It pushes her hooves forward to kiss frothy shore
Then observes her kick up heels, returning for more

With exuberance, she trots back into the swells
Tossing her mane while prancing upon crushed seashells
I like to see her happy heart's motivation
To feel pounding joy of sunny day sensation

Though I am an observer, standing on the sand
I respect her sentiments of affectionate stand
For all forms of love find a way to display
Their natural high, like a horse in ocean spray

Cherie Leigh Sumner
Denver, NC

[Hometown] *High Point, NC* [Occ] *writer, poet, author, artist*
My greatest hope is that what I create in life will give others some kind of emotional response. Then, I feel I have achieved success.

The Lost

There's not hardly a day goes by that I don't tear up.
The loss of the eight of you is so great.
It makes my heart ache. Each of you had such a sweet smile.
You all lie in rest in the field; it all seems unreal.
I hope to myself it's only a dream, for I can picture
your faces in my mind and hear laughter.
But I know as tears stream down my face that I am awake.
To face another day without you all . . .
But my memories of each of you are in my heart
and will never part.

Elizabeth Bowman
Clintwood, VA

Just Us Two

For years I've searched but not to find
that perfect hand to intertwine mine...
A picnic under a tree so great, yes I do
remember our very first date.
Time moves fast each day we spend, so
glad to walk with you to the end.
We'll start our lives together as one, an
everlasting journey that will never be done.
So take my hand and say "I do" for with
this life, it's just us two.

Matt Zubiller
Glen Cove, NY

[Hometown] *Glen Cove* [Ed] *medical* [Occ] *sales*

The Wonderful Guy

As you look ahead, what is it do you see? Could it be your future or maybe something else? So you turn your head to the right, something caught your eye. It was not clear what is was. It was there and now it's gone. Then you turn your head to the left. There is nothing to see. What was there is gone. Do not know what is was. Then you wonder did I see anything at all? Something was there and now it is gone. It could have been something of a dream as you wake up you do not remember a thing. No that does not seem right; it's in the middle of the day and the sun is shining bright. You keep looking for something that is not there and now you are wondering did I see anything at all. Then out of the blue there was a man standing at the corner of the street wondering what you were doing as he was watching you.

Lu Ann Pederson
Bethel, MN

[Hometown] *Bethel, MN* [Ed] *customer service* [Occ] *hospitality—hotel associate* [Hobbies] *read, write, visit relatives, spend time with grandchildren* [GA] *publishing a book*

Nature's Colors

The sky this morning, painted,
A tapestry up high.
Tho' man will color canvases,
Nature stirs the mind.

Violent reds to subtle blue,
Yellows caution, too.
The hues of life remind me of much,
Of all that God can do.

At night the speckled purple sky
With diamonds stretching far,
Images from ancient times,
A story in each star.

Nature's colors long endure,
Enlightened eyes can see.
Man is but a minor mass
Of molecules conceived.

Grandeur seals this morning's scene,
A man stands humble, small.
Colors found in heavens above
Inspire thoughts for all.

Kerry G. Lundmark
Shoreview, MN

[Hometown] *Shoreview, MN* [Ed] BA/MBA
I turned seventy this year. As I begin my eighth decade on this planet, I think on how poetry has been in my thoughts for over a half-century. Moments for reflection come at unplanned times. A painted sky caught my eye and my thoughts went to a poem.

Just Imagine

Sky of blue and no clouds, the sun
of gold and no rays. Moon of silver and
no beam, stars of sparks and no twinkle.
Trees short and tall and no leaves. The
bushes and buds and blooms.
Creeks and rivers but no flow, the ocean
and sea but no shore. Mountains and
hills but no valley, air of wind and
no breeze. Rain and thunder but no storm,
the silk threads and no clothes. Leather
and canvas but no shoes, the plants and
seed but no food.
All that music but no tune, grief and sadness
but no tears. Funny jokes and gestures but no
laughter, and there's the house that is no home.
So many no's and we wonder why, ask that
of God and you will hear "Listen my children
and I will tell you." Each of these no's have
been fixed with acts of love and kindness shown.
So take this love and share with stride each and
every day. For God is love in all our lives
through each and every way.

Lola B. Clark
Sanford, NC

[Hometown] *Cumnock, NC* [Ed] *SFD Central High, SFD Business College* [Occ] *teller, Sanford Savings & Loan* [Hobbies] *poetry, jigsaw puzzles, word search books* [GA] *Editor's Choice Award, Outstanding Achievement in Poetry from the International Library of Poetry*
The three hobbies listed I enjoy. Doing the jigsaw puzzles are time-consuming and a feeling of success is shared by having them framed, hanging on my walls, or using as gifts to family and friends. Also handle my poems this way. My son, Joel, daughter-in-law, Heather, and my granddaughter, Mariella, I truly adore and love. They will always be special to me.

Roses

Through the window on the table
 is a token of tomorrow.
It's a tried and true remembrance
 of a love that used to be.
Every peddle has a story
 of this love that should yet be there.
While they signify the soft and tender
 moments from the past.

They can testify the torture
 in the hearts they represent here,
In the dryness and the wrinkles
 from the withering of time.
Now for them there's no tomorrows;
 they have died for lack of water.
But for love and tender caring
 they'd have bloomed eternal fourth.

While the hour yet approaches
 as the final day is dawning,
Such a love was saved the morrow
 of the hells of rath and scorn.
As the scene of pure emotion
 tried to blind the lovers' senses,
Only moments from the breaking point
 they grasp one anothers hand.

Vaughn Carlson
Yerington, NV

[Hometown] *Yerington, Nevada* [Ed] *mech. eng.* [Occ] *retired* [Hobbies] *photography, mineral/fossil collecting, poetry* [GA] *contributing to the betterment of mankind*
What I write is a microcosm of my education, what I've lived through, and who I am. I write to release hurts, impart knowledge and understanding. Or relate stories of humor. I pray it's found to be enjoyable, entertaining, or of value.

Impact

It is amazing how much of an impact
A person can make on you and your life
It is amazing how much you can love a person
How much they love you back
I love you cannot be said enough
I love you cannot be overused or overwhelming
It is amazing how much of an impact
Someone can make on you
A friendship can turn into more than a friendship
It can turn into a deep, deep friendship
A friendship that makes you feel
That you never want them to leave you
While there are difficulties in life
You still have that person you love so much
While they love you back just as much
You never want to let them go
Over the moon can relate to many things
It can even correspond with friendships
While there are fights and arguments along the way
There are times for you that are silent
There are times when everything is great again
While missing you may come in waves
We know that you will always be watching over us
You will be in our hearts forever
We will always love you forever
As you were and will always be family

Laurie Ann Monica Ransweiler-Dain
Akron, OH

[Hometown] *Cuyahoga Falls, OH* [Ed] *associate's degree* [Occ] *teacher with LeafHomeWaterSolutions* [Hobbies] *writing, singing, piano* [GA] *being published and invited to this and becoming a teacher which has been my dream!*

I wrote and dedicate this piece to my friend Doris who recently passed away. She was such an amazing person and we will miss her so much. She worked with us at Spins Bowl Akron in Akron, OH. I absolutely love to write and it means everything to me to be able to be where I am in my writing. I am so excited. Life is full of ups and downs, but I always have my writing. I will always love you and miss you, Doris, and I dedicate this piece to you as you meant so much to me.

Broken Promises

When the bottle is stronger than your love
you turn where you find faith
because they like being drunk
Last night was it, no more
Starting over will be easy
because it cannot get any worse
Meeting new people
Learning to trust again
Lonely nights are not good
Praying for daylight
because I am getting on with my life
New job
New place I can call home
Thanks to God, Father, Holy Ghost spirit
Met him for coffee
No longer turn to food for comfort
Even sang at church
being at peace with God
Then the phone rings
Please forgive me I will change
No, not this time
I am on my own two feet

Lora Graham
San Augustine, TX

Feelings and Thoughts on the Ending of Summer 2012

by Nin Butterscotch AKA Nina Goldworth
As you enter the grounds of Arrow Park (Resort),
Three famous busts of Poets greet you:
Alexander Pushkin, (A great Russian Poet)
Taras Shevchenko, an Ukrainian Poet — also very fine,
and Walt Whitman an American, thought quite sublime
Memories of a lavish buffet and thoughts
of a castle-house (it being hostel-like)
The hotel lead down steps which were ivory-like
to a plush forest; so pine-like in odor to breathe remedy
That made for a calm feeling.
danced within a rec room with cedar walls…
As my butterly instincts emerged;
Once the summer was ended,
I'd not had my fill of floral scents and whippoorwills;
The new season of poets brought remembrances
dipping my feet in a cool Arrow Park lake
with a refreshing jaunt to look forward to
or going on a row-boat or canoe
with BBQ's and cake!
I relive moments now when people truly knew my name
knew I could've conquered the world and fame!
wrestled with the discovery of how human-kind is undermined —
particularly by incomprehension of amour's truest invention;
That is when summer closed her door to love's intention!

Nina Goldworth
Woodside, NY

[Hometown] *Manhattan* [Ed] *Bachelors ELA Culinary Certification* [Occ] *Writer* [Hobbies] *Cooking, poetry writing, volleyball, eukrastic ideas* [GA] *Who's Who of Best Poets 2021*
Thank you for publishing my poems in Best Poets 2015, 2019, 2020 and Who's Who 2021. I Co-host the New York Open Mic for the National Writer's Union. For those interested in participating, it happens the first Thursday of every month in partnership with NYPL Muhlenberg Branch. I am also in the process of completing a metaphor/simile anthology involving thirty-three writers and five artists, due to be published in the beginning of 2023. Looking forward to giving my fellow poets recognition and reward for their versatility and talent.

Fantasy World

Living in a fantasy world
where everything there is real to me
I can pretend and be whomever I want to be

I can pick and I can choose
the man I think is right for me
and hopefully I will pick one
who will respect and not take
advantage of me

Even a one-night-stand will do
because once we are done, we are through

Living in a fantasy world

Gail Hester
Los Angeles, CA

[Hometown] *Los Angeles, CA* [Ed] *degree in travels* [Occ] *writer/caregiver* [Hobbies] *writing, baseball, volunteer work* [GA] *publishing my own poetry book titled* Ruby Jewel
Published author and writer of poetry book titled Ruby Jewel *you can find some of my other work in Eber & Wein Publishing Best Poets of 2019, 2020, 2021. Graduate with a degree in travel. Enjoy volunteer work; became a caregiver for over ten years. Worked for professional Jazz basketball on their board of directors for three years. Lover of basketball and baseball. Inspired by my son Dr. Kim W. Hester. My poems are inspired by feeling and experiences in my lifetime.*

Led

The searing blast hit with the ferocity of a storm
The intensity of hellfire and black smoke, a firestorm
I could not see, or hear, my mind was drifting away
Blinding, soothing white light permeated the day
My soul struggled to get up and detach from the pain
It reached up, then collapsed under the strain
Thoughts returned to my youth as horrible as it felt
The abuse, mental anguish, unheard cries for help
Then my wife and children that dealt with my problems
Not knowing if returning to them would help be solemn
My body felt cocooned, plastic on and inside my body
All about was rushing air, I felt disembodied
Random thoughts throughout my life, mostly military
Lives I positively affected, others were my adversaries
My soul again tried to reach up to the portal it saw
It failed, this time slamming back into the dark maw
Charges of immense power coursed through my being
Wracking my body, up and down, I felt like screaming
Faint sounds of voices and machines permeated the air
A voice and a feeling of comfort, I was almost aware
I awoke from the nightmare surrounded by my friends
Alive and completely intact, I was ready to make amends

Barry Lloyd Grissom
Fayetteville, NC

[Hometown] *Fayetteville, NC* [Ed] *associate's degree in math, myriad of military related schools.* [Occ] *retired* [Hobbies] *online gaming, spending time with my wonderful family, and of course writing* [GA] *finishing and publishing my book* Is It Easier to Kill or Write a Poem?
I was born in Akron, OH in 1966. I have served in the military for over twenty-seven years in Army Special Forces. I am married to my beautiful wife, Maritta. I met her in Lima, Peru. She is my better half and is also my source of strength and aspiration. I have two wonderful kids, David and Elizabeth. I am passionate about my writing and want to share my imagination with the rest of the world.

Thank You, Jesus, Thank You, Lord

Mind is not as sharp as it used to be.
It would be remiss in this clarification if I
Didn't mention my feeble sexual inconsistencies.
Not walking as fast as I used to walk.
Not searching for possessions lost.
I have come to a point in living this life,
That I realize now who is in charge.
Before I sleep, I thank them.
When I wake, gratitude is due. As I hurriedly
Approach the instant beyond this living,
I thank them over and over again!
Thank you, Jesus! Thank you, Lord!

Marshall Thompson
Buffalo, NY

[Hometown] *Buffalo* [Ed] *Emerson Voc. High School, Bryant and Stratton Bus. Inst.* [Occ] *Buffalo Fire Dept. (ret)* [Hobbies] *writing* [GA] *my love of the Lord*
There is not a whole lot I can add that my poem has not clarified. I would like to add that my deceased mother is partly responsible for this gift. The many poems that she wrote and that she would recite from memory, as I slowly fell asleep. Thank you, mama. I love you. Thank you, Lord, I love you most!

Life of My Trucker

He spends many days and nights out on the road, miles and miles away from home, Grumpy, tired and all alone, to deliver supplies you need at home. He deals with dispatchers and brokers too, who push him past his time but they don't mind, still can't tell time. Traffic is cutting him off and riding his tail this bumper-to-bumper traffic is hell. Make it to his destination on time, or he will sit a very long time with no extra pay running out his time for the rest of the day. Breaking down is a longer delay to get back on the road and finish his day only to make it home the next day with little pay—it's been a long day. This is only part of his day. You would have to ride to see what it's like—what a Trucker does day and night. The most important part of his day is everyone gets home in one peace. I support what he does alone and waiting for him to safely come home. Only a few hours then off he goes to deliver the next load. The life of a trucker you will never know.

Tracy Elaine Brown
Kingsburg, CA

[Hometown] *Kingsburg, CA* [Ed] *human resource management* [Occ] *HR consultant/housekeeper* [Hobbies] *writing, drawing, sewing, baking, crafts* [GA] *having my 6th poem published*
I'm happily married to the love of my life twenty-nine years. I have two best friends; I would do anything for them and their kids and the same goes for them. I love walking on the beach picking up sea shells as my hubby fishes. I'm a pet mom of five pit bulls and three of our cats plus three wild cats one of them a momma and her four kittens. This inspires my writing poetry. I also like to wait until the very last minute to write when there is a deadline.

Cardboard People

I've seen too many cardboard figures
masquerading as human souls
exciting all the inner triggers
that make me feel cold
and vacant inside, like an empty room
pressuring me into feeling the doom
that's inherent to a civilization in flux
where the lure of power and big "bucks"
are the driving force for personalities
living in our society. . .
as exhibited by you and me.

Donald Gene Millner
Durham, NC

[Hometown] *Durham, NC* [Ed] *retired manager* [Occ] *engineering/tech. writing* [Hobbies] *writing poetry, collecting music* [GA] *my kids and grandkids*
Donald G. Millner is a retired engineer/engineering manager and training developer/training manager. He currently resides in Durham, NC and is enjoying a life of leisure as a parent and doting grandparent.

One Word Mom

One word: Mom
Mom this or that
Never-ending
But everlasting

Hearing it over and over
Day in and day out
In so many different ways
Screaming, crying, loving, asking, or even angrily

At the end of the day
That one word is what I want to hear
I am Mom
Silence is not an option

Mom is my name—that one word
It is my identity
So please children do not stop
Keep saying my name

One word is who I am
It holds so many meanings
Love is the most important
Mom equals love

Debra Lynn Grumbo
Evansville, IN

[GA] *being a mom and wife*

Mist

I am silent unless you hush and
risk a muddy ear

my start is the stop of leaves or leaving
seldom seen

Ah me, I roar past mountains cresting and splashing

slowing to help a forest friend
become a wildflower

steady over the ages
seasons blending and bending
I, rivulet
or heart

Rozann Kraus
West Stockbridge, MA

[Occ] *mentor and helper* [GA] *survived her childhood to know how to love and nurture in peace Rozann Kraus has taught at Yale and BU. Embracing each day anew, she dances, runs, swims, writes and tries to heal the planet. She lives with her glorious multi-generational family near a wonderful town and trees.*

To Walk Again

We start out walking
Our bodies all in tune
Exploring this expansive world
One cautious step at a time.
Learning to walk again
A second time in a lifetime.
Once when I was small
And decades later after the falls.
An MD said, "Arthritic damage
The cartilage is worn."
After a work life of service jobs
The original hip joints' function was gone.
First, a titanium hip replacement,
Then a walker, and now a cane.
God's, family and friends' support
All helped me to walk again.
Today, gray hair and a bionic hip,
For these, I am grateful.
Again, I am out exploring the world
One cautious step at a time.

Joni L. Brossart
Frederick, MD

[Hometown] *Frederick, MD* [Ed] AA FCC, *food service* [Occ] *retired/homemaker* [Hobbies] *writing, guitar, cooking, baking, and walking* [GA] *marrying my soulmate*
Life changes after an operation. After three falls and a diagnosis of arthritis the MD recommended an anterior hip replacement. Life has changed. Adaptation is the key. God has blessed me time and time again.

I Know Him

He sat on the stoop as I passed, this old man;
His eyes are on me; I do not know Him.
He told me to "go home before the rain."
One drop of rain touches my face as I entered my door.
A storm is coming.
Morning , the storm has passed.
A feeling of warmth surrounds me.
Still, I see this old man sitting on the stoop.
He told me to "go the other way to work."
I don't know why, but I listened.
No one's at work, a fire blazing!
I passed the old man this evenings,
His eyes are on me; my eyes are on Him,
He smiles, I smile,
I look into His eyes; He looks into my eyes;
at that moment I know who He is!

Catherine Johnson Broussard
New Orleans, LA

Catherine Johnson Broussard is an African American poet, author, and activist living in New Orleans, LA. "I always had a need to write. As a child, I remember writing on pieces of paper knowing that I must share my words." Mrs. Broussard's first work of poetry was published in 1982, thereafter her poems have appeared in several books and publications. Mrs. Broussard has a master's degree is social work from Southern University at New Orleans.

Peace

What I want most in the world is peace
Wish the turmoil would finally cease
For all to live in freedom and not hear
Bombs, air strikes and live in fear

Everyone be able to have their own faith and pray
Everyone deserves a carefree day
Everyone should have freedom in every way
Everyone should have peace wherever they lay

No country should ever control another
In a sense, all men are our brother
Holocaust happened and I thought never again we'd see
Such atrocity to people and take away their liberty
But it is happening again in faraway countries
Suffering and being separated from their families
All they want is freedom and to live in a democracy
Our prayer to God, let peace and harmony be

Frances Ann Richter
St. Louis, MO

[Hometown] *St. Louis, MO* [Ed] *some college and certified medical assistant* [Occ] *retired administrative secretary* [Hobbies] *variety guild, dancing, Zumba, traveling (all states and Europe)*
I was listening to the news and so distressed about the Ukraine situation I wrote this poem. I dedicate this poem to my granddaughter Rachel who has brought me only peace and happiness.

The Buffalo Woman of White

The buffalo woman of white is a lover of the plains
A mystery to the life of man
She holds Mother Earth in her caring hands.

A powerful light resides in the birth of buffalo
And when the natives head out to see the buffalo graze
They bless the land indebted to the buffalo calf woman.

Buffalo, be still; let the natives chant in their way.
Come hither, say the ancient plains
Make peace and memories among our brothers.

Before the hunt, let us also bless the herds
Beyond what others may at times understand.
Let the Shaman call the wise old ones to guide us.

Past the days of winter's source
To test us when we make our sight
Unfolded in the wisdom
Of the sacred buffalo woman of white.

Mariah Ann DeLorenzo
Homeland, CA

I am thirty-six years old and have been writing poetry since third grade. I attended Los Angeles Pierce College in Woodland Hills, CA. I received a degree/certificate in preschool and a certificate of honors dean's list award for academic excellence. My interests are in creative writing, reading, music, choir, art, and most of all, being constantly engaged with writing poetry. I wrote this poem and dedicated it to my Great Aunt Sandra. She embraces the Cherokee native American Indians and other Indian tribes of our great nation. The native American Indian culture, sacred songs, ceremonies, and traditional ways are all inspiring.

You

I've heard people say
"The stars are the most beautiful
Objects in the universe"
I'm guessing they have never looked into your eyes.

A supernova
A hot gaseous mess
Oh heavenly body
A constellation

I've heard people say
That an angel's laugh is
The most beautiful sound on Earth.

I've never heard an Angel laugh
But darling, your voice sounds like Heaven
And I'm dying to hear more.

Rebecca Valentine
Dale City, VA

[Hometown] *Dale City* [Ed] *currently pursuing a degree in horticulture* [Occ] *herbalist* [Hobbies] *plant enthusiast* [GA] *two-time published author; work has been featured in* Best Poems of 2021 *by Eber & Wein Publishing*
I wrote this poem because of a crush I had on a girl at the time. The all-girls school I attended was queerphobic, among both students and teachers. I felt discouraged to be my true self and turned to poetry to express myself. I found an outlet that allowed me to be myself.

Beheld Near and Far

I think it's found inside a buttercup,
or maybe it's untied from barley sacks
that spill their bodies out upon the floor.
I'm sure it is beheld on beaded leaves
just after rainfall covers oaks at sun-up;
a glint that shines a bit, then settles back
in shade or shadows to open the door
to other worlds. Its song will drip from eaves
in ticking minutes held in space to sum-up
the endless ages found within a star.
I am always amazed when it supports
the webs of spiders, setting me ajar
with its inherent show that sparks like quartz:
a soundless sound that falls both near and far

Ronald H. Peat
Auburn, CA

[Hometown] *Auburn, CA* [Ed] *BA, MA, MFA* [Occ] *retired, art instructor* [Hobbies] *the visual arts* [GA] *living to 80 years old*
RH Peat lives in California, Sierra Nevada Mts. Published: USA, New Zealand, India, England, Canada, and Japan. He's operated Open Mics, taught poetry workshops, read works on radio and TV. He's been listed in top 100 in Writer's Digest Annual Poetry Competition; operated poetry readings - sponsored by Poets & Writers Mag.. Published regularly in anthologies. Published book: Abyss of The Moon *(LCCN # 2010909546) It's found on amazon. Won awards for his poems in competitions. Operates a closed workshop on the Internet @ Writing Forums.com — members from several countries including, USA, Australia, Canada, Portugal, Canada, Holland.*

The Unbreakable Red, White, and Blue

You can rip her down. You can tear her to shreds.
Curse her name and set her in flame.

Still she flies. Like a Phoenix from the ashes our stars and
Stripes will rise. You won't believe your eyes. Unshakable,
unbreakable and stronger than before. She will continue to soar.
If there is one thing you cannot do it's break the red, white, and blue.

You can hate her and disgrace her. Even attempt
to deface her. You can try but I promise you won't erase her.

Old Glory has seen it all over the years. She's drenched in blood, sweat
and tears. She's been through many battles and fights and through it all she still stands tall an inspiration to a nation. Our freedom and liberty
are sewn into every stitch. Try as you might, you can't take that away!

She will take your abuse and your misuse. We spit in the face
of your hateful manner because no matter what she will always be our
star-spangled banner. We will raise her high and fly her with pride.

She will never forget all those who gave for her and all those who died. She knows every name
and won't let their sacrifice be in vain. In the end
you won't win, and your tyrannical reign will end. We the people won't back down. We are not color, we are not race, we are Americans and this is our place! If there is one thing you cannot do it's break the red, white, and blue!

Still she flies. Like a Phoenix from the ashes our stars and
Stripes will rise. You won't believe your eyes. Unshakable,
Unbreakable, and stronger than before. She will continue to soar.
If there is one thing you cannot do it's break the red, white, and blue.

Mariah Sue Larsh
Libby, MT

Greenery

If you don't know the Lord,
Then take the time to explore.

Missin' out on the world,
Created to be adored.

God's greenery, so serenery,
The ocean so blue with sheenery.

Hot springs with a spew of steamery,
Laughter with wings that he sings to me.

Even hereafter when my bell rings,
I'll cherish all the beauty he brings.

Tropical winds and all,
how I love to collect leaves that fall.

Admiring the greenery in trees,
Short, fat, skinny and tall,
I love and appreciate it all.

God, thank You for your greenery,
You've enticed in Your big blue ball.

Sarah Pauline Moon
Los Angeles, CA

"Greenery" is inspired by the natural beauty in nature that God has created for us.

Symbiotic

Independence is important
It is definitely a must
But what is life
Without someone to trust

A building will collapse
If it's foundation isn't strong
And a ladder won't work
If it isn't very long

A sink without water
Will serve no use
Just as a light bulb can't shine
If it is too loose

But we all tend to fear
The co-dependence of this
And if we keep cutting cords
Forming connections we will miss

So it is okay to be close
It is okay to depend
Everyone needs
At least one friend

Skyler Alexa Metviner
Brookfield, CT

[Hometown] *Brookfield, Ct* [Ed] *Pace University* [Occ] *teacher* [Hobbies] *reading, painting, doing puzzles, playing board games, spending time with my dogs, and watching horror movies*

Dio

We thought you'd live forever
But legends never really die
The place you are is better
In our hearts you'll always lie

You chose to be a dreamer
And always make your mark
A light in the darkness
A rainbow in the dark

You were always a mystery
Who made us stand up and shout
You are the king of rock and roll
Of that there is no doubt

In loving memory of Ronnie James Dio
(1942–2010, would've turned 80 on 7/10/22)

Brad Berreman
Lino Lakes, MN

[Hometown] *Lino Lakes, MN* [Occ] *sports writer* [Hobbies] *writing, poetry, fantasy football*
I'm a sports writer by trade, a poet by hobby for a couple decades now. My affinity for the hard rock/heavy metal genre of music inspired the poem "Dio," my submission for this anthology.

The Wise Man and the Fool

In a town off the river's bend,
Two brothers lived apart.

One took to a simple job,
The other, a scholarly art.

The first brother was mocked for his work.
Often he was named a fool.

The second brother was praised for his studies,
A wise man with philosopher's tools.

One day the brothers would part for some time,
But the second was soon to come back home.

For more successful is the fool with friends,
Than the wise man who shelters alone.

Mary Grace Gutshall
Round Hill, VA

Stuck in the Past

Following the tracks of my tears.
Do I really belong here?
Here, running from my fears of today.
Or my fears from yesterday?
Why is it we trap ourselves in the past?
Why do we try to make struggles last?
Is it because at that moment it felt safe?
Were we afraid to move from that place?
How do we step beyond shadows of doubt?
How do we make those choices count?
Can we banish demons of bad mistakes?
Can we stop reliving our own outtakes?
Nothing changes once the day is done.
Nothing changes without the sun.
We can't rewrite our original reaction.
We can't change our first interaction.
Take those memories, store them away.
Step into the present, don't hit replay.
Remember all the lessons learned.
Avoid the heat, don't get burned.
Live for the present, live for the new.
Keep clear thoughts within your view.
Make amends with the past long gone.
Make a decision, sing a new song.

Melanie Kay Graves
Zephyrhills, FL

[Hometown] *Willowick, OH* [Occ] *retired* [Hobbies] *reading mysteries, writing poetry* [GA] *published a poetry book*
Writing poetry allows me to create relaxing images for the reader. Hopefully, the reader can step away from the mundane for a brief moment in time, and unwind.

Wasteland

How do you survive
in a wasteland city without
the person that holds you
rooted to the Earth? Desolate
and dry, this town sucks any hope
from your already fragile heart.

How do you thrive on your own
when you crave the touch of
the person you are certain
is your soulmate? A person so
perfectly designed for you.

But one must grow on their own
to be able to water a relationship
that can sustain the heat of
a burning world.

Jenni Schwartz
Las Vegas, NV

[Hometown] *Chicago, IL* [Ed] *Bachelor of Science in entertainment design* [Occ] *makeup artist*
Jenni is a professional makeup artist based in Las Vegas. She has been an vid reader and writer since she was a young girl. She is so excited to see her work published in a physical book!

When I No Longer a Warrior Be

When I no longer a warrior be
I hope someone will replace me
In the honored ranks of those gone before
To defend our nation from our enemies once more

For we have foes that are everywhere
Who for our values have no care
They strive to destroy all that we've done
And plunder all that we have won

So young ones all
Grab our flag as we fall
And carry on the warrior tradition
For it is ever a valued mission

T. H. Henning
Haymarket, VA

[Hometown] *Haymarket, VA* [Ed] *Penn State BA, med.* [Occ] *retired*
T. H. Henning is a veteran of the US Air Force. He's authored and published five poetry books, two fiction novels, and two non-fiction books.

Spiritual Morning

I'm dreaming about a spiritual morning
A beautiful feeling of hope
And it's bringing this dawning

I carry a very meaningful saying
It lives in my heart and soul
And I find it by praying

That saying is "Hey—every day
You've got to start with a spiritual morning
It will show—the whole world will know
That your heart feels a spiritual morning"

I'm living in a way that fulfills me
As I face the world with open eyes
Everything thrills me

Before I caught on, I was just missing
The joys of love, and the joys of kissing
Once I found my spiritual morning
Love came to me like a gift without warning

And now we start with a spiritual morning
Every day with a spiritual morning
We found our way—it'll stay now
A spiritual morning

Nina M. Beck
Redondo Beach, CA

[Hometown] *New York, NY* [Ed] BA *in music/jazz pianist* [Occ] *library clerk* [Hobbies] *personal finance, bridge, listening to jazz music* [GA] *winning the Metropolitan Jr. Girls Golf Championship in 1973*

Bridges

I'm hollow—
Shattered vase empty on the floor; I once held air.
Oftentimes stale, but a breeze when bodies moved
me always came.
I counted the tics of the clock hands that often
looked down at me anytime I tried to open up.
It's face filled with every moment I missed the mark;
Bullseye center hold the pointing fingers that circle
in every direction I teeter and off the edge—
I've already slipped. But the fear of failing
has my splintered frame begging for any part of me
to reach out, looking for life above
as I lay below—
a pale comparison of what I once was.
And this trip—I sleep with this very crossroad weekly
and shame walk toe to toe as if that will make it
any more clear—wipes clean the prints left behind
as if that mattered once one is unusable; that
idea was born of my own innocence.
So pottery then—
broken and unfinished on the floor instead:
expendable all the same.

Latoshia Carrie Hopewell
Seymour, TN

Communication has always been a challenge for me, and due to that I found myself in a journal many times. Pages have a way of accepting what I have to say a touch better than ears, in saying that I have the world's greatest family and friends and want to thank them all for always being my muse. You all cure more than writer's block, and I am blessed and thankful for my creativity with the pen and all those who have helped brighten my life. I have overcome life in its raw form within my own and have come to love every single moment that has hurt or healed. I've walked so many paths through my words and I plan to sight see the rest of my days.

Bass Man

Drops of blood drip down her body,
they both know that this happens, now and then,
when he plays too hard and rough.
He takes a soft towel and wipes her body down.
He wraps his hand around her neck;
he squeezes, gently but firm,
his other hand moves over her body.
He mouths the words: *"bum, bum, bum"*
She lets out that low sexy moan that drives the crowd wild.
She responds only to his touch,
he bites his lip as she lets out another sexy moan.
The crowd yells, *"more, more, more"*
She is firmly in his arms as they move to the rhythm of the music;
they sway back and forth, their bodies intertwined.
They are in the groove, listening and watching.
He looks down at her and smiles.
He knows that he loves her.
He teaches with her;
he creates music with her.
She knows that she is not the only one,
but, she knows, he can't rock without her.
He is a man, living his dreams
on stage, with his band of brothers,
moving and grooving to the songs of his youth.
He is in a 70s hard rock band.
They call him, Barry the Bass Man

Tammy Mustapha Johnson
Sergeant Bluff, IA

[Hometown] *Sergeant Bluff, IA* [Ed] *BA in education and English, MA in bilingual and ELL education* [Occ] *high school teacher* [Hobbies] *writing, reading, and working with the Junior Optimist Club* [GA] *receiving the award from the Morning Optimist Club for working with our youth*
I am an avid seventies hard rocker. I get my inspiration from watching the musicians from the seventies era. Count's 77 is the band that I follow.

The Planetary Songsters and Songstresses Sing Noe

The sun,
Some yonder pale warming star
Hums like a fine-tuned engine
While Mercury creaks
Like an old house about to fall.
Venus echoes deep like a foghorn
Under a flickering fiery system of clouds
As Earth makes the buzzing busy noise of people going to and fro.
Mars is at the bottom of a bottomless sea
Moaning like a sunken ship forever
Separated from red skylight,
As Jupiter chimes a movement
That only a deaf Beethoven could
Ever hear (in his head).
Logical, orderly Saturn now screeches
Out in unbridled pain
While Uranus hosts a frozen, forsaken wind that sounds lonely.
Neptune hisses like an insane sea serpent
And tearful, tiny Pluto, our outcast disenfranchised one, then tolls out the Final bell of all this insignificance glorified.

And I'm speechless.

Why do the planets of this minor solar cell
Wax so spooky?

The terrible, trembling fear of God is all over me now.

Shirley Mandel Satterfield
South Boston, VA

This poem was inspired by the images and sounds that were sent back to Earth by the Webb telescope and the glory of God as displayed in the heavens.

I Want to Smile Again

What's that I see?
Is it light? Is it really light
I think it's light but my eyes are so accustomed to the darkness, it's hard to tell.

I've been in hibernation for a long dark winter
but now the sun beckons me to emerge from
this cave of the blind
And I am hungry.
I must seek sustenance. I must look for salmon
for my soul
My whole being is dehydrated for the water of truth
and right and dignity are calling my name.

I want to look into eyes again
And see the smiling countenance of others
I want to rip this infernal rag from my face
and breathe God's sweet air again.

I want to use it to smother the lies that
assault our ears and threaten our freedoms
I want to say Father forgive them
for they know not what they do.

I want to live in an America I once knew
not perfect but always striving to be a place
for everyone, not just the rich and powerful
who disdain us and use us for fodder.

Can we have such an America again?
Yes we can! Speak up and demand
Get out of our way Woke folks
We've got a plan!

Pat Dukes
Columbia, SC

The World in My Hand

When I was little girl growing up
Life was so easy and amazing
I had no worries, I could live my life
without any problems
I was a little girl who was always
optimistic and creative
I wanted to show the world
all my talents and potentials
I wanted the world in my little hands
I had big dreams, big hopes, and big ideas
As I grew into adulthood, I realized
life can be complicated but
you still can have your dreams, hopes, and ideas
I knew, I had to stay focus
I knew, I was still the same person
I was as a little girl—a person who will
always be optimistic and creative
I must live and become the best of me
Living in stress is only a distraction
Being happy and stress-free is the best option
Knowing that I am important, and I can still
have the world in my hand
I must be able to explore a path of life and
have fun doing it
When I started counting my blessings,
giving thanks, and living life
I know, I could do wonderful things in the world
I still can have the world in my hand

Caramel Lucas
Fern Park, FL

[Hometown] *Orlando, FL* [Occ] *published author/poet, creative writer, podcaster host, standup comedy* [Hobbies] *writing, dancing, telling jokes, traveling* [GA] *became a bestselling author*

Life can be very difficult sometimes but you have to realize you have an option. You can let life take control over you and live a life that is dealt to you or you can take control of your own life and live a life how you want to live. You can live with peace and happiness; it's all up to you. It's the choice of life.

Breaking Silence

Breaking silence
at noon is sometimes full,
as if a river could not wait
to flood its banks and
create new shores.

Yesterday it was
more of a pain, as if
peace could never
be found inside or
outside of the chapel.

On Sunday the shepherds
graze their sheep farther
down the field into
the orange groves,
trimming the weeds.

Wishing for sanctity, I say
"It is I,"
causing any ripe fruits to blush.
Their sunlit colors become
softer to my silent touch.

Kathleen-marie Snipes
Chapel Hill, NC

[Hometown] *Chapel Hill, NC* [Occ] *writing* [Hobbies] *reading*
Life entwined with nature has a beauty that I hesitate to intrude on, but sometimes draw or paint, or when I was younger dance about. My silence allows me to observe above how demure is a family of orange trees. Finally, when I say a few words, the spell breaks, while my voice seems to echo back from everywhere.

Anatomy

Beginning from the bottom my calves seize, my knees buckle and my thighs are still. Something has gone wrong with the wiring. Something has broken. And finding the instruction manual? It seems to have been shredded. My hips have locked me in place. My stomach is twisting into knots. My chest is almost as tight as we were before the fateful night that crumbled my mainframe. But it wasn't our fault; it wasn't my fault. Or was it? Am I to blame for these fractures? Have I been the downfall of my anatomy? Or was it you? Did you do this to me? My arms aren't moving; my hands are balled into fists. I can't breathe, but because of who? My heart beats so fast. Sometimes I wish I could self-destruct. My manufacturer never added the option. Continuing up, my brain is a mess of sliced wires, electricity jolting through sending sparks to the darkness of my mind. Someone must have taken a knife and critically destroyed me. Thinking straight is no longer an option. My features aren't operating the way they used to. But who is there to blame? They taught me in school to be independent, to learn things and grow. What they failed to teach was how to possibly repair a break of this magnitude. They never knew they'd need a repair manual for a shattered heart. I feel myself falling down further and further. Spiraling into the unknown. What comes next? If my anatomy is shutting down what is there left to do? I am blinded and deafened by the heartache my entire frame crumbles before. I am shutting down. My world begins to falter. My mainframe is crashing. Into the darkness I dive until tomorrow morning I'll wake up again just to put on a new face and act like we found those manuals long ago.

Molly Rae Everett
Waterford, MI

[Hometown] *Waterford* [Occ] *cashier* [Hobbies] *reading, writing, adventures, and Netflix*
Hi! I wrote this poem at a time of despair, loneliness, and ache. I wanted to show emotion, yet also compare the body to a machine. Every day seems to feel like the same robotic movements at times, but we keep going forward. I love this poem very much because I wrote it from the depths of my mind, the darkest feelings brought to light. Poetry has always helped me to express myself and to feel better. Thank you so much for reading!

Alive

Our faith rests upon fact not fantasy:
Ventricle pierced by a soldier's rude spear,
Jesus was dead when removed from the tree.
Atonement made for those with ears to hear
The good news: mercy purchased, such a price;
God's holiness, wrath, justice: satisfied!
The Lamb of God, the perfect sacrifice;
Forget not: 'twas the Father's Son who died.
Hear His promise to all whose souls He bought;
Remember His triumphant cry, "Tis done!"
Yet, leave Him in the tomb and all for nought:
Dead Saviors can redeem the souls of none.
As Jonah came forth from the ocean deep,
From the whale's belly, so the body lay
Within the tomb until that hallowed hour
When suddenly opened those once dead eyes,
Ev'ry nerve and muscle charged with pow'r,
As a butterfly from chrysalis flies,
Jesus burst forth from the bondage of death.
See the elation on His thorn-scarred face
As He inspires that long-awaited breath;
Passing through grave clothes, they collapse in place;
Passing through those cold stone walls most hated;
Bodily raised. Not a spirit. Alive!
Resurrected, not resuscitated!
Crucified! Buried! The third day: Alive!

Richard G. Rinker
Columbia City, IN

[Hometown] *Fort Wayne, IN* [Ed] *nurses training/ESL teacher* [Occ] *RN (cardiac nursing), retired* [Hobbies] *writing/built, owned, operated Tea and Coffee Shop for 17 years* [GA] *medical missionary India 8 years*
Bible-oriented nature-lover since childhood. High school English teacher encouraged my pursuit of writing. Enlisted Navy: gunfire control technician during Cuban Missile Crisis. Discharged; took creative writing courses, worked as orderly at local hospital, applied school of nursing: accepted as first male student. Practicing RN forty-five years; medical missionary, India, eight years. Home, certification ESL instruction; taught Burmese immigrants. Operated Tea & Coffee Shop with wife. This poem inspired by the fact that the most significant event in human history—the bodily resurrection of Jesus Christ—is being denied: E.g., Jesus wasn't dead on the cross; he merely swooned.

A Prelude for a Constantly Changing Weather

Discontent as winter is seemingly more bold (2015)
Where some places are exceedingly snowy and cold
Where cold and snow don't stay persistent and linger so
Where skies stay darkened and linger much more
Contentment came as the midday sun peeked out
And bestowed a glittering splendor on the frosted snow
Winter entwined with spring in a deceptive way
Disenchantment as spring seems more unreal and late
Warmer places, surprisedly has sudden snow chill
And threatened the blossoms and daffodils
Touches of rain drops, then came torrents of rain
Spring's buoyancy came in, scattered rainbow beams
Everything became sun-drenched and spring became real
Disenchanted as summer begins to intensify its ways
Steamy, sleepless cities, humid with rainy days
Other places like California, the rain seldom stays
Farmers contented with drought-stricken fields (2016)
Kneeled prayers for rain were generously fulfilled
Strengthen the farmers and the crops yield
Summer entwined, brought humid, hammock days (2017)
Oh' fall how enchanting your breathless ways
How stunning the beauty of your autumn flaming blaze
How heavy laden the frequent haze, I'm simply dazed
Left are fields, harvesting God's bountiful yield
Left are snow dusted pumpkins and leaves gone astray
God's handiwork comes alive in His awesome seasons

Ada E. Koth
Gilroy, CA

[Hometown] *Highmore, SD* [Ed] *high school/college corresponding* [Occ] *jack-of-all trades, homemaker, caregiver* [Hobbies] *writing, collecting cookbooks,making different salads, reenactment photography* [GA] *my first poem ever written (2013) for my ill hubby, and my two kids*

As a senior citizen (with controlled indulgence and persistent determination). I've overcome diabetes and oncoming obesity. My unwavering passion for writing, in my early youth, where I temporarily escaped into an imaginary world of short stories and plays. Later on I became honored to be involved as a ghost writer for a classmate, family and friends. Also, editorials in several newspapers that were totally loved and enjoyed by many readers. I dedicate this poem to my nephew Rich and niece Gloria, who both have experienced ill health these past years and last but not least, a nephew, Jeff Koth, also.

Away with War

Today the sun shines through clouds of darkness,
its blazing light illuminating the cloudiness below.
Peace is like the sun dissolving the clouds.
War is like the windiness of tornadoes
with ammunition that blows away all in their path.
Can we stop war as it topples both Ukraine and Russia?
Their leaders are scrambling for the winning position.
Tornadoes of war moving will long be felt by both sides.
World countries watch in horror as precious people die
and the ruination of lands and surroundings abound.
All the fire power sent by nations wanting war's end
only fuels the struggle.
Winning wars lie in people's hearts seeking finishing
talks among its opponents.
The world prays for the repartition of people's lands
only waiting for those to be had.
Will our chants for peace bring end to devastation,
prepare to rebuild, and mend fences among themselves?
Speaking with each other is the key to winning.
Prayer for opening of heartfelt dialogue is the answer.
Who will initiate this with an olive branch?
We all must take part in this! Can we do it?
Will we bring peace to the world instead of war?
We must rebuild our world with major changes
of the heart, then actions of the hand.
I believe we can! Let us together do away with war!

Brenda Kay Miller
Hoboken, NJ

[Hometown] *Hoboken, NJ* [Ed] *Bachelor of Music in education, Master of Music in vocal performance, opera performances in Graz, Austria for the American Institute of Musical Studies* [Occ] *retired voice and piano teacher* [Hobbies] *reading mysteries and action novels, writing poetry and prose, composing music and drawing* [GA] *joining the Soka Gakkai International, chanting Nam Myoho Renge Kyo*
Brenda Kay Miller was born in Canton, OH, and is a retired voice and piano teacher living in Hoboken, NJ. She has conducted choruses and orchestras for churches, elementary schools, junior and senior high schools, and the Soka Gakkai International; groups at largest numbering 800 voice choruses and 100-piece orchestras. Presently, she composes music, does artwork, and writes poems and prose. As a Nichiren Buddhist, she chants for peace, culture, and education. Since war is abhorrent, Brenda was inspired to write this poem to encourage people to dialogue for ending wars and more importantly for discussion to avoid causing wars.

How to Weave a Poem

A poem will not weave
Without a climax
Words must knit
Or be deceive
To reach the climax
The mind must turn
The heart will twist
The soul choose words
Of twist or turn
Only the soul
Can do both
Knit and console
It is remote
There is a trick
Who twist or turn
The soul decides
Which knit will coincide
The mind has turn
The heart has twist
The soul words knit
For poem to fit
Mind and heart relax
As the soul weave
Of the poem in contact
To reach its climax
The mind
Has reached the heart
Both search the soul
That weaved the poem whole

Therese Jacques Gamache
Chepachet, RI

[Hometown] *Chepachet, RI* [Ed] *high school* [Hobbies] *writing poems* [GA] *to sell my books and thank the Lord for the gift*

My first poem was "My Mask." My son Joseph said a person may appear on the exterior to be what he or she is really not at all—Joseph Gamache (1958-2001). A few years later, when I was not mourning, the poem, "My Mask," came in my mind. Joseph and I wrote religious songs. I have them on cassette tapes. The Lord gave us about sixty songs. I said in October 17, 1996 my son Joseph wrote in his book, "My mother said: Great people are known but greater people are unknown."

Albums

Spread out music of memories, they are
Dreams that can't die. Numerous photos
Under the light glowed, some feelings
Glittering sunshine in the mirror
That once brother soldier bring doll,
Caring proud gift book for be the
Best in the school… Rising happiness
When father comes from hospital home
Took advice from loved sister know
Mom has died… first love turning in
Pain when twin baby boys died…
Upward again, separate ways alone…
Studying hard finish collage, great job,
Own art shows. New dreams, new country
Travel everywhere, the dalliance of my
Angel, beautiful landscape new country,
The moon shines mystical. Love again all
Stars come out to bright light;
Daughter is born… years… past due.
Then lived in a house where roses
Grow to roof… rays of sunshine,
Atlantic, new continent, Florida, smell
of Everglades, all night dancing in
Key West… hurricane, silence no smile
Together go, Wilde West flashing Neo
MS lights, oasis in desert start again Albums of Life!

Vesna Hanhart
Las Vegas, NV

[Hometown] *Las Vegas* [Ed] *college nutrition* [Occ] *painter, writer* [Hobbies] *tarot card reading, chess, poker, biking, swimming* [GA] *learning many languages, creating my beautiful paintings*
I have lived in Las Vegas, City of Lights, since 2011 and in the USA since 2000. I am a nutritionist, artist, painter and writer, photographer, live poker and chess player. I love reading books, like my father, a military person and mortgage broker. I am an investor and house plan builder. I enjoy having the chance to help friends in need. I have a strong personality, I am energetic, have a love for family, my daughter. I have lived in many countries and have created many art shows. I love animals: horses, wolves, chow-chow dog (first turned sixteen years old) and Hachiko who is nine. I enjoy walking, going to the movies, and seeing national parks.

Lover's Lament

Stars above can fade, can die, for they no longer have
her eyes in which to shine. Dusty trails can turn
to mud, for her feet, alongside mine, won't tread.
Birds can stop their sweet songs, for her ears open
once, no longer hear their sounds. Spring's rains can
fall cold, its winds bustle, blow, for no love making
lying naked in Spring's new grass transpires.
Summer's hot nights go unmeasured, they no longer have
her passion's heat with which to compare degrees with.
Poems can now be written by some other poet as writing
them I'd hoped her heart I'd win. Paintings can now be
painted by some other painter for she, my muse, was
my lone, my one, my only, inspiration. Plants wilt,
grass turns brown, without her no life's waters be
found. She was my sun, the light I followed. She was
my future the horizon I steered toward sunrise to
sunrise, always my day's only thought. She settled
my mind in peace. She was my high note always singing.
She was each breath I relied on for life. Her touch to
feel, my skin longs. Her smile warmed me through.
She had a style of which priceless crystal is made.

She's left me now in life's deepest canyon. Without
her guidance I'm lost, alone, and can not found be.
Lost in time's passing without love, without a reason,
without the purpose this lonely heart needs to go on.

Hugo T. William
Eugene, OR

[Hometown] *Manitowoc, WI* [Ed] *Catholic grade school, 1-8; public high school, 9-12; and the Universities of Wisconsin & Oregon* [Occ] *retired postal letter carrier; now an eleven times published novel writer* [Hobbies] *writing poetry and adventure novels in different genres* [GA] *The insight and direction I gave to many young men through coaching little league sports and scout mastering a troop for years.*

Following a walker around limits one's ability to live my previous out-of-doors life, but it has allowed me to concentrate my efforts on my indoor writing. I've written twenty-seven books including five books of poetry—two published; two books of short stories - one published, and twenty adventure novels—eight published thus far. I've always found it funny when someone tells me to get out more, when all I have to do is sit back, close my eyes, and I'm there wherever I want to go. One might say that my past travels have been extensive, exciting, full and wonderfully fulfilling.

4 Little Bundles

God gathered samples of Heaven
and wrapped them in very small bundles.
God sent them down to me
to cheer my spirit and bring new life
and joy to me to make my life worthwhile.
God made 4 perfect little angels just for me.
He gathered together the most beautiful treasures
of Heaven above.
He put sunshine in tiny little faces
as soft as satin and smooth as silk.
God picked the most perfect beautiful
tiny pink rosebuds, that had been
Kissed by the dew and put them on tiny little
mouths, that smile so sweet at me
and fills my heart with love.
He took a handful of sparkles from the
bright shining stars above,
and sprinkled them like diamonds
in eyes as blue as the clear blue sky.
As I hold these tiny bundles of love close to my
heart—I can feel the breath of life
Whisper ever so softly on my cheek,
like the cool freshness of the very first
snowflake falling softly to earth.
Fran 6-19-1965
Lorraine 10-28-1970
Chris-Tina 6-11-1976
Tyler 6-15-1983

Frances V. Clawson
Newland, NC

[Hometown] *Newland, NC* [Ed] *high school* [Occ] *retired CNA* [Hobbies] *Bible study, Old Time in home prayer meetings, family, outside nature, writing poems* [GA] *salvation — Mother, G. Mother, G. Grandmother - CNA-9 poems- book published*

I wrote "4 Little Bundles" for my daughters Fran, Lorraine, Christina, and son Tyler. Later God sent me four more little bundles, two grandsons Austin and T.J., a granddaughter Lacey and great-granddaughter Cora. I can never thank God enough for these precious gifts of love, my husband and I look forward for more little bundles. God has blessed us in so many ways. He has also helped me to have nine poems and plaques published by Eber & Wein. I also have a book published Every Nook and Cranny *for purchase at Amazon.*

Morning Birds

Morning birds sing your song
Sing so sweetly after dawn
Remind me please
Remind me yes
There is joy and there is rest
Bellowing forth from your sweet breast
Yes! hope arises with the sun
Ushered in by your sweet song
Oh, I hear the melody
Does God have something to say to me
Joy does come in the morning
Hope floats down like dew
Sing your songs sweet little birds
I will listen to you
Listen to the messages coming from above
God does speak in many ways
Bringing forth a brand new day
Oh how glorious is your little song
Whispering softly to hearts that long
Long to hear the voice of God
Flowing eloquently from your song
Are you singing just for me?
Making that sweet melody
How precious I must be
That the creator would send you for me

Ginny Ann Crespo
San Jose, CA

[Hometown] *San Jose, CA* [Ed] *San Jose City College, cosmetology* [Occ] *cosmetologist* [Hobbies] *playing pickleball with my husband, sons, and friends; Tahoe in the summer and enjoying the outdoors* [GA] *raising four sons with my husband*

Being a mom is the most precious gift I have been given. Life was going along as expected, when all of a sudden, a crises hit my beautiful little family. This poem was inspired from that crises. I started to notice things that I did not pay attention to before. I'm sure the morning birds sang their song long before I ever heard them. What comfort they brought me. When I heard them sing, I just knew, a new day was dawning and if God cared for the little birds, he cared for me and my family also.

Index of Poets

G

H

I

J

K

L

M

N

O

P

R

S

T

U

V

W

Y

Z